The Resonance Code

Volume 1: Maps

Empowering Leaders to Evolve Toward Wholeness

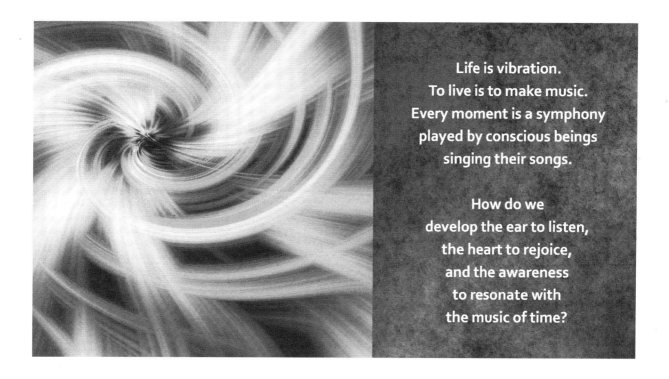

Life is vibration.
To live is to make music.
Every moment is a symphony
played by conscious beings
singing their songs.

How do we
develop the ear to listen,
the heart to rejoice,
and the awareness
to resonate with
the music of time?

Spring Cheng, PhD
with Joseph Friedman and Joe Shirley

Author contact: thecode@resonancepath.com

www.resonancepath.com

Printed by Kindle Direct Publishing

Cover photo: Four Sisters mountains in Sichuan Province, China

To my parents,

And all the mountains, rivers, and oceans

That have nurtured and guided me.

Notes:

1. The pronouns in the book alternate between "he" and "she."

2. The images used in the book are either created by the authors or drawn from online sources either in the public domain, free to use, or published under a Creative Commons license. Image credits and sources of images are compiled in Appendix II.

3. Also see Appendix II for Endnotes documenting sources of key information and quotes throughout the text.

Contents

Voices from the Lab

The Resonance Code Research Lab (RCRL) is a small group of intrepid explorers who have held a container for the birthing of this work. You'll learn more about them in the body of the text. Following are a few of their voices describing their experience and what they would like to share with you, our readers, as you begin your journey into The Resonance Code.

Expanding Wisdom Beyond the Rational

As a leadership coach, one of my favorite metaphors for helping clients build awareness is inviting them to "go to the balcony" to gain broader perspective, to see more of what is going on and more of what is possible. Inviting attention to the larger, universal wholeness of perspective expands the potential container I can help my clients create in these balcony moments. My 16-month journey with the Resonance Code Research Lab offered me many such moments, helping me see limitations in my perspective when relying on traditional mental models. Perhaps more important, it has fired up an expansive view of *wholeness* and a hunger for mining new frontiers of "knowing" through practices of broadened attention.

The RCRL shines a spotlight on the value of ancient-Eastern as well as modern-Western wisdom traditions and shows how neither is complete without the other. An example is the Western preference for rational, logical, scientific reasoning. While this has led to great advances in the last 500 years, it is also limited and has led to some of the greatest problems faced by global society. This approach alone is not leading us to a sustainable future. The RCRL helped me reframe the meaning of "irrational" from un-intelligent to a vast source of wisdom that resides in the still-unknown. The Resonance Code introduces these expanded sources of wisdom and invites us to find the tango rhythm between scientific reasoning and new ways of knowing.

The Resonance Code is an invitation to expand our attention beyond rational thinking. We can wake up the parallel sources of wisdom from our heart, soma, and intuition, and employ these sources as co-creators with our logical, rational-mind thinking. Additionally, the RCRL reminds us that we are all interconnected, and provides experiential exercises for tapping into the wisdom living only in this place of wholeness.

In recent years, leaders have become increasingly alarmed by the societal challenges of increased VUCA (volatility, uncertainty, complexity and ambiguity), often viewed as problems or challenges. Through the RCRL, I have deepened an appreciation of VUCA, as the provocative unknown, a vast frontier for learning, growing, and transforming — both individually and collectively. I appreciate VUCA as a catalyst for solutions to resolve our greatest global challenges.

Expanding wisdom beyond the rational-only perspective into the sea of VUCA requires expanded self- and systems-awareness. The Resonance Code provides frameworks and practices for tapping into this deeper individual and collective wisdom.

When I met Spring at a 2016 workshop, I was stopped in my tracks, hanging on every word she uttered from her quiet demeanor, knowing I had met an especially insightful person. When she invited me to participate in 'Voyage into the Unknown', my immediate response was, "Sure... what's that?" Sensing her presence in every interaction, it is clear that her life's purpose through this work is answering a special call from the universe. This voyage has only just begun! If this work intrigues you, I encourage you join the

voyage by diving into this book and participating in a future RCRL. I trust you will appreciate these tools and perspectives in support of your vital participation in the emerging present.

Kris Miller, Executive Leadership Coach and Consultant, Collective Leaders Project

Dancing Elegantly with the Emerging Present

I met Spring in April 2017, when I was at a time of transitioning on many fronts. Professionally, I was taking stock of twenty years working as the CEO of my consulting firm. Having been an entrepreneur and educator in the field of personal, organizational and social transformation, I was contemplating what this professional field needs in order to evolve to its next phase. My own spiritual journey also had entered a new phase. I have been on the path of Sri Aurobindo's Integral Yoga for a decade. I am a native Chinese and have lived in the West for 27 years, and I started to inquire into how my Chinese spiritual and cultural heritage might contribute to my personal spiritual evolution as well as the to evolution of the global culture of the world.

In the past two years, Spring's way of being and her body of work, crystalized in this book, have exponentially expanded both these fronts in my life. My participation in the Resonance Code Research Lab has led to a profound shift in both my inner landscape and my outer engagement with the larger world. Spring's work taught me how to evoke resonance in life and the world through cultivating my own wholeness. Through practicing The Resonance Code, I learned how to amplify resonance when venturing into the unknown, dancing elegantly with the emerging present. I learned to perceive and act upon the subtle connections between the outer environment and my inner, private domain, especially at times of VUCA, (volatility, uncertainty, complexity and ambiguity). Moreover, this work invites playfulness, fun and creative expressions while working on serious issues of transformation and evolution. As a result, I learned to engage my process with joy and playfulness by opening my innate artistic creativity.

The Resonance Code is unique and rich in several aspects. Spring integrates Western human development theory and practice with Eastern ancient wisdom traditions, Taoism, and Chinese medicine. Her work combines scientific rigor with holistic, intuitive seeing and sensing. She diligently cultivates this work through her own lived experienced and deep resonance with the bigger life forces calling forth the birthing of this work. What she teaches is not abstract intellectual theories but practices and experiences that she lives every day.

I also had extensive experience with Feelingwork, the companion method to The Resonance Code, developed by Joe Shirley, Spring's life and professional partner. Feelingwork is a profound practice indispensable to experience inner wholeness and engender transformation from within. It complements and enriches the experience of resonance.

I see that this work offer tremendous insights and liberating practices to several types of audiences.

- Consultants and coaches in the fields of leadership development, organizational transformation, and social evolution
- Leaders and policy makers aspiring to evolve the cultures of their organizations toward wholeness
- Spiritual seekers aspiring to source their personal transformation within by contributing to social transformation without
- Global-minded Chinese who aspire to internalize the richness and depth of Chinese cultural and spiritual heritage and apply the wisdom to their engagement with the global world.

I recommend this book as a journey for self-discovery and self-mastery. Let the rhythms of your inner and outer experiences rise as you read the book. Engage with the reflections, exercises, and practices. I am quite certain, after this journey you will arrive in a place different from where you entered. I also highly recommend you to meet the

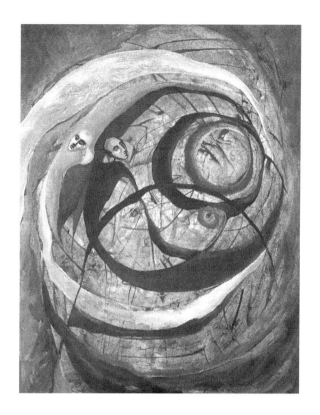

authors personally through attending upcoming offerings of Resonance Path Institute. They are rare and loving individuals to be around.

Tong Schraa-Liu, founder and CEO of TSL & Partners, an international consulting group and think tank headquartered in Amsterdam, with active presence around the world, particularly Canada, China, Ethiopia, Germany, India, United Kingdom, and the United States.

A Framework Both Simple and Complex

My journey with the Resonance Code Research Lab has resulted in receiving a beautiful way of understanding more about my experience, and ways to share about it, with a group of people who all have been learning how to speak the same language. My mind is fascinated with mapping out large-scale perspectives of how everything in this world fits together, and until recently I was very perplexed that most people around me did not seem to share my keen fascination with these patterns. The Resonance Code has given me a framework that is both simple and complex enough to describe my experience to myself and has given me more courage to share with others. By engaging with the I Ching through several different perspectives, I understood that the dark and the unknowable are just as important as their bright and shiny counterparts. I am so glad that now this new way of relating and engaging with both the large and the unknowable fields of reality will be shared by more people and we will be able to use this understanding in all of our explorations.

Alexandra Isaievych, an artist and a dancer inspired by the large scale cosmic patterns and energies, exploring the interplay of dark and bright. (Images on pp. ix and xi are Alexandra's paintings.)

The Next Frontier and Hidden Promise

Weaving themes and inquiries,
legacies and future visions
Walking the path of the unknown,
of mystery and awe,
of emergence and resonance,
Climbing the craggy cliffs with just the right
balance, in just the right gear,
having no fear of fear,
We ascend the asymptote,
each step informed by sages of tomorrow.

On the way down we surf the golden numbers.

The premise of The Resonance Code in itself had a profound impact on me, from the moment it was clear we were together embarking on an astounding, awesome, and utterly thrilling expedition to update the ancient code of I Ching into something fit for purpose in today's world. We are human operating systems deployed in dizzying lifestyles. As our nature and environment, economy and cultures, media and technology, all spin out of control; as waves upon waves of noise and poison threaten to saturate and drown us; these humble efforts give our very existence hope.

From these early days, most memorable are the steady stream of "Resonance Moments," cosmic alignments aka "inexplicable synchronicities" occurring throughout and between the group video sessions, and our deep meta-diving — inquiry into inquiry — remains embedded in my core. In doing group readings, we co-created and refined a technique to generate individual and collective readings simultaneously. To me, this was groundbreaking. Observing the trajectories between our respective and co-generated hexagrams and progressions, and inconceivable patterns of repeating hexagrams and other relational movements, helped us mine and alchemize the disparate senses of the readings into harmonized gold.

Throughout it all, from the start of the Voyage cycle to what you hold before you, are Spring's prolific and exquisite mind and heart, emerging and flowing in written and graphic form. Deceptively simple and concise, her visual representations of incredibly profound concepts and structures reflect ancient Taoist wisdom and elements of Chinese culture, creatively interwoven with modern Western disciplines of science and psychology, threaded with a touch of magic. Spring's concepts command such a full range of disciplines, and her ability to traverse heavy matters with a light touch is mindblowing.

Deeply connecting with Spring as walking and flying and dancing partners in the scheme of

Resonance Code Research is an experience I continue to cherish as it unfolds. Bringing her monumental work to the overwhelming inquiry into climate change — and the consciousness shifts required at all levels moving forward as humanity — is a privilege, and potent opportunity.

I Ching is already a huge and powerful toolset, and The Resonance Code has emerged as a complementary framework for augmenting the evolution of people choosing to integrate with nature. I'm confident in The Resonance Code's vast potential for entities and group inquiries of any scale. For me this is the next frontier and hidden promise of the Resonance Code: a regenerative process for addressing a world in flux. I remain curious and excited to witness and support the evolution of The Resonance Code into a robust system to promote positive collective change.

Charles Blass is a curator of pattern languages, mapper, and producer working in media, arts, technology, and regenerative culture.

Introduction

Voyage into the Unknown

In this book, I introduce you to a navigational system that enables you to explore a new territory. This territory does not lie in a virgin corner of the Earth. Nor does it reach far into distant outer space. Its entrance lies right within our heart and mind. It is the inner terrain of our psyche, which holds all of our mental and emotional activities, instinctual and sensory experience, conscious and unconscious awareness.

My co-authors and I have traveled extensively in this terrain. To navigate, we have drawn from many diverse disciplines of knowledge, ranging from one of the Earth's most ancient wisdom traditions, Taoism, to the cutting edge frontiers of complexity theory, whole systems design, human development, and leadership development.

This work has brought together the life energy of all three authors. Our combined total of eight decades of professional life includes fields such as organizational transformation and leadership coaching, psychosomatic work, biology, Chinese medicine, and statistics.

We also have led an "expedition team," the Resonance Code Research Lab, to explore the terrain together. Through this book, I will

share with you navigational tools, map-making technologies, and stories of our journeys.

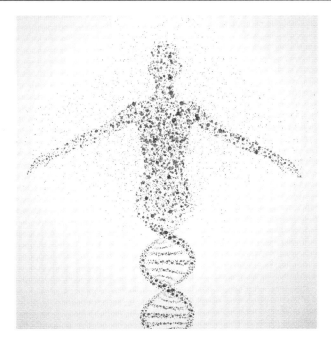

In this terrain, I will take you to a new vista to witness ourselves as participants in the evolutionary process on Earth, both as individual human beings and as a collective species. I hope the view from this vista will evoke the deepest and most expansive compassion toward all we humans have gone through. I hope that the felt sense of compassion will become an inner compass that helps you and your community navigate the challenges of today's world while guiding you toward a vision of a thriving future.

Evolution means the gradual process for something to develop from a simple to a more complex and diversified system. The most studied example of evolution is how life on Earth has developed from unicellular organisms to multicellular organisms, and eventually to the exquisitely complex systems exemplified by the human body. A human body is an ecosystem made of 68 trillion cells, 38 trillion of which are bacteria cells forming the microbiome. This system is diverse, with about 200 human cell types and more than 2000 species of bacterial cells. Imagine the intelligence involved in organizing such a vast and complex system!

When we are born, each one of us is endowed with such intelligence encapsulated as a human body, a precious gift of Earth's billions of years evolution. As long as we are healthy, we don't have to figure out how to make our heart pump blood rhythmically to sustain our entire life, or coordinate the 86 billion information-processor neurons into a super-computational network. Evolution has figured out these bodily processes and automated the body's complex functionalities — from hormonal secretions and metabolic pathways to chemical signal transduction and electrical current transmission. Yet we humans have a special role to play in the unfolding of Earth's evolution.

Looking at the past 200,000 years of human history, our social organizations have evolved from scattered clusters of hunting-and-gathering bands to today's interconnected global community of 7.5 billion people, of whom 4.5 billion carry a cell phone. That means more than half of the world population can connect with an instant phone call or text message. We are becoming the "nervous system" for the body of Earth. It took evolution three billion years to develop the kind of neural network seen in mammals. Within 200,000 years, evolution has re-created this complexity on the social, technological and consciousness level

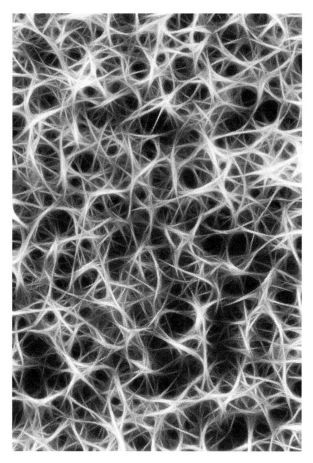

Artistic Rendering of a Network of Neurons

through human civilization, speeding it up 10,000 times. What privilege we humans have to be the leader and primary witness at the front row of this evolutionary process!

pandemic depression and mental illness to loss of biodiversity, from geopolitical conflicts to a gross inequality gap, from the threat of nuclear war to trade wars. More people die from suicide than the number of people killed by wars, murders and natural disasters. We have become the biggest threat to ourselves. Meanwhile, the emergence of new technologies such as artificial intelligence (AI), brain machine interfaces, bionic and genetic engineering are forcing us to reexamine what being human means at the most fundamental, existential level.

It feels as if the old contract that defined humanity's role in evolution is reaching its expiration date. We are now drafting a new contract giving ourselves a new role in Earth's evolutionary process. To draft this contract, we have to answer these questions: Who have we been? Who are we now at this moment of time? How can we chart a new course so we can continue participating in evolution?

At the same time, our humanity and the environment have paid, and continue to pay, a very high price to reach this point of evolution. Today, our globally interconnected social organism is facing a wide range of serious challenges ranging from climate change to the disastrous breakdown of ecosystems, from

The drafting of this contract will happen on both the collective and personal level. It will be the cumulative result of how each one of us responds to the challenges we are facing, propelled by both our instincts and our soul's desires.

Because evolution has transitioned from the biological realm to the conscious realm, drafting this contract requires maps of the inner terrain of our psyche. To a person participating in her own conscious evolution, these maps are as fundamental as the knowledge of DNA code to a biologist studying biological evolution.

How do we chart those maps? More importantly, how do we chart maps that will represent the range of diversity in the terrain of our global, collective psyche?

Chinese culture is one of Earth's oldest civilizations and has maintained its continuity for thousands of years. Throughout this era have been many crucial thresholds where the forces of history could have destroyed it or torn it into pieces. Yet it survived and found its way through round after round of birthing, thriving, chaos, and re-birthing.

Much of the DNA that has given the Chinese culture its vitality and resilience is contained within a knowledge system called I Ching, also known as the Book of Change. In the west, I Ching is usually known as a divination system — a compilation of philosophical commentary and moral advice associated with a six-digit binary

pattern called a hexagram. However, few people in the world today, including the majority of Chinese themselves, know that I Ching started out as a set of maps and numerological patterns, the earliest record of which might be as old as 5,000 years, the same age as the earliest written languages.

These maps contain an intuitive understanding of the architectural structure of a cosmology where time, space and the human psyche are considered as a continuous whole. This idea has been recently re-embraced in the west through the discoveries of quantum physics. The text version of I Ching, from which most English translations are sourced, was derived from these maps 2,000 years later.

Here are two of the 64 hexagrams in the I Ching. Each consists of six broken or solid lines forming a six digit, binary code. A hexagram is an ancient form of computer language. When the mathematician Leibniz invented the modern binary system used in computers today, the I Ching provided an important insight.

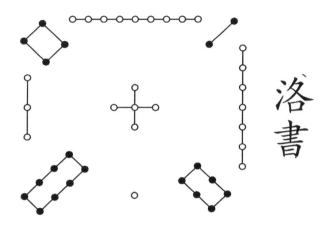

Luo Shu, one of the ancient cosmology maps which function as the kernel knowledge of I Ching

In 2008, I encountered these maps. Back then I had only a rudimentary understanding of Taoist cosmology. Yet that encounter catalyzed an alchemical reaction between my understanding of Taoism and my training in biology and data science. I had an intuition that these maps contained a source of vitality and regenerative power that would be important for the evolutionary process of today's world. I felt an enigmatic and irresistible attraction toward these maps and numerological patterns. For the first five years, I experimented with these maps and numerical patterns on my own, without having any way to share them with another person through language. The information annotating these maps was written in archaic Chinese characters or puzzle-like numbers that few people understood. Yet they evoked distinct felt-sensations in my body. I could feel them through the structure of my bones, rhythms of my heartbeat, and the flow of my blood.

Being in contact with the raw energy of I Ching with my naked psyche brought about a life-altering shock wave that shattered everything I knew about life and myself. I went through round after round of initiatory tests in those four years. At times, I felt as if I was dying and being reborn hundreds of times in my adult body. It was only through the force of grace that I was able to pull through that initiation.

In 2012 I met Joe Shirley, who became my life and creative partner. Joe brought me many gifts that became critical ingredients in my creative process of developing The Resonance Code. The most important was his life-work, Feelingwork, a sophisticated, high-resolution mindfulness mapping process which had a mysterious echo with some aspects of Chinese medicine, even though Joe himself had little prior knowledge of eastern philosophies. Using Feelingwork, I started to systematically map how these raw energies registered as somatic experience inside as well as outside of my body. My understanding of these maps and symbols grew rapidly. I began to acquire a vision of the subtle energy binding people, events and happenstances of the world as a live, animated, inter-connected web.

Meanwhile, I started my own coaching and consulting business and became involved with several communities interested in social change. Through these activities, in 2016 I met Joseph Friedman, a senior leadership coach and organizational development consultant who also happened to have four decades of experience studying I Ching! Meeting Joseph was the definitive moment when the ancient knowledge of I Ching was no longer bound in my somatic sensations but started to unleash itself into modern English. As soon as Joseph and I met, we began an intense collaboration where we started making dozens and hundreds of drafts of new maps with the intention to upgrade this ancient knowledge and make it available to the field of leadership and organizational development.

After a year of intense collaboration and experimentation, we were ready to scale our work. In November of 2017, I opened the course, Voyage into the Unknown, an invitation calling for pioneers to research and experiment with the maps Joseph and I had back then. A group of people answered the call. They consisted of coaches, consultants, artists, activists, and community conveners. They were spread across the east and west coasts of the US, as well as three different countries in Europe. Two of us were Chinese women living abroad.

The originally-planned, three-month course turned into six months, and then a year, and finally 16 months. During this process, our group has transitioned into the Resonance Code Research Lab (RCRL). We meet over video conferencing and when we began, most of us had never met each other in physical space. Yet, with this minimal physical contact, we have been able to tap into a powerful collective presence that has touched us in ways unique to each person's life. This suggested to me the potential of using this work as a binding force and activating agent to cohere a community and catalyze collective spirit and intelligence.

The RCRL members have midwifed The Resonance Code by staying present with the unknown and being committed to what their hearts and souls know to be true. The work presented in this book has blossomed because of their pioneer spirit and passion to explore uncharted territories of humanity.

RCRL - Resonance Code Research Lab

Beth Massiano	Joe Shirley	Tong Schraa-Liu
Saratoga Springs, NY	Seattle, WA	Amsterdam, Netherlands
Joseph Friedman	Charles Blass	Kris Miller
Ashland, OR	Zürich, Switzerland	Washington, DC
Spring Cheng	Riina Raudne	Alexandra Isaievych
Seattle, WA	Tallinn, Estonia	Los Angeles, CA and Ukraine

During the first Voyage into the Unknown, the current RCRL members circumnavigated the globe of the human psyche, from ancient China to modern Euro-American continents. The materials presented in this book are the maps and knowledge we have brought back from our 16-months-long research and experimentation.

The language, maps, and patterns are some of Earth's oldest wisdom, newly re-born into modern English and concepts to empower leaders on the edge of evolution in today's world. My colleagues and I hope that with these maps we humans will find our way toward becoming integrated and conscious participants in the vast tapestry of evolutionary processes on Earth.

My intention with this book is to present a high-level conceptual architecture of the psyche in a digestible volume. I'd like to note that each concept introduced in this book is coupled with a range of experiential exercises and inquiries that I did not include in order to keep the volume concise. If you are interested in in-depth exploration of these materials, please check out the course and trainings offered at our institute. RCRL needs more explorers to join the expedition.

I invite both your heart and mind onto this journey with me. Chances are in your adult life, when you pick up a non- fiction book, your rational mind is in the driver's seat. That is great. A strong rational faculty is a tremendous resource for this trip. However, I also ask your rational mind to consider sharing the driving with your heart, trusting your heart's intelligence and strength. The road is long, winding and quite complicated. It will require the teamwork of both!

To assist your mind and heart to collaborate, I have integrated text with many images, graphs and charts. I invite you to take time with these non-verbal elements, digesting them along with the meaning of the text.

There will be times when the terrain is too steep for the rational mind to grip the wheel. As long as your heart is still engaged and open, that is okay. This book is really an invitation to you to come and experience our work in person. Our experience tells us that once someone has a more visceral experience and felt sense of the terrain, it will be much easier for the rational mind to catch up.

Following this introduction is the Prelude, in which I tell some of the personal stories behind The Resonance Code. Chapters One to Four present

a model of the architecture of the psyche and a series of maps associated with the architecture. Chapter Five presents the evolutionary threshold we can cross given the knowledge presented here. In Chapter Six, I give a brief introduction to Feelingwork, the companion method to The Resonance Code.

With that, let us begin this journey together!

Prelude

When the Motherhood
of Earth Rises to Sing

Twenty-three years ago, I waved goodbye to my parents in Shanghai, flew across the Pacific Ocean in my first-ever airplane ride, and arrived on the campus of The University of Pennsylvania. I was a shy and quiet Chinese student, overwhelmed by the complexities and foreignness of the crime-ridden inner city of Philadelphia. Despite that, I was living the dream I had held dearly since I was 11 — I became a doctoral student at an Ivy League school! At that time, the highest achievement I could imagine was the standard American dream — middle class, respectable job, cars and houses — all of which was far beyond reach in the 22 years of life I had in China. That was before China had taken off to become today's mega-capitalist-consumerist giant. I grew up in a socialist planned economy. Nobody around me had a car, owned a house, or had their own business.

At that time, had someone told me that I would become the lead author of a book presenting an intellectual architecture that reinvents I Ching, one of Earth's oldest books, and introduces Taoism and acupuncture theory in leadership development, I would have laughed out loud and thought that was the most ridiculous joke. Intellectual architecture? What is that? I Ching, Taoism and acupuncture? The dark taboo and shame of Chinese culture? You gotta be kidding me! Leadership? Not interested. That's for men, or women who want to compete like men. Back then, these primary elements of this book were like three desolate mountains shrouded behind thick clouds in the remote corners of my awareness.

Yet over the more than two decades of my life in America, I have discovered a secret chamber in my heart. In this chamber was a very faint voice humming a song. At first this voice was very weak, almost inaudible. Yet, the tune it was humming, for me was like the sound of a running brook to a desert traveler. I instinctively traveled toward its direction so that I could hear this voice louder and more clearly. Sometimes, traveling toward the song meant facing painful choices of tearing down my life structures such as jobs or marriages. Yet in my heart, the longing for being close to this song is more powerful than any other desire I have. One step after another, I found myself embarking on a wild journey guided by this song.

I call this song, *The Song of Earth*. Its life-giving and soul-nourishing melodies have awakened powers and desires in me I did not know I had. It has given me the vision to see those mountains, aroused an unquenchable passion to climb them, and led me to the resources required to take the journey this far. The Song of Earth is the creative source of the work presented in this book. In this chapter, I want to share a few stories of my journey following its muse.

Story One: Earth, East and West

What does the name "Earth" mean? Of course, it points to the 6×10^{24} kg mass of planet under our feet and all the ecosystems it supports. Earth is a universal concept in every language. But is that all?

What Earth means to me is more than that. I derive this meaning from both the Five-Element theory of Chinese medicine and my experience of coaching people with The Resonance Code. Chinese language, in its classical form, symbolizes simultaneously the external, concrete world and the internal, subtle awareness that allows us to perceive the concrete world outside. The character for Earth, 地, on the concrete level points to the outer Earth, the ecological context from which our material existence differentiates. Everything we eat to build our body mass comes from this outer Earth. All the material things we rely on to meet our basic needs originate from it. That is why the outer Earth is often associated with

mother, because it reminds us of how our body differentiates from our mother's body.

Yet for me, probably a more essential meaning of the word Earth points to an inner Earth, which is the *experiential context* from which our sense of self differentiates, the vast territory of raw, felt-sense, and somatic experience before we filter, sift, organize, and abstract ourselves into symbols, language, and meaning.

Humans inhabit only a thin layer of the outer Earth. Likewise, our conscious awareness occupies only a thin layer of our inner Earth. At the bottom of this layer are the more ancient cognitive faculties such as senses, feelings, emotions, and instinctual impulses. At the top of this layer are more modern faculties including thought, logic, and rationality. This top layer produces concepts, labels, categories, and myriad knowledge systems out of the building blocks of language.

Modern culture requires our attention to be focused on the top layer of awareness. We spend a lot of time shaping and reinforcing self-identities constructed by language and the value systems woven by language. This is often done at the cost of isolating the self from the life-giving soil of our inner Earth.

For the first 12 years I lived in America, I did exactly that. I had constructed an identity as a biologist and paid a dearly high cost for it. I spent five years completing a PhD in molecular biology and biostatistics. Then I became a research scientist working for a cancer research center and subsequently a pharmaceutical company in Seattle. The further I went in my career, the more I learned to shut down, compartmentalize, or minimize some of my most deeply felt experience, because I did not have the agency and power to hold my inner Earth without threatening the painstakingly constructed self-identity that I needed to survive as an immigrant.

One such experience was when I was half-way into my PhD thesis. My work required me to do an enormous quantity of animal experiments. Day in and day out, I put lab mice and rats into gas chambers to kill them, and dissected neurons from their spinal cords for research. After a while, something in me felt horribly wrong and deeply violated. I remember watching my hands doing the act of killing as if I was watching someone else's hands, as seeing them as my own evoked a dizzying sensation of repulsion. Yet in the academic environment, disclosing this experience was dangerous to a young, fledgling graduate student. Sentimental feeling is something to be ashamed of, especially for a female scientist. Once I revealed a hint of my unease. Immediately my advisor refuted, "we are making medicine to alleviate human suffering. Animals do not have sophisticated feelings. As a scientist, you should not let your sentimental feelings influence your judgment."

I did not agree with him. My intuition was that animals were far more conscious. My impulse was to ask him, "If you knew there were other ways to better human health that did not involve unnecessary suffering to other animals, would you choose that?" But I remained silent. I was a third-year graduate student. My advisor was a distinguished scientist, a member of the National Academy of Science. He had tremendous authority over me. To hold an honest conversation with him on this subject required a command of English and understanding of the topic that I had not yet developed.

Under the intellectual framework of western science, his logic was rational and correct. But my native upbringing in China endowed me with a strong connection to my inner Earth — I did not invalidate my feelings just because they were scientifically incorrect. At the same time, I was aware that it was not the time for me to probe deeper into my "irrational" feelings. I was in the US with an immigration visa — there was a tremendous pressure to comply so I could survive in this foreign country. The only choice I had at that time was to defer to the scientific authority. With enormous effort, I tucked my feelings into a secret chamber of my heart and finished the animal experiments that allowed me to write my thesis and graduate.

In fact, over the course of the next twenty years, there has been a growing body of scientific data suggesting that animals indeed have far more sophisticated capacities for feelings, emotions and even empathy and altruism than we had thought. Today some scientists have begun to ask the hard questions — how do we take into account the suffering we impose on experimental animals? Will it skew the results of experiments and our understanding of human medicine? My heartfelt feelings at the time were indeed pointing to something valid before I knew the words to speak it or the evidence to prove it.

Unfortunately, in the field of science, especially medical science where huge financial interests are at stake, it is a deeply ingrained conditioning to privilege intellectual validity at the cost of denying, minimizing and compartmentalizing the

felt-sense experience from our inner Earth. This practice highlights one of the key foundations of western intellectual architecture, the implicit assumption that the intellectual mind and rational faculty is more intelligent than and superior to feelings, senses, and instincts, the more ancient layers of awareness closer to the core of the inner Earth. This assumption is in direct contrast to the Eastern intellectual architecture, which holds an intellectual mind and rational faculties as part of the *ecological system* of the inner Earth. In this ecological system, a more sustainable way to develop greater intellectual capacity is to grow deeper and wider root networks to integrate with the more ancient cognitive faculties, instead of rejecting or marginalizing them. This is at the heart of what this book will present.

The implicit assumption of the intellect being the more superior faculty has fueled the development of western science and propelled incredible technological achievements in the last 300 years. However, I believe humanity has evolved to a point where maintaining this assumption is now blocking us from further development of our intellectual understanding of the world around us. Without drawing rich nutrients from the core of the inner Earth to renew itself, the intellectual framework of the world will continue to lead us toward a disembodied and dysfunctional relationship with both our inner and outer Earth.

Over the course of my 13-year career as a biologist, my heart had been gradually disengaged and filled with sorrow and anger. I chose this career because I was enchanted by the complexities and wholeness of life, especially by how organisms transmit and organize genetic information through DNA, the central question of molecular biology. Yet, the further I engaged in my science career, the more I felt resentful that I was a part of an enterprise that treats life as something to control, dominate, and extract profit from. Modern western science is obsessed with employing the reductionist approach to reduce the wholeness of life into material constituents, locking the wholeness of life outside the door of laboratory.

My observation is shared by many leading western thinkers and philosophers. Carl Jung wrote, "(Scientific) experiment consists in asking a definite question which excludes as far as possible anything disturbing and irrelevant. It makes conditions, imposes them on Nature, and in this way forces her to give an answer to a question devised by man. She is prevented from answering out of the fullness of her possibilities since these possibilities are restricted as far as practicable ... The workings of Nature in her unrestrictive wholeness are completely excluded."

My heart twisted in knots watching myself cutting, fracturing, and killing the wholeness of life in my day job. I felt as if I was an intellectual prostitute, selling my intellectual ability for immigration status and financial security. Although I was able to perform quite successfully and sailed through my career, I hardly enjoyed my work and struggled a great deal emotionally.

I interpreted my emotional struggle as my being not very intellectually bright. I thought myself lazy as I always just did the minimum required to get by without much ambition to push beyond that. I felt shameful about my laziness. It was only years later, when using my intellect with my heart engaged, I discovered that I had much more intellectual aptitude than I thought. My struggle and lack of ambition were not because I was lazy or not bright, but because my intellect and inner Earth were caught in irreconcilable conflict. Now in my coaching practice, whenever my clients disclose a part of themselves they devalue or feel shameful about, I know they are on their way to discover hidden gifts they did not know they had.

My story is just one example of how scientific authority rejects and invalidates one's inner Earth. Today, any established authority that upholds man-made standards that do not tolerate ambiguity and uncertainty can be a force that marginalizes the inner Earth. This authority may be of any nature — scientific, moral, cultural, political, religious, or spiritual (yes, even spiritual!). As I demonstrated in my story, there is often a very good reason to respect the existing authority. That reason may also be an expression of the inner Earth which needs to be embraced. In fact, rebelling against an existing authority might equally deny the uncertainty and ambiguity necessary for the wholeness of life to unfold. In other words, there may be no simple "right" action. The skills and knowledge presented in this book will help you develop the capacity to hold ambiguity and uncertainty, and transform the conflict between existing authority and your inner Earth into bridges and connections that allow creative choices to emerge.

I hope my story can help you to connect with some territories of your inner Earth that you have not allowed yourself to visit, because you have told yourself that they were wrong, irrational, shameful, immoral, or unenlightened. Perhaps you have been afraid to visit those places because forces in those places threaten to disrupt some aspects of the status quo — your profession, identity, marriage, belief systems, or spiritual associations.

You are right. Visiting those places without the right skills, knowledge, and resources can be disruptive. Yet, barring parts of you from your consciousness can be even more disruptive in the long run. Nothing can be more draining, painful, and harmful to our physical and emotional well-being than compartmentalizing, minimizing, and denying parts of ourselves. Nothing is more costly than spending our own life energy to suppress the wholeness of life expressing itself through us.

Every time humans have ventured into a new territory, we have made new discoveries that propelled humanity to grow and develop further. This time, the new territory lies within ourselves. I hope with this book you will find tools and maps that will enable you to embark on an expedition to those remote, wild, and beautiful places in your inner Earth so that you can reunite with the whole of yourself.

Story Two: Taoism, the Forbidden Love

The conflict between my inner Earth and my scientist identity actually had a deeper origin. Inside my heart hid a secret lover whose name I dared not utter ever since I was a young girl. This secret lover was Taoism.

Tao in Chinese means the way or the path. It is the pathway through which the outer and inner Earth relate, generate, and inter-penetrate one another. It is the trajectory of the interplay between the outer and inner Earth. This way of conceptualization that straddles the internal and external is a critical element of the Eastern intellectual architecture. It has given rise to the practice of Chinese medicine, acupuncture, and a wide spectrum of social practices including a long tradition of leadership development in ancient China.

When the Taoist sages engaged with the plants, animals, and physical features of the outer Earth with an awareness deeply rooted in their inner Earth, they perceived a subtle "music." Music in the audible range is a phenomenon of Resonance. When a guitarist plucks the strings, she activates a host of vibrational frequencies. The wood body of the guitar vibrates in resonance with those frequencies. This subtle music the Taoists hear results from how they use the instrument of their psyche as a resonator, like a musical instrument.

Lao Tzu in Tao Te Ching wrote, *there is a grand music in the universe, a music inaudible to the ear.* Taoism teaches that when we attune to this subtle music, our physical body, sense of self and soul can all be cultivated to become instruments to amplify this music. In doing so we may elicit signals of Resonance with the world around us.

Resonance infuses us with a sense of aliveness. We become aware that everything happening in life — birth and death, creation and destruction, happiness and suffering, is all congruent with the universal cycles of unfolding and enfolding happening around us. Resonance will not guarantee us to be successful, happy, perfect, or even safe, but it will transform our fear of death, pain, failure, and imperfection into graceful acceptance and sustained momentum for conscious evolution.

This understanding of Resonance as the source of life is not unique to Taoism. Many indigenous traditions around the world shared a similar understanding of Resonance. However, the extent of this knowledge has been limited due to the earlier developmental stages of human civilization. Without a globalized economy and a universal means of communication, Resonance could only be established in a localized system, within a mono-cultural/linguistic environment. At the same time, the process of evolution constantly disrupts equilibrium in established systems so that the scope of Resonance can expand into larger contexts with stronger coherence and magnitude. This disruption has occurred to almost all indigenous cultures around the world.

When the old Resonance system is disrupted and the new one has not been established, we experience a period of chaos and dissonance. I was born in the midst of the Cultural Revolution in the 70s, a period of chaotic dissonance that swept the whole of China. Taoism, Buddhism, and Confucianism, the three pillar foundations of classic Chinese philosophy that had nourished the culture for thousands of years, were all treated as the greatest shame and taboo. This collective self-rejection and self-denial started when China's collective spirit was crushed by a series of wars between China and the western world (and Japan),

Taiji Symbol of Taoism

beginning with the Opium Wars in the mid-nineteenth century.

When I was little, teachers and parents told me the following narrative. Taoism was superstitious nonsense which had poisoned the Chinese mind throughout history. Under its Influence, the Chinese mind got lost, wandering the fantasy land of metaphysics instead of pursuing natural science like the West had done, rendering us inferior in our technological development. Because of our inferiority, we were defeated and brutalized by the colonizing forces from the West and Japan. In order to protect ourselves, we needed to burn the old books, toss the teachings into the trash, and follow the West's lead to develop our own natural science and technology from the ground up.

Under this narrative, I grew up starving for the soul food that had nourished my ancestors' minds and spirits for thousands of years. The education system privileged and prioritized western science far over Chinese classical education. The majority of people in my parents' generation knew nothing of the traditional teachings. Many people had hardly ever heard of I Ching, the seminal book that seeded the origin of Chinese culture. In my soul, the sense of deep malnourishment was devastating. When I was a little girl, with next to no resources, I went out of my way searching for the nourishment of traditional knowledge, looking for moldy books that somehow survived the annihilation, buried in the most dusty corners of libraries or piles of waste paper in recycling centers. I felt like a homeless child, rummaging for food around trash cans, savoring whatever scraps and pieces of knowledge I could find that would reveal even a tiny bit of the taste of my ancestors' wisdom.

I remember when I first saw the Taiji symbol as a teenager, I fell into a deep trance. The symbol came alive in front of my eyes, like two "fish" swimming head to tail circling one other. The image pulsated with mesmerizing mystery and erotic attraction. I turned to adults to seek explanation. Yet no one could tell me what yin, yang or Tao was. It was maddening to experience something this profound without any mental framework to guide my young mind.

Yet true knowledge is infused with life force. Life force is like water, always finding a pathway to flow through, getting around big boulders or seeping through the tiniest cracks of even concrete dams. Even though knowledge primarily lives in meaning made through language, it also transmits through other vehicles such as sound, image, somatic experience, and abstract symbols. Even though the traditional means of knowledge transmission had broken down when I was growing up, I was still immersed in an ocean of sounds, images, traditional customs, and archetypal symbols that carried the energetic vibrations of the knowledge. My parents and extended family, even though they could not speak about traditional knowledge in an intelligent way, were a rich source of embodied examples of my cultural heritage. My intellectual mind was deprived and starving, but my inner Earth was not. It was absorbing, digesting, and processing deep veins of nutrients left behind by my ancestors. It was preparing for me a rich bed of experiential resources, waiting for the time to come when my mind would wake up to hear The Song of Earth.

Story Three: The Song of Earth, Return of Resonance

Fourteen years after I first landed in the US, I finally broke free from the cocoon of the American dream. The internal pressure to hide, compartmentalize, and deny my inner Earth finally reached a critical threshold and exploded in a chain of life-changing events. As a result, I quit my scientist job and embarked on a new journey, resolving to reconnect with my ancestral heritage.

This life transition asked to me to step into an extremely vulnerable place. My Chinese family including my former spouse did not have the capacity to provide emotional support. In fact, my decision was devastating to my parents. They felt betrayed. They had sacrificed immensely to support my emigration from China. My American dream was their pride and hope too. They could not understand why I would give up such prestige and financial stability to pursue something that to them had no value.

At the same time, life opened its abundance to me. As I resolved to reconnect to my ancestral lineage, I discovered two incredible resources in Seattle, Taoist Studies Institute and Seattle Institute of Oriental Medicine (SIOM), both providing world-class education and training in Taoist cultivation and Traditional Chinese Medicine. I had no idea that they were here before I quit my job! Like an orphan reuniting with parents, I dived into the knowledge I had been craving since my youth. SIOM, where I studied Chinese medicine, is the one school in the world that has kept the most intact and faithful representation of a wide range of East Asian medicine modalities. This school is one of the few formally accredited acupuncture schools in the world that not only teaches but further develops an ancient healing art referred to as palpatory skill. This skill is no longer taught in mainland China because it is too "unscientific." With palpatory skill, we are trained to listen and attune to the subtle feelings and sensations arising from the inner Earth and use our own hands as instruments to connect with patients' energy, to diagnose and heal. Finally, I was able to reconnect with my hands. This time I used them toward healing instead of killing.

This life transition was far beyond a mere professional shift. It was an earthquake of loss and chaos that shattered all my old life structures and shook me to the core. My marriage with my Chinese husband painfully dissolved. Right at a time when I needed financial stability, I lost a third of my investments in the 2008 stock market crash.

Two American elder women who had over the years took me under their wings and "mothered" me as my life mentors died of violent cancers one after another. I was immersed in an ocean of grief and fear stirred up by all the losses.

In this most vulnerable and uncertain time, for the first time in my life I became involved with a Western man in an intimate relationship. He had a brilliant intellect and a broad knowledge of Western philosophy and history. After having lived in the West for 14 years, it was the first time I experienced Western culture through the doorway of personal relationship and interior feelings, which was as much of a culture shock as when I first arrived in US! I realized that the chasm between Eastern and Western cultures was much more than just the visible things such as language, behavior, and customs. There is a Grand Canyon of differences in the realm of invisible, subtle awareness. These differences range from the most fundamental concepts such as what constitutes the sense of "I" or "we", what the verb "is" or "need" means, to how we think about sex, body, and family. Most of these differences never came up in conversations with my American friends and colleagues in the 14 years I had lived in the US. I had no idea that I had lived with this invisible Grand Canyon between me and American culture.

At that time, I had not yet developed the awareness and skills to communicate with my partner and build bridges to cross this Grand Canyon. As a result, this romance brought me three years of tumultuous emotional upheavals. Yet as painful as it was, it served as an alchemical cauldron for deep personal transformation. It was as if I was propelled to drill as deeply as possible toward the core of my inner Earth, through many layers of the collective unconscious. To find the raw material and energy to build bridges across the Grand Canyon, I needed to be in touch with a more ancient sense of self before eastern and western cultures had bifurcated in human history.

It was a time when I felt the ground of my reality was shaking and the sky was falling. Everything I relied on as reference points either abandoned, betrayed, or hurt me. I felt devasted and broken. Yet precisely in that brokenness, The Song of Earth pierced through the cracks, starting to sing to my heart. Song, like language, is an abstract representation rising from the soil of the inner Earth. Musical notation consists of mathematical symbols that denote vibrations with different frequencies. If one's awareness vibrating between the inner and outer Earth were to turn into a form of "music," what would the musical notation look like?

Right around the time when I ended my science career, I encountered I Ching, the book that is most revered and shunned, most loved and least understood in Chinese history, the source of the Chinese culture's long and meandering river and its vast network of tributaries. The Western man I was involved with introduced I Ching to me. Through him I discovered that I Ching had been much more respected in the West than in modern China. That was extremely poignant to me. It was the violence done by Western armies on the Chinese soil that initiated China's collective self-denial and rejection where we ripped our soul from our collective body. Now it took a Western man and an alchemical romance to bring I Ching, the soul of Chinese culture, back to me.

In the western world, I Ching was mainly known as a book of spiritual wisdom or a divination tool. An I Ching book usually focuses on the verbal translation and philosophical discussions. Yet when I first cast my eyes on I Ching, my attention was immediately captured by the elegant mathematical structure underlying the symbol system. All the knowledge and experience I had acquired to that point — science, statistics, computer programming, Chinese medicine and Taoism — converged into a bright flash of intuition. I saw the possibility for a new,

coded language for Resonance, a language that could possibly expand the ancient knowledge of Resonance into a global scale beyond the constraints of Chinese culture.

I Ching Hexagrams: A Six-Digit Binary Symbol System. Each hexagram consists of six lines. Each line is a binary symbol, being either solid —— *or broken* — —.

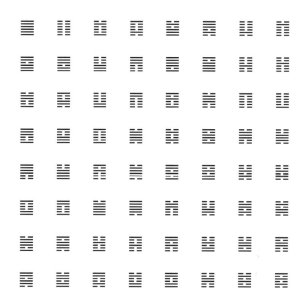

As awareness vibrates between the inner and outer Earth, an energy passes between the two. Our conscious activities, thoughts, actions and feelings are this energy's vehicle. I Ching contains an abstract symbol system that allows our intellectual mind to perceive this energy in just the way that musical notation allows trained musicians to "see" music and enables them to play together. When our intellectual mind can see this energy, we gain the capacity to collaborate and co-create with one another through consciously evoking synchronicities. Never had I in my wildest dreams imagined that in my first encountering of I Ching I would see the possibility to re-invent it with new language, language that is not bound by the archaic symbols and metaphors of ancient China but pulsates with the rhythms and dynamics of modern life. With this new language, it would become possible to re-weave the web of Resonance in a way that could serve the globalized, multi-cultural civilization we have today.

Why do we need to reweave the web of Resonance? As humanity today has gradually lost touch with our inner Earth, our sense of self has become uprooted from the inner soil. An uprooted sense of self is at its core impoverished, and the culture formed by this impoverished self takes on the quality of cancerous tissues to the larger ecosystem. From this place, we extract resources and energies from the ecosystem to fill the black hole of our materialistic needs with devastating consequences. We subjugate the outer Earth to the probing, drilling, and testing of whatever power we have forged in our scientific labs, and demand her to give us answers that we can use to extract profit. We become deaf to the music between the inner and outer Earth and unknowingly find ourselves trapped in a maddening escalation of dissonance, wondering why things are going so wrong.

Today both our outer and inner Earth are in urgent crisis. With the outer Earth, the crisis can be summarized into two things: climate change and the Anthropocene Age. The most recent report (2018) from a panel of scientists gathered by the UN describes a world of worsening food shortages and wildfires, and a mass die-off of coral reefs as soon as 2040. As for the Anthropocene Age, Nigerian author Bayo Akomolafe gave a stark portrait, "corrosive spillages and a frightening excess of broken ecological boundaries, damaged ecosystems, poisoned oceans, plastic landscapes, deforested landscapes... rising carbon emissions, rising sea levels, oil spillages, loss of biodiversity."

This ecological crisis of the external Earth is a mirror of the equally devasted, polluted and chaotic landscape of the internal Earth. Today more people kill themselves every year than the combined total killed by war, natural disaster and murder. Depression, the primary reason why someone would commit suicide, affects nearly one in ten adult Americans. Increasingly large percentages of young people are subjected to various mental disorders, and the rate of youth suicide is escalating in many countries. The toxic effects of mass murder, nuclear weapons and political polarization are infecting our daily life like poisonous gas.

The Chinese word for crisis is composed of two characters: 危, pronounced as "way," means dangerous; 机, pronounced as "gee," means opportunity. It is hardwired into the Chinese language that crisis and opportunity go hand in hand. Further, the scope of the danger is considered to be proportional to the scale of opportunity, and the amount of fear triggered by the danger suggests the magnitude of change required to seize the opportunity.

On the other side of this crisis is an evolutionary leap that is waiting for humanity, a leap as giant as the invention of written language or transitioning from hunting-and-gathering to agriculture, except this leap will take place in a much shorter time span. More and more people around the world are tuning into this evolutionary leap and working toward preparing for it. For me, the opportunity presented here is for humans to reconnect with the inner Earth and establish Resonance, a consciousness of wholeness synchronized on a planet-wide scale, this time with much stronger coherence and magnitude, to weave humanity into a more vibrant whole.

At the time I was struck with the intuition of The Resonance Code, I was a student practicing Acupuncture during the day and Taichi in the evening. Although I held the vision of The Resonance Code, nowhere in my consciousness could I fathom what it would take to produce it. The job of inventing The Resonance Code from I Ching could be described like this. Imagine one day in the future, all there is left about music as we know it are a few digital recordings. The knowledge of musical scales and notation is lost. There is no single musical instrument left. One day, you come along and listen to the recordings of Beethoven's symphonies. You feel so inspired that you somehow get this crazy idea that you will reinvent the musical scales and the instruments. Then you will teach others to play these instruments with the scales you invented so that they could make new music and orchestrate new symphonies with these instruments! In order to do that, you have to decide what a scale is and re-make every instrument from scratch. How many notes will there be in a scale? How many keys should you put in a piano? How many strings should a violin have? What is the shape of a flute?

At that time, my rational mind, still steeped in the reductionist mindset, would completely short circuit and shut down if I tried to imagine the scope of this work. To my most optimistic estimation, it would take several decades if not several life times to crack the code of I Ching. "Someone else will have to do that, but not me." My mind was set on the goal of practicing acupuncture for at least a decade.

However, what I started doing right away was engaging I Ching in an experiment. I had already intuited that each hexagram represents an evolutionary lesson that is emerging in the present moment. Since I was going through an extremely unstable and changing time across all fronts of my life, it became the perfect "lab" for me to observe how subtle patterns of change might correlate with the hexagrams.

Instead of focusing on the existing I Ching text, I directly attuned to the energy inherent in the hexagrams and documented my internal awareness as well as external events and changes associated with each hexagram, observing their correlations and coming up with my own conceptual frameworks that would allow a much more personalized interpretation of each hexagram. I imagine this was how experiments involving the hexagrams were first conducted by the ancient Chinese in I Ching's earliest days.

I did that for three years without ever expecting that one day this would be my work. I did it because I felt an irresistible attraction toward the I Ching. This careful experimentation provided me with meaning and joy during a tumultuous and challenging time of my life. It became a new reference point. I felt that I had finally become the kind of scientist I was born to be: a scientist who experiments with the whole of myself — my sexuality, embodied experience, identity, mind, and soul. My heart started to attune to The Song of Earth again!

Story Four: The "Child" of The Song of Earth

As my journey reached this point, I had most of the necessary ingredients to start an alchemical experimentation between the past and the future. My embodied awareness had drilled deep into the past and my vision had shone light on a far distant future. Yet before I could stoke the fire of my creativity, my rational mind needed to catch up.

After I graduated from acupuncture school, I started to construct my second professional identity as an acupuncturist. Soon, though, I crashed head-on into a new conflict between my inner Earth and my emerging identity.

In Chinese traditional culture, a medical practitioner could simultaneously play multiple roles ranging through philosopher, politician, shaman, family counselor, and community leader. This integrated role was necessary as the healer was treating the whole person — body, mind, and soul. The social infrastructure back then accepted this role and supported it financially. This integration is impossible in the modern, western medical system, whose reductionist mindset strips acupuncture from its spiritual and cultural depth, cutting it into small pieces in order to stuff it into a convenient box in its own system.

In the US, an acupuncturist's scope of practice is largely dictated by insurance companies. Counseling and psycho-emotional intervention are completely outside the sanctioned scope. Acupuncturists are compensated by insurance for treating only a tiny fraction of medical conditions. This reflects the insurance industry's utter ignorance and disrespect toward the integrated approach of holistic medicine — no matter what symptoms a patient presents, holistic practitioners always see the symptoms in the context of the whole. If the integrated role of the traditional healer was like a tall-standing tree connected to the forest of community through its root system, acupuncture as a profession in the US feels like a small, potted plant, placed in an inconspicuous corner in the giant mansion of the western medical system.

I remember being in shock and rage when I discovered that I would be paid by the number of acupuncture points performed on a patient. I felt insulted and humiliated on behalf of my ancestral heritage. Can you imagine Mozart coming to China and playing piano on the street to a crowd of people deaf to his music? Not only that, they see his playing as a mechanical activity and decide to pay him by the number of times his fingers pound the keys? Not only that, they make rules to tell him how to play so that they can streamline the payment procedure?

The rage and grief I felt started to quickly build up pressure inside. I was frightened to realize that this second identity was about to crumble too. But where could I go next? Into what soil could I re-sow the seeds of my beloved wisdom tradition so that it could grow into a strong, tall-standing tree again? On what stage could the essence of Taoism and Chinese medicine be truly appreciated and seen? Even more importantly, how could this knowledge renew itself and evolve into deeper understanding?

It was at this time that The Song of Earth sang to me in an unequivocally clear voice, extending a big, warm invitation to step into a new unknown territory. This invitation first came in the form of a lover and partner who has the stamina, skills and passion to co-create with me in order to cross the Grand Canyon between the East and West! I met Joe Shirley through a series of beautiful, synchronous events. The unfolding of these events was so well orchestrated that it felt like they were masterfully arranged by a romantic and creative divine event planner. Immediately, Joe and I realized that The Song of Earth was inviting us to enter a partnership on multiple levels, from

intimacy to domestic partner, from professional collaboration to conscious evolution of the soul.

Joe offered me a key to unlock and transform the vast resources buried in my inner Earth. This key is Feelingwork, the expression of Joe's whole life's creation. (Chapter 6 will give a brief introduction to Feelingwork.) Feelingwork is a process in which one turns attention to the inner Earth to release the energy in its bound-up, reactive forms and facilitate its transformation into more constructive and creative forms. It prepares one's mind to transcend from the linear, mechanical, and reductionist mode into a fluid, organic, and systemic mode, re-activating the inborn, natural wisdom of what Joe calls the feeling mind. With Feelingwork, the experiences I was accustomed to pushing away from my awareness — the pain, shame, remorse, failure, anger, resentment, fear, victimhood, or hopelessness — could now be welcomed back, transformed into fuel to catalyze productive engagement with my creative work.

As I started to engage with Feelingwork, a wellspring of power and energy was released like a gushing geyser through me. I started to develop The Resonance Code in ways that continued to blow my reductionist mind! I started to understand that I was recruited by The Song of Earth to give birth to a body of work that has a life of its own. My job is to steward its birthing and growth, like a mother nurturing and attending her child.

To "mother" this body of work, I needed to learn how to fly. Whenever I reached a point where there seemed to be no path forward, the power from The Song of Earth would show up, encouraging me to drill deeper toward the core of inner Earth, experiencing the parts of me that had been previously minimized, invalidated, and denied so I could release them. The drilling often took me way down into the collective unconscious. Then this power would urge or even drag me to rise up and leap into the unknown, making a bold step that I had been afraid to make. As I leapt, the outer world responded to my inner change with an unequivocal "yes," presenting the right people and right circumstances that miraculously emerged out of nowhere, pointing me to a direction or resource that I could not previously see.

I experienced that as I gradually committed to The Song of Earth, it also gradually amplified its message to communicate with me through people and events around us. For example, at the time when I was torn between my desires to hang on or give up my acupuncture practice, a teacher in a workshop told me, "the world does not need one more acupuncturist, but the Earth needs someone to do acupuncture on her body." When I was stuck in my reductionist mindset and thought I would never have enough time to create The Resonance Code before I ran out of resources, Joe said to me, "Don't just produce work. Create time!" When I was feeling vulnerable and hesitant about bringing the ideas of Taoism into the field of leadership development, my friend Chris Clark, an organizational consultant, came to me and said, "I just finished reading Tao Te Ching. It feels like a letter written by Lao Tzu to human evolution." All these people acted as my Zen masters, delivering a koan to me at the crucial moment. How does one do acupuncture on the Earth? What does creating time look like? How can I translate the letter of Lao Tzu in way that expands our understanding of human development? These questions were like the thunder of spring time, waking a part of me slumbering in hibernation, propelling me to explore new possibilities and engage in new experiments.

I think of Rainbow Circles

Along this journey, I gradually found my way into the field of leadership development, coaching, and consulting. It was then I met Joseph Friedman, a senior consultant who had been working in the industry for several decades. He also had a decades-long relationship with I Ching, having done his first reading when I was just a year old. Meeting Joseph was an inflection point where the development of The Resonance Code started to accelerate and intensify. Joseph and I soon started to engage in a close collaboration. With his long experience of coaching practice, leadership development, and immersion with I Ching, Joseph provided me a priceless space of generative listening in which the architecture of The Resonance Code emerged one piece after another in front of our eyes. He soon became another devoted father of this "child," not just nurturing it but also gently guiding the development of this child with his expansive wisdom and laser-precise intuitions.

Last year, this journey culminated in the first Resonance Code course called Voyage into the Unknown. The course attracted more intrepid scientists who were courageous enough to embrace the unknown. Later, the course evolved into the current Resonance Code Research Lab. The Lab researchers have formed a collective space where we further the research and development of The Resonance Code. Now this "child" not only has parents but also a small village around it.

Story Five: When Motherhood Rises into Leadership

To me, every step of this journey felt like a vertical climb on a featureless cliff face. How do I give voice to the silence of the unknown? Again and again I was pushed to the limit of my capacity and courage. Out of despair and fear, I would often lament, "Why me? Why has this work knocked on my door? I am nobody. I have no backing from an established institution. English is my second language. I have no formal academic training in social science. I am consuming all my financial resources to fund the ongoing research. Why didn't this work find someone who is more experienced, with more credentials or more resources?"

More than once, I was resentful that The Song of Earth had put me into such a vulnerable spot. In those moments, I let myself break down and cry, asking Mother Earth to hold me. Like Antaeus, the child of Earth and Ocean in Greek mythology, falling toward the ground is my way to replenish my strength. Tears flush whatever inner blockages are in the way. As those blockages dissolved, again and again I heard a voice echoing from the dark abyss of the unknown. "Your being 'nobody' and having no visible power is the condition required to give voice to a power sourced from the dark unknown. To further evolve, we humans have to learn how to be in right relationship with the unknown, as there will come a time when relying on what we know alone will no longer be sufficient for survival!"

My sense of disempowerment as a "nobody" is deeply rooted in my internalized archetype of a Chinese/Asian woman. As a Chinese woman, the fiercely ingrained conditioning is to follow and support. Growing up, most of the leaders I knew were men. And the women leaders I knew mostly adopted an over-masculinized way of leadership, toward which my innate feminine instinct held a strong resistance. I had no template for leadership that honored feminine creativity, particularly feminine creativity embodied by a Chinese/Asian woman.

As it is for other women of color, the voice of Chinese/Asian women is seldom heard in public. There are few Chinese/Asian women role models in the public arena, particularly in fields dominated by males such as science, politics, and business. Whenever I was among strangers, I was keenly aware of the stereotypes cast upon Asian women — demure, domestic, and deferential. In those circumstances, I, as my own self, am invisible and voiceless. But this voiceless stereotype is not just about Chinese/Asian women. Since Asian women together account for more than half of the motherhood of humanity, this stereotype is also a symbolic representation of the Motherhood of Earth which has been muted and taken for granted in modern culture.

The voiceless nature of the Motherhood of Earth is reflected in the modern narratives of human development and human evolution. These narratives heavily focus on progress measured by intellectual development and technological advancement. There is an emphasis on individual agency and sovereignty. These narratives neglect that in order for innovation and new knowledge to emerge, there needs to be a healthy and generative social environment, as well as a healthy and abundant natural environment. The kind of knowledge required to steward, sustain and regenerate the well-being of the natural and social environments is a knowledge sourced in the feminine. It is rooted in somatic intelligence and intimately woven with the organic and spontaneous processes of life. Thus it is trans-rational and can not be approached solely through intellectual means. Fixated on the narrative of progress, we have been neglecting developing this aspect of human agency. We have become deaf to the wisdom of Earth and have disempowered the feminine voice in both men and women.

The narrative of our own evolution is an extremely powerful tool. For humanity to evolve further, we are destined to move into territories of the unknown. The narrative of human evolution serves as a beacon by which we can shine light into the unknowns of both the future and the past. When we see the future more clearly, we know which direction we are heading. When see our past more clearly, we know where to regenerate resources and nurture ourselves back into wholeness. I feel strongly that this beacon needs to originate in a much more intimate exchange between the feminine and masculine voices.

In my view, the knowledge of Earth and feminine wisdom is severely under-represented in our current evolutionary narrative. This is no surprise as the conceptual frameworks of human evolution have mainly been written by English-speaking intellectuals in the western world, the majority of whom have historically been male. The work I present in this book is sourced form the trans-rational knowledge of Taoism and extracted from the Taoist legacy of the somatic transmission. My intention is to set a foundation for a new conceptual framework and invite an interplay between the feminine and masculine perspectives to co-create and co-shape the narrative of human evolution. In human history so far, motherhood has been tightly coupled with procreation. This is particularly so for Chinese culture. Today a Chinese woman who chooses not to procreate will withstand tremendous prejudice and denial of her womanhood. Even in American culture, there are still a great deal of unexamined assumptions. More than once, for example, I have encountered conversations where people hinted that because I have not had the experience of bringing up a child, I missed the most important lesson in life and I will never understand what a selfless, maternal love is.

I have chosen to express my feminine creativity not through biological reproduction but through my mind and soul. Like many women who have chosen this path, I have had to come to terms with unconscious judgment and projections from our culture. Because I chose to forgo the external reference to validate my motherhood, I also chose to enter an ongoing inquiry of my internal motherhood, an inquiry which has always been uncertain and ambiguous, and probably will continue to be so in my life.

Creation happens through the interplay of feminine and masculine energies. This interplay, like a dance, may be led either by the feminine or masculine. In a full and enlivened expression of creativity, feminine and masculine energy will share leadership in a spontaneous, fluid exchange that is highly sensitive to the circumstances and timing. Motherhood leadership arises when this dance is led by feminine energy; fatherhood leadership when it is led by the masculine.

home -making

The only "dance" in human culture where feminine energy plays an unequivocal role of leadership is the reproductive act of birthing. Many "dances" we do in our social enterprise, like the establishment of science, politics, business and spirituality, are led by masculine energy and reflect a strong influence of fatherhood leadership. Even when women take leadership roles, these women leaders are subjected to an even greater pressure to perform and lead in a masculine way because they are obligated to prove themselves to the patriarchal hierarchy. For most of us, we simply cannot imagine what a motherhood leadership looks like. In my personal sensing, I see that motherhood leadership is already powerfully rising and surging throughout the globe. Collectively, though, our culture struggles to see it because we haven't had a mature conceptual template for it. In this book, we will describe a new conceptual lens

to recognize motherhood leadership and the awareness pathways that consciously cultivate it.

To distinguish masculine and feminine energy, we can reference how differently these two energies express themselves sexually. Masculine energy emphasizes externalizing, projecting its energy outward in a sustained, linear effort that climaxes at a peak. Feminine energy emphasizes internalizing, attracting energy inward in a periodic cycle with multiple peaks and valleys. Masculine energy distinguishes itself in its intensity and explosiveness, feminine energy in its duration and wave-like, sustainable power. While for most of us, our physiology is embodied in one sexual polarity, our psyche and soul contain the potential for both polarities. This is the kernel teaching of the occult Taoist practice *Nei Dan*, Inner Cultivation, where both men and women practitioners train themselves to develop both poles of their psyche consciously, so that they can offer their body and soul as vehicles of the Tao, the interplay between the polarities. This bi-directional polarity model is also the key feature of the new framework for human development this book proposes.

Now that human evolution is no longer dependent on how many babies a family can produce, how do we raise the vibration of motherhood leadership, so we can consciously express it in other social endeavors? In the aftermath of our overly-masculinized creativity having exhausted our planet's natural resources and disrupted its ecosystems, how might we consciously bring the sustainable, long-lasting cycle of feminine energy to restore a generative equilibrium?

A female's womb is the biological embodiment of feminine creativity. A womb is an internal, empty space, providing the necessary materials and conditions for gestation, pregnancy, and birthing to happen. A womb goes through the process of building up and tearing down every month — the menstrual cycle. This constant cycle of construction, deconstruction and the bleeding associated with the deconstruction are all necessary to the renewal of fertility.

Our intellectual mind is one of the most important faculties through which we collaborate in social enterprises. How do we develop a "womb" within the "body" of our intellectual mind? If we hold the intellectual mind as superior to other faculties, we cannot hold an empty space necessary for the development of a "womb." Opening and surrendering to the power of the unknown, the uncertainty, and the ambiguity, is a prerequisite to develop the feminine aspect of our intellectual faculty.

Since our self-identity and ego are associated with our intellectual concepts, developing an empty space in our intellect will affect these core identity constructs as well. When we build into our sense of self a "womb" that embraces the unknown, we become able to consciously experience the eternal cycles of fertility, periodically riding through cycles of constructing and deconstructing our self-identity and ego. With this new awareness, we become free to engage with things we are now conditioned to feel ashamed of and avoid, such as failures, mistakes, and breakdowns, experiencing them freshly through the lens of this cyclic renewal. In doing so, we develop a much greater capacity to nurture, accept and care for ourselves.

Developing feminine energy in our intellectual mind does not mean suppressing or neglecting the masculine aspect. Instead, it actually enhances and empowers the masculine energy to reach for a much higher ground of knowledge than is currently possible to imagine from where we are now. At the leading frontier of science, researchers are now integrating knowledge from quantum physics, biology, and cosmology, piercing a layer of reality that challenges all of our basic assumptions of life, time, and physical space. The newest research suggests that those reality-bending observations made in the quantum realm, such as quantum entanglement, nonlocality and future-influences-past-events may exist in the macroscopic scale as well. Many leading-edge scientists have transcended the reductionist, materialistic view of life and started to postulate physics models to explain the subtle energy of life. For example, Mae-Wan Ho, a Hong-Kongese woman physicist postulated a new definition of life that speaks about Resonance in the language of physics, *"The organism is, in the ideal, a quantum superposition of coherent activities over all space-times, constituting a pure coherent state towards which the system tends to return on being perturbed."*

What is most important for this time in which we live is to develop new social structures where men and women come together to co-create through our minds and souls, synchronize our body-mind-soul ecosystems, and prepare for the evolutionary leap that is calling humanity. Through millennia of human cultures, there have been massive amounts of shame, taboo, and inhibition associated with sexual energies. We need to transform them so we can re-embrace our most powerful, enlivened, and charged creative life force.

The evolutionary threshold, quickening through climate change and the Anthropocene Age, is inviting humanity to reconnect the motherhood and fatherhood leadership of humanity at higher octaves of expressions, making new music in ways we cannot even imagine right now. This book is a harbinger of this new phase of human evolution that is about to unfold.

Story Six: A Message Delivered by the Arrival of a Child

My dear reader, thank you for reviewing this journey with me. I hope my stories may spark you to visit your inner Earth and all its remote, wild, and beautiful places, or to travel to the drilling site of your own ancestral heritage so that you may discover the inner resources to fund your most daring vision. Or perhaps you have contemplated how the threads of motherhood and fatherhood have woven through your own life.

Twenty-three years ago, I travelled from China to the United States and studied how Earth has recorded its biological evolution into DNA material stored in cells. Now I have begun a new cycle of learning. The Resonance Code is the "DNA" material I have extracted from my life-long experiment with my cultural heritage, both its past glory and current chaotic dissonance. The research we are doing at our Resonance Lab suggests that The Resonance Code may be engaged as a DNA code to assist our conscious evolution.

I am filled with gratitude to my second homeland, the Pacific Northwest, where my journey has been supported by the fertile soil of land and the loving spirits of the people on this land, with their rich history and culture. Before you begin to read the main body of The Resonance Code, I will share with you this last story.

My choice of expressing my reproductive instincts at a higher octave has been a gradual, volatile process, coming in and out of focus depending on the weather of the partnership I was in. After the relationship between Joe and I had matured, the intention of this choice became more and more clear. Right around that time, my cousin and his wife, with whom Joe and I share a communal house, discovered that they were pregnant.

I will never forget the moment when I learned about this pregnancy. I was working as an interpreter and cultural consultant for six Chinese families in an international Non-Violent Communication family camp. It was the first time I worked closely with children and parents where the conscious development of both generations was the center of attention. The children I was working with in that camp showered me in their fresh, enlivened life energy, filling my heart with a joy that I had never experienced before.

It was Joe who phoned me and told me about the news of the pregnancy. The awareness of this new life coming into Earth and into my own house brought a powerful surge of ecstasy washing through every cell of my body, bathing me with the sweet nectar of cosmic creativity. It was at that moment I fully understood and accepted the privilege of being in a woman's body, this incredible somatic experience of being a full participant in creation. And, simultaneously I more than ever saw clearly that my soul chose to let go of this privilege and pleasure. Instead it chose a path of uncertainty and ambiguity. I felt the shattering pain of giving up the most precious part of myself, knowing that my soul had committed to a different creative process where I will blaze my own trail every step of the way.

I was knocked to the ground by experiencing both the ecstasy and pain simultaneously. I wept out of both joy and sorrow. I knelt in front of my destiny and surrendered. In that surrendering, my sense of self dissolved and I felt my body expanding across time. I was immersed in the ocean of experience of my mother, my grandmothers, and all my feminine ancestral lineage, the infinite ocean of their joy and sorrow, the giant waves of hope and loss, the swirling currents of love and grief. And I heard a choir in a gentle and longing voice, rising like a cool breeze blowing from the shore. This choir is joined by the voices of my father, grandfathers, and the masculine lineage, whose arms link together as towering mountains embracing the ocean. In the midst of this choir, I heard a message in the voice of children coming from the far distant future.

"We, the future of humanity, are coming into Earth. We come with power that you cannot imagine. As you turn your awareness to your inner Earth, you will learn to listen to us. In that listening, you will open the pathway for our power to arrive. We need your support to materialize this power on Earth. We need your shoulders to stand on. Please, lay the ground for us, for the continuation of humanity."

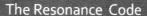

Chapter One

Awareness, Time, and Resonance

The subject matter of this book is the inner terrain of the psyche. By the psyche, I mean the space that holds all of our mental and emotional activities, imagination and intuition, instinctual and sensory experience, conscious and unconscious processes.

As you go through your day, your psyche constantly exchanges information between you and the outside world. The information may be on the behavioral and cognitive level, in the form of actions, thoughts, and spoken or written words. It may be on the sensory level, in the form of sight, sound, smell, taste, and touch. It might be on the psychological level, in the form of feelings, emotions, and instinctual impulses. Some of these activities and processes are conscious while a large portion are semi- or unconscious.

Awareness is wherever you direct your attention to either the conscious or unconscious activities within the scope of the psyche. It is the "vehicle" we drive to explore the terrain of the psyche.

What is going on inside our psyche is invisible. We make the contents of our psyche visible by projecting it through our language, behaviors and choices we make in our lives.

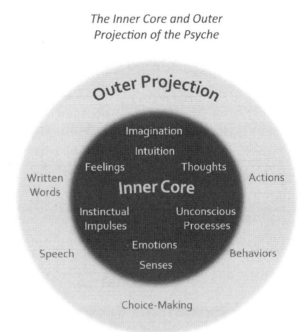

The Inner Core and Outer Projection of the Psyche

It is important to note that language is an important medium to transmit information cognitively. Yet, at any given moment, our known, existing language patterns can only cover a tiny sliver of the infinite world of the psyche.

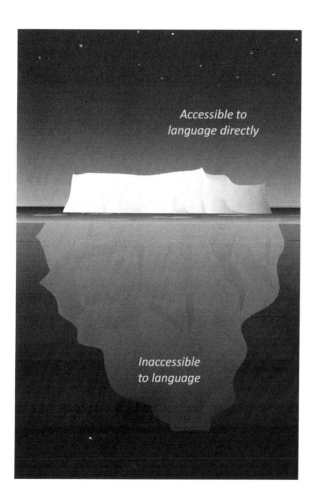

Accessible to language directly

Inaccessible to language

Language cannot convey the rich nuances of our sensory experience, such as the sight of full-colored foliage on a crisp New England autumn afternoon, or the taste of a sumptuous meal shared and prepared with a loving family. Our daily colloquial speaking pattern usually provides very low resolution about our feelings and emotional experience. Even in verbal communication, the majority of the information is conveyed through the tone of voice, facial expression and body language. Anyone who has traveled to a foreign country or tried to communicate with a foreign language speaker may have a direct experience of that.

However, we can deliberately use language to pave new roads into those remote corners of our internal landscape. I will share some examples throughout this book. I will also specifically present how to deliberately use our linguistic faculty as a tool to dive deep into a territory of awareness called *the feeling mind*, which usually does not receive the light of our attention. Accessing the feeling mind and focusing awareness on our sensory and emotional experience is essential to develop the kinds of skills presented throughout this book.

Since evolution is a process in relationship with time, our awareness of time is crucial in our navigation of evolution. Our psyche registers the flow of time as past, present, and future. For those of us who are actively engaged with modern civilization, most of the time we drive our vehicle of awareness on a well-built highway. The sign on one side of the highway points to the PAST; the other to the FUTURE. Yet, past and future are imaginary points at which no human can possibly arrive in their flesh-and-bone body. They are reference points held within our psyche between which we are having a constant experience of the present moment.

Most of the time on this highway, our experience of the present is either programmed by the conditioning of the past, or strategized toward a future predicted and planned through the analytical function of the rational mind. In either case, the present is static.

This highway is constructed of habitual patterns to direct our awareness. Humans have developed these patterns over tens of thousands of years as an evolutionary strategy. They have offered us the sense of safety and stability that set the stage for

civilization to evolve and accumulate knowledge about its evolution along the way.

The Future

The Unknown

The present is either programmed or controlled.

The Past

However, to only obey the program of the past or mold into a rigid, mental picture of the future blocks us from accessing the fullness of our human potential. Once in a while, we take an exit and step off from this "highway." We experience the *present*. Not the static present, but a *present* as an all-encompassing, timeless experience of all there is. This is the felt experience of wholeness. From this place, we see that the highway we are used to, the static present that is programmed or strategized, the knowledge we have created and accumulated, is actually wondrously cradled by a wide open field of the unknown. It is through roaming this timeless field of the unknown that

we can access the full power of our imagination, intuition, and divine inspiration.

Albert Einstein once said,

Imagination is more important than knowledge. Knowledge is limited. Imagination encircles the world.

In this book, I refer to the experience of the present as the *emerging present*. It is the womb through which human creativity and adaptivity take shape. It is the bigger context of our awareness that gives rise to the imaginary reference points of past and future.

During the process of human evolution, it used to be that only a handful of geniuses or the luckiest few had the chance to step into the emerging present and bring back ideas and inspirations to spawn the social or technological innovations of our civilization. However, many signs are telling us that we are about to cross a new evolutionary threshold, where more humans are being asked to step off from the highway of the static present and step into the field of the unknown to embrace the emerging present.

Spring's Evolutionary Narrative

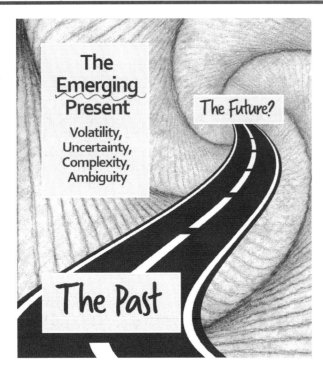

The Emerging Present

Volatility, Uncertainty, Complexity, Ambiguity

The Future?

The Past

The signs of this evolutionary threshold can be characterized as a term called VUCA, an acronym standing for Volatility, Uncertainty, Complexity, and Ambiguity. The VUCA we are facing today has two main sources. One source comes from human relations. More than ever in human history, cultures, ideologies, and belief systems are confronting, clashing, and influencing each other more frequently and transparently. The issues we are facing today are so complex and unpredictable that our experience of the present is less and less knowable and controllable. The second source comes from humanity's relationship with Earth's ecosystems. Our civilizations, heavily oriented toward growth and productivity, have depleted natural resources and disrupted the equilibrium between human life and Earth's ecosystems.

Even though VUCA brings out existential fear and frustration, it is entirely natural, and congruent with the evolutionary threshold we are facing. Modern culture has maximized individual choice-making and agency far more than any of our previous generations could even imagine. Simultaneously, it greatly strengthens the web of inter-connection through technology and commerce at larger and larger scales. The polarizing pressures to be more self-governing and more interconnected are exactly the conditions needed for us to evolve toward wholeness. As a result, more and more humans are being catapulted from the old highway of a static present into the wider field of the emerging present. Meanwhile, our human systems are becoming more alive, dynamic, and unpredictable than ever.

Leaders of large organizations and anyone who has devoted themselves to engaging with human relations at meaningful depths are facing challenges with unprecedented complexity. These challenges defy the conventional strategic approach based on linear, analytical methods. They often have many variable and inter-connected parts. It is nearly impossible to gather comprehensive and updated information about all these parts; categorize them neatly; and derive plans, formulas, or models to guide actions that all can agree with. Often by the time we do that, the situation has already evolved way beyond our models and plans. VUCA presses us to find new perceptual lenses and thought paradigms to perceive, observe and engage with these challenges.

These times are both terrifying and exhilarating. Terrifying in that everything that is familiar today can change tomorrow. Exhilarating in that we are now facing a new evolutionary threshold. If we can collectively navigate our VUCA environment, we will be poised to harness the colossal potential in the emerging present and experience unprecedented innovations brought forth by an explosive surge of imagination and creativity.

The work I present in this book suggests that we may begin to see VUCA as an invitation issued by Earth's evolutionary process to become whole. In becoming whole, we will gain the conscious choice to step off the conveyor belt of the static present and enter into the exhilarating field of the emerging present.

Evolution is asking us to learn how to embrace the unknown of the present, dance with the uncertainty and complexity, and improvise with the creative potentials emerging every moment with fluidity and resilience. It asks us to add these new reference points of playfulness, creativity, spontaneity, compassion, and authentic human connections into our inner compass.

Yet the old patterns of the static present are deeply ingrained in our psyche. Embracing the unknown means we have to brave our deepest fears and face our darkest inner demons. It also means that we need to reveal our most devastating wounds to ourselves so that we can heal them properly with the power of wholeness. Any of these tasks poses a daunting challenge to our psyche. How do we step off from the old awareness highway and explore the wider terrain? What are the new ways to organize our conscious activities that will enable this new adventure?

The knowledge and practices I present in this book synthesize information from a wide range of disciplines, providing a whole new schema to view and relate with the human psyche. I will introduce ways to train one's awareness to operate in this new schema of the psyche, so that we can collectively gracefully navigate through the complex terrain of evolution and embrace the gifts of the emerging present.

This book is written for the leaders who are taking a pulse of both the enormous uncertainty and the exciting opportunities of today's world. What we mean by leaders certainly includes those with defined leadership job titles and responsibilities. But we see leadership not just as an explicit role one takes on. We see leadership as a way of being, choice-making, and relating with the world that is not dependent on one's explicit role. Chances are if you allowed this book to find you, you are either already such a leader or preparing to become one.

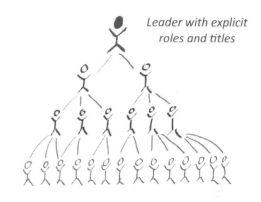

Leader with explicit roles and titles

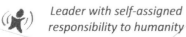
Leader with self-assigned responsibility to humanity

The materials in this book represent a combination of experiences working with leadership and executive coaches, organizational consultants, and other transformative change agents. We are also inspired by leaders showing up in all walks of life, such as mediators, therapists, healers, permaculture designers, community conveners, and teachers. Many of these leaders feel called to take on a large responsibility for the world because of a felt sense of compassion toward humanity. Through their intuitive sense, they are drawn toward a more whole and beautiful picture of humanity with which their hearts resonate. To them, the satisfaction of following the heart's and soul's calling is a more primary drive for action and choice-making than financial return or external recognition. These leaders are standing at the emerging edge of human evolution, exploring new frontiers of humanity. Our work offers tools and knowledge to serve these leaders.

Leaders on the emerging edge of evolution understand that the change we want to see outside has to happen first within ourselves. Our leadership needs to be grounded in a continuous, dedicated, transformational process of self. Then we can become effective instruments to influence other people and systems around us through our embodied examples and lived experience.

Around 450 BC, Confucius stated an idea similar to this kind of leadership:

DeGruding

To change the world, we must first change the nation; to change the nation, we must first change our family; to change our family, we must first cultivate our own selves; to cultivate our own selves, we must first set our hearts right.

This kind of leadership requires a type of perception that can perceive the subtle connections and mirroring between one's external environment and internal psyche. This leader sees his choices and behaviors in his private life and family relations as integral to the development of his leadership. With this perception, a leader may develop the agency to influence the outside environment through changing his internal psyche, and lead through continuously evolving himself toward a greater wholeness.

There is a reason why we have collectively chosen to insulate ourselves from the complexity of the emerging present. Improvising with the emerging present requires a kind of psycho-emotional, gymnastic finesse, coordinating emotional and mental faculties, balancing heart and mind, while tuning into the infinite amount of information available by expanding awareness beyond habitual thought and action.

However, human civilization has accumulated a wealth of knowledge and wisdom along its evolutionary journey. Our cultural heritages offer vast treasures. My work is sourced from the wisdom tradition of ancient China. The ancient Chinese perceived human consciousness as an integrated part of a continuous whole that encompassed both the internal, subjective experience and the external physical world. This kind of perception is in drastic contrast to our modern civilization, which primarily focuses on the physical and material aspects of life and treats our subjective experience as separate and inconsequential to the outside world.

Knowledge rooted in this kind of perception, such as Taoism and Chinese medicine, primarily

Traditional Chinese painting uses elements of the landscape as symbols to express internal, subjective feelings.

concerns how physical materiality and non-physical awareness synchronously vibrate and mutually resonate with each other.

This synchronous vibration between inner subjective experience and outer objective events is what I call Resonance in this book. In the physical world, resonance is a relationship between two systems in vibration. The simplest example occurs in music. When a guitarist plucks the strings, she activates a host of vibrational frequencies. The wood body of the instrument then starts to resonate with these frequencies, generating overtones. The timbre of the sound is dependent on the intrinsic natural frequencies carried by the instrument.

Let's translate this relationship between the string and the guitar body to an example in the human world. Imagine a group of riveted students sitting with a wise teacher. The teacher's words, embodied presence, passion, and vision are like the plucked string, sending out a complex set of vibrational frequencies. The students' hearts, minds, and somatic awareness are the body of the guitar, responding to the frequencies transmitted by the teacher's embodied words. As the natural frequencies in the student are being activated by the teaching, new insights and understanding are awakened in the student. Resonance happens.

As the students respond, their questions and insights generate new insights in the teacher. The Resonance amplifies itself into an abundant flow of learning in both the teacher and the students. This is the hallmark of Resonance: mutuality.

The phenomenon of Resonance is as ancient as humanity. In the earlier part of human history, an individual's livelihood, sense of self, and even sense of their body was intimately embedded within their family and tribe. This primal Resonance, a felt sense of connection between one person and their collective group, was as instinctive as the schooling of fish and the flocking of birds. At the same time, the resonant connection in traditional societies was largely invisible to the conscious mind.

I grew up in China when this felt sense of Resonance was still intact in the culture. Chinese refer to the experience of Resonance as qi (or chi).* The traditional healing arts such as acupuncture, and the Taoist somatic-spiritual cultivation practices qigong and tai chi intentionally cultivate qi and apply it to healing and self-cultivation. These traditional practices have been central pillars for most of my life.

All indigenous and native cultures around the world have shamanic traditions with Resonance as the basic ingredient. Yet connecting Resonance and the modern intellectual mind is a path seldom trodden. Without a rigorous inquiry process empowered by intellect, the practice and theory of Resonance must stay under the umbrella of a monocultural tradition and cosmology, unable to meet the challenges of today's global culture.

* *The word qi does not have a direct, corresponding translation in English, because it is not a concept in western culture. In English, the word qi is often interpreted as energy or vital force, which results from one's experience of Resonance. Yet equating Chi with energy obscures Resonance as the deeper source.*

Growing up in the midst of the tumultuous impact of the Cultural Revolution, I have also been personally affected by the most disruptive aspects of my own culture, such as the devaluing of individual freedom, critical thinking, and objective analysis. Through those experiences, I have recognized the limitation of Chinese traditional knowledge. Its deeply subjective and internal nature, without being matched and regenerated by an externally-oriented awareness, has imploded under its own weight. Its knowledge, without being translated into something relatable and digestible to the modern, rational mind, has lost its potency and relevance. Since I moved to the US, I have been learning and absorbing nutrients from Western thinkers and knowledge systems, experimenting with how to integrate these two halves of myself. Collaboration with my co-authors Joe and Joseph and the subsequent work with the Resonance Code Research Lab is the culmination of this effort.

With this book, I will be leading you on the trail that my team and I have built along a steep ridge that lies between the knowledge traditions of the East and West, the ancient and modern, embodied felt sense and intellectual mind. My heart tells me that to meet the challenge of today's world as a global culture, we need an integrated approach between these divides.

Working with Resonance in leadership could look like this: a leader develops her whole self as the instrument to resonate with the frequency of creative potential that wants to be realized in the present moment. This preparation is crucial in the same way as the preparation of a piece of raw wood being shaped into the body of a guitar.

As she translates the potential into ideas and visions, and models the potential with her presence and action, her qi becomes the embodied vehicle of that creative potential. This embodied qi elicits Resonance in the people and social systems around her. In turn, the leader opens herself to resonate with the responses that come back to her, allowing herself to be led. This mutual Resonance effect initiates a positive feedback loop to actualize the potentials of the present moment.

Cultivating Resonance will enable the kind of leadership needed for today's world. Leaders who have been trained to rely on expertise and rational analysis find those approaches insufficient to meet the most complex challenges. Leaders who have been trained to issue directives and manage through control often find those means ineffective, even counter-productive. Today's leaders need access to a deeper source of power.

This book introduces maps, models, and practices to help leaders develop skills to intentionally amplify Resonance.

The system presented in this book is called The Resonance Code. It is a knowledge system rebirthed from I Ching, also known as The Book of Change. I Ching is a seminal book in Chinese philosophy that provides the source of many branches of Chinese knowledge, from philosophy to medicine, from social ethics to military strategy, from the arts to mathematics. At its core is a pattern language coded with a six-digit, binary numerical system, called hexagrams, of which there are 64. History suggests the base of these codes originated as eight trigrams created 5,000 years ago by the legendary king Fu Xi.

In the west, I Ching is best known as an oracle system. Carl Jung, the Swiss psychologist, was fascinated with how I Ching seemed to reveal a kind of time-space connection that Western science has pierced only recently with quantum physics. He defines this time-space connection as synchronicity. "Synchronicity is the coming together of inner and outer events in a way that cannot be explained by cause and effect and that is meaningful to the observer."

When we develop a vision to see Resonance as the fundamental process of how things and events of the universe relate with each other, synchronicity becomes a phenomenon as natural as a violin singing under a violinist's bow. Through The Resonance Code, one may intentionally train one's perceptual lens and intellectual mind to perceive Resonance, thus tapping synchronicity as a resource.

Fu Xi with the eight trigrams.

Now we are ready to explore the structure of the psyche that supports its engagement with Resonance. Before that, though, I want to introduce you to the three different voices I have woven into this book. Each of these voices speaks to a distinct layer in the psyche.

The first voice is a story-telling one. You have met this voice in the Prelude and will meet it again later in the book when I recount people's stories of engaging with The Resonance Code. This voice invites you into the personal journeys that have given rise to this body of knowledge. Knowledge is a tree growing out of the soil of experience. I hope this voice may inspire you to find the richest "soil" inside yourself to plant this tree of knowledge.

The second voice is an architect's voice. It speaks through images, charts and geometrical shapes. This voice speaks to the part of your mind that perceives patterns beyond language and cultural barriers. These patterns represent archetypes that are universal to the process of life.

The third voice is a rational voice. It presents the conceptual framework and articulates the rational connections. This rational voice is an ardent servant and devoted lover of its counterpart, the trans-rational side of humanity. Its purpose is to build a stage on which the sensuous story-teller and the imaginative architect can co-create, learn, and play with one another.

When you read this book, I invite you to notice what each of these voices evokes in you and how you respond to them. Now let's begin.

Chapter Two

The Architecture of
the Psyche as a Resonator

Resonance is a phenomenon between two systems in vibration. To perceive and elicit Resonance, our psyche needs to function like a resonator that can amplify vibrational signals. Starting from this chapter, I will lead you through a process to construct an architecture of the psyche that supports its function as a resonator.

What I want to point out now is that currently the vibrational quality of the psyche is obscured, especially in the developed world, because the rational mind at our current evolutionary stage is dominated by linear, categorical thinking. Categorical thinking puts things into boxes and organizes the boxes into tree-like hierarchical structures. For example, biological evolution is often presented in this fashion. Incidentally, this is often how we construct and live inside a conventional organizational structure.

Categorical thinking is a crucial aspect of the development of our cognitive function. It greatly reduces life's otherwise overwhelmingly complex information into digestible bits for our mind to engage. It is a fundamental pillar of our civilization. Yet, with its strength comes a limitation.

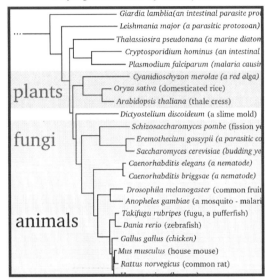

Phylogenetic tree of Eukaryotes

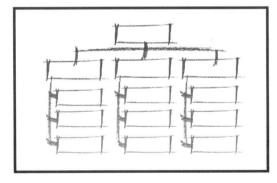

A Conventional Organizational Chart

The limitation of categorical thinking is that it obscures the inherent continuity and connection between the "thing" in one box and the "thing" in the next, leading to an overly reductionist and binary approach to challenges arising in complex systems.

Its limitation can be seen in today's socio-political scene where people tend to put themselves and each other into polarized boxes such as progressive versus conservative, or anti-X versus pro-X. Such labels are necessary to make clear distinctions that guide actions. Yet treating these labels as if they were reality blocks us from feeling into the humanity that connects us despite the labels. It fixes our attention to how wrong it is for anyone to choose a box different from ours. (Because surely the box we choose for ourselves is the only right one!)

When we stop seeing the humanity connecting us all, we lose important opportunities to influence the system as a whole: Resonance and synchronicity. To pass beyond the limitation of categorical thinking requires us to expand into vibrational awareness. This moves us beyond the incessant categorization and labeling into a multi-dimensional integration and synthesis of the ideas and concepts that are dividing humanity.

The relationship between vibrational awareness and categorical thinking can be illustrated through a guitar string. Let us examine how musical notes are generated on a single guitar string.

On a guitar, each string is tuned to a fundamental frequency. For example, the bottommost string is tuned to the note of E2 (82 Hz). When this string is plucked, it produces a sound at this predominant frequency.

An acoustic guitar usually has a fretboard with 19 frets. Frets are little sections that divide the string. When we pin the string down at a fret, we inhibit part of the string from vibrating. Now when we pluck the remaining string that is free to vibrate, we will produce a musical note at a frequency higher than the base note of E2. In fact, we can produce a whole scale of musical notes on the same string, just by incrementally inhibiting part of the string from vibrating.

If we are fixated on categorical thinking, our attention can be caught by the differences in the notes created by the fretboard. Yet as different as each note is to each other, it is the same string that is vibrating. Moreover, every note plucked on the string activates the natural frequencies inherent in the wood, eliciting resonance from the whole body of the guitar.

While categorical thinking directs our attention to distinctions and hierarchies, vibrational awareness directs our attention to how each part contains the template of the whole and how the whole can resonate with the vibration of just a part of itself.

In our social life, a fully developed vibrational awareness will see similarities and connections between polarized parties, even people who are enemies. In fact, people who are enemies are often similar in ways they themselves do not yet perceive. One of Tibetan Buddhism's teachings is to treat your enemy as your parents and children. This is not a behavioral or moral code. It is a direct observation made from a mind informed by vibrational awareness.

Good musicians need the categorical mind to make fine-tuned distinctions between different musical notes, and vibrational awareness to work with harmony and compose expressive, rich textures for their music.

As leaders, we need the strength and precision associated with categorical thinking. And we need the vibrational awareness to see the underlying connections between polarized parts, so we can amplify Resonance at the whole-system level to initiate change and cultivate collaboration.

Categorical thinking reduces the whole to its smallest constituents and analyzes those constituents. Vibrational awareness sees the pattern that repeats itself in parts and the whole.

Now we will begin constructing the architecture of the psyche as a resonator. This architecture has three planes — Dense, Middle, and Light — anchoring our relation with past, present and future respectively. The ability to direct one's awareness fluidly and proficiently along all three planes is the foundational skill to perceive Resonance and intentionally amplify it.

Dense Plane — Automated Circuitry

The Dense Plane contains the more ancient neurological faculties. They include primal instincts that concern our survival, death, and sexuality. The latter two are both transformative forces for regeneration. They also include sensory functions such as sight, hearing, taste, smell, and touch, along with a wide range of neurochemical and hormonal pathways that underlie our emotional responses. These faculties comprise the interface between our cognitive functions and our biological intelligence, evolution's intelligence automated in the body. Because the activities of these faculties on the Dense Plane are either automated or semi-automated, I also refer to them as the automated circuitry.

Automated circuitry is influenced by sensations and somatic memories of individual history. It is also influenced by ancestral experience possibly through the mechanism of epigenetics. It is the somatic interface through which we are connected with the collective unconscious, as our automated circuitry also carries the imprints of our cultural and linguistic programming.

A large portion of the automated circuitry is programmed during our early childhood by parents and cultural conditioning, before our own cognitive capacity develops. Automated circuitry is crucial in reducing the complexity of life into simpler patterns, and passing collective knowledge and experience across generations. Without this mechanism, we would be flooded with large quantities of raw, unorganized information. We would not be able to develop complex functions that build upon past experience. On the other hand, if we do not develop the capacity to re-program outdated automated circuitry, then we become the puppet to a puppet master.

For example, if a girl is brought up by parents who strongly discourage girls to display bold personalities, she will carry that somatic imprint as an automated circuitry before her cognitive mind develops. It may be an underlying feeling of powerlessness or insecurity. Even as she grows up and adopts a more feminist ideology, when she puts herself in situations that call forward her leadership, she will encounter those feelings. And she will experience the internal conflict between her automated circuitry and her intellectual belief. In another example, if as a young child someone is conditioned to associate intense moral judgment or fear toward people of color, that automatically programmed, somatic response of fear may still be retained in his body even when later on he intellectually adopts an egalitarian philosophy that views all races of people as equal.

To consciously transform our automated circuitry requires special awareness skills to engage with the Dense Plane. Simply denying it or trying to rationalize it away is largely ineffective or even counterproductive. Automated circuitry is the somatic foundation for higher cognitive functions such as the intellect and rational thinking to build upon. It is the soil, our inner Earth that requires our utmost care and respect.

Feelingwork is the primary tool that my co-author Joe Shirley has developed that enables this skill. At Resonance Path Institute, we use Feelingwork in conjunction with The Resonance Code in our coaching practice.

Light Plane — Pattern Perception and Soul Awareness

If we were to imagine that awareness occupies a spatial architecture, then the Dense Plane is the foundation and the Light Plane is the penthouse. Through the Light Plane we perceive archetypal and transpersonal patterns which are abstract and subtle. These patterns inform our beliefs, world views, and templates for life.

We naturally perceive subtle patterns all the time. When we listen to a piece of music, we quickly discern what genre it falls into. When we watch a movie, we get a sense of the artistic style of the director. When we walk into room full of strangers, we quickly scan the "vibe" of the space and find a conversation or a corner of the space that draws us. When we make associations between things with metaphors or similes, we are perceiving an energy or a quality shared between different things. We constantly read these patterns and respond to them through our daily activities.

It is when we apply this perception of subtle patterns onto our sense of self that we are in touch with the part of us that is larger and more expansive than our finite, physical existence, akin to what people refer to as soul. We call this perception the soul awareness. With soul awareness, our sense of self is not just confined within our physical boundary. We feel as if we can be simultaneously here and there. We also are not confined by the particular time window defined by our biological life span. We feel as if our sense of self may stretch beyond our short life.

The Light Plane allows us to be in touch with the possibilities of the future, including the unfulfilled longing or unresolved karma of past generations. These possibilities ignite our passion to actualize what we intuit as possible. This passion infuses us with a powerful sense of purpose and meaning.

Since soul is a concept important for our discussion of the Light Plane, I'd like to discuss several different approaches to soul awareness to illustrate perceptions and agencies focusing on the Light Plane. Throughout history, humanity has developed a wide range of approaches to soul awareness, from religion to spirituality, from mysticism to shamanic rituals, from mindfulness to psycho-somatic disciplines (such as yoga or tai chi), from artistic pursuits to philosophical inquiries. All of these approaches share a common

A Mandala depicting a model of the universe according to Tibetan Buddhism

Rainbow and the Worm. Ho's research describes a living organism as a quantum coherent system spanning all space-time. This means that each individual life is a field of many possible states, unbounded by its apparent physical coordinates and time stamp. The sharp boundary we perceive separating this body from that one, along with our perception of time as a linear, incremental procession, is only a function of many conditioned thought and perceptual lenses.

activity: perceiving, organizing and presenting complex, subtle patterns of how people, nature, objects, and events are inter-connected. Conventional science based on the Cartesian view of the physical world has long rejected ideas such as soul. This is changing. Currently, scientists at the frontier of quantum physics and biology are making new discoveries describing life as a quantum field that exists both here and there in space, and now and then throughout time.

Mae-Wan Ho, a Hong-Kongese scientist, explored the physics underlying living organisms, synthesizing knowledge from physics, biophysics, biochemistry and philosophy in her book, *The*

Because of the wide variety of pathways to soul awareness and many implicit assumptions associated with soul, I would like to make two key distinctions regarding what I mean by soul awareness. These distinctions are crucial to the work of The Resonance Code.

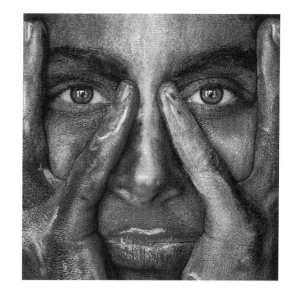

Soul Awareness as an Extension of Sensory Experience

First, in Resonance Work, soul awareness does not point to an immaterial realm located outside the reach of our earthly flesh. What I mean by soul awareness, rooted in the Taoist tradition, is a natural extension of the range of perception of our very own sensory apparatus.

Our sight, hearing, and kinesthetic senses are perceptual apparatuses that read and interpret different vibrational signals such as light, sound, or movement into physiological signals.* Each one of these sensory channels has "default settings" regulated by our neurophysiology. Through certain types of mindfulness practices, one can develop the capacity to modulate these default settings to sense into subtler domains of perception beyond the default.

Imagine having a neuronal system sensitive enough to perceive vibrations beyond the range of flesh and blood. The boundaries demarcating one body from the next, one object from the next, become washed over by waves upon waves of vibrations of different kinds. One starts to sense the entire universe as a giant musical instrument that vibrates. One's own self becomes a single molecule of the wood that vibrates with the whole instrument. The inter-connectedness with all living beings is not a concept or belief anymore, but a felt-sense experience. If that is the case,

---

*   The other two senses, taste and smell, are sensitive to chemical processes. The chemical interaction of molecules is governed by electromagnetic forces, another form of vibration.

Yes × just as we can extend awareness towards × into the light plane, we can extend awareness down × into our bodies × thru them the Earth.

the heavenly bliss we are looking for is held right within the innermost petal of our own body!

Soul Awareness and Morality

Second, an implicit cultural association links the word soul with the function of upholding a high moral standard. Under that assumption, by conforming our behavior and actions to a moral code we develop a noble soul.

No doubt being in touch with our soul awareness will bring out the loftiest part of ourselves. However, it is important to note that humanity is at a profound moment of change where we are exploring what it means to be living in an increasingly inter-connected and diverse global culture. The morality we know today is mostly localized, shaped by rather homogeneous, culture-specific ethics, values, and ways of living. For example, the traditional Chinese culture has a moral code that places collective interest far above the individual's, whereas for the modern developed world, individual freedom and sovereignty has been given the utmost priority. Even within the same country, such as the US, the moralities of different ideological factions can be drastically different from each other.

Today's diverse and inter-connected world is pressing us to examine all the local moral codes we have inherited and learned. As leaders, we are challenged with the question: what kind of moral code shall we hold for ourselves and for the community we are serving in order to adapt to this fast-changing, ever-emerging, global world?

In the process of discovering and inventing The Resonance Code, I find myself having to "violate" many deeply-ingrained moral codes inherited from my culture. For example, I needed to put my individual drive and intention way above my family's. As a result, I have withstood tremendous moral pressure from my extended family network and peers from my native culture. At times it felt like a rupture of my soul.

It was through cultivating the sensory perception that sees my soul simply as a subtle pattern that resonates and responds with the changes in my outer environment that I was able to free my soul from the placenta of its old moral codes. And I now naturally find myself entering a bigger inquiry. How can I continue to steward my soul as I evolve as a global citizen, and what new moral codes are emerging to serve my soul's journey as a participant in global evolution?

PLAY

Ref to LT's description of the child learning

Where we most readily experience soul awareness is in the activity of spontaneous play, the most natural activity for every child. Play is the primordial and universal activity in which one engages with the archetypes of the universe in the most natural and sensorial way.

In spontaneous play, we experience an integration between our Light and Dense Planes.

When we are fully immersed in playing, we do not think about how to pay the bills, prove ourselves worthy, or win the competition. We totally surrender into the flow, the spontaneity and the intensity of the experience of playing. We are rewarded with a full-bodied sense of rapture, which is a sign that we are practicing soul awareness by being fully awake in our body through our sensory experience. Perhaps that is why Rudolf Steiner allegedly said, "We are fully human only while playing, and we play only when we are human in the truest sense of the word."

Each pathway leading to soul awareness provides unique perspectives and gifts. And each has its own limitations. The spiritual pathway comprehensively organizes societal functions, yet its power tends to be corrupted by misuse, intermediary interpretation, and directives. Art provides a heart-felt access. However, it is not yet possible to rely on the language of art as the predominant tool to coordinate social collaboration. Science provides methods and terminology that can be shared across cultural boundaries. Its rigorous inquiry process can reduce the likelihood of the corruption and misuse of power. However, the rational mind steeped in linear, categorical thinking can be overly rigid and disembodied. I believe a more wholesome approach to Light Plane soul awareness will come from an inter-disciplinary integration between all three: spirituality, art, and science.

The Resonance Code is a nascent attempt to meet this challenge. It presents a set of Light Plane maps that describe energetic patterns, the features of the terrain of the psyche. It also presents a navigational system to enable leaders to amplify Resonance in their leadership. The Light Plane maps and navigational system of The Resonance Code are integrated with the complete architecture of the psyche. Like a tree, in order to grow tall and reach more light, the roots need to reach deeper for nutrients in the Dense Plane.

We have established the upper and lower planes of this architecture. Notice that these two planes are polar opposites of each other. The Dense Plane is embodied, finite and vulnerable. The Light Plane is abstract, infinite and invulnerable. Without Dense Plane awareness, the soul becomes a disembodied, empty, dried-out shell, longing to be enlivened. Without soul awareness, the body will be weighed down by its monotonously deadening automation, starving for purpose. Life is the alchemical interplay held between these two poles. And we need a Middle Plane to stoke the fire of this alchemy.

Middle Plane

The Middle Plane primarily consists of our conscious activity based in language. It includes both our linear, categorical-thinking-based rational mind and our non-linear, empathy-based heart mind. The dominant modern culture boasts a powerful, linear rational mind, rapidly developed in the last 300 years. This rapid development has operated in a paradigm that separates human culture from the natural world. This paradigm interacts with nature as gross, material objects to be organized into categories.

The linear rational mind has greatly enabled modern civilization's capacity to use and control the physical resources of the natural world toward meeting our material-based needs. At the same time, it has contributed to an unbalanced and unhealthy materialistic approach to life, where everything, including our own body, as well as nature's body, has been reduced to materials. We are now living in the midst of the disastrous impact of this approach to our ecosystem.

Meanwhile, we have become conditioned to perceiving ourselves through the lens of our linear rational mind, with which we construct the ego as a conceptual model of ourselves. We construct our identity based on our professional skills, social relations, and status. We try to make sense of aspects of our personality by taking personality tests or typing our psychological profiles.

The conceptualization of self can be an invaluable tool that enables us to see in ourselves that which otherwise remains invisible. However, like all powerful tools, over-using the linear rational mind and over-categorizing the self is counter-productive, especially for us as leaders facing the complexity of today's world.

In an ideal situation, the mature linear rational mind, well integrated with the Dense and Light Planes, will mediate between the somatic automated circuitry and the soul awareness, between our somatically stored memories of the past and the possibilities stored in the quantum field of the future. It will lead us into the infinitely creative potentials of the emerging present.

The heart mind is another dimension of the Middle Plane. It is our heart's natural capacity to feel empathy with human experience, beyond the linear rational mind's judgments and categories. Biologically, our heart is like the director of a symphony, establishing rhythms for the biological processes of the body through pumping blood and sending electrical impulses. Psychologically, a mature heart mind is adept at regulating its opening and closing.

The heart mind is to the linear rational mind as our senses are to our body. The linear rational mind constantly makes a conceptual model of the reality we inhabit so we can make sense of it. Due to diverse cultural and social backgrounds as well as individual uniqueness, we each make our conceptual models from vastly different perspectives. With a heart mind, we can develop the "ear" to listen to other's conceptual models of reality that are different than ours, and find connectivities that integrate different perspectives. A mature heart mind also knows how to set healthy boundaries with others. Developing the heart mind is crucial in catalyzing and enabling collaborations required in today's culturally diverse environment.

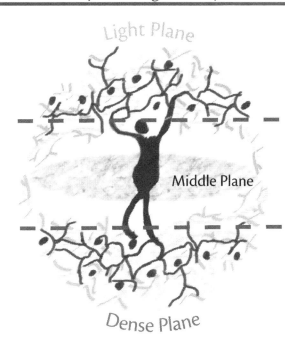

- Archetype or mythology
- Transpersonal connection
- Soul awareness
- Those elements that provide meaning, purpose

- Self-Identity
- Value of self measured through financial means
- Relation with the material world
- Social connections built upon self-identity

- Health and wellness
- Instinctual drive for life, death and regeneration
- Relations with family
- Ancestral origin
- Sensuality
- Sexuality

Now that we have established the three planes, I invite you to experience them in yourself by consciously directing your awareness to them, one at a time. With the following questions, you may reflect on your experience of self in the three domains. It may be helpful to journal or talk it out with a friend. You may identify parts of your experience that satisfy you and parts that don't. The parts of your experience that evoke a sense of longing, or carry a quality of tension indicate how you may choose to evolve toward more wholeness.

Dense Plane

How are you experiencing yourself in your body? Do you feel vital and enlivened, with a sense of well-being? Do you like your body? How are you fulfilling your sensory needs? Note that some aspects of our current culture can provide an overwhelmingly high dose of sensory stimulation. Yet large quantities of sensory stimulation cannot replace quality. One useful indicator for the quality of sensory experience we have is the touch we give to and receive from our fellow human (or non-human) beings. In the case of human touch, do you experience touch in its pure quality that conveys authentic connections, without being associated with sexual or other pragmatic implications? Do you experience that outside the context of your primary relationship? *

On the instinctual level, what is your relationship with your sexual drive? What is your relationship with death? Dense Plane awareness also points our attention to the "ancestral" body that we are part of. What is your relationship with your family lineage?

Middle Plane

How do you experience yourself through your social identity? Do you feel valued by others? Do you feel safe and confident about who you are? Are you fulfilled by sense of self? How is your relationship with the material world? Are you comfortable in working with the material world? Do you feel a sense of abundance or lack? How do you feel within the social and professional networks surrounding your identity?

Light Plane

If you could write a book or make a movie to tell the story of your life, what would the title of the book be? In this story, what kind of archetypal elements are at play? What mythology, legend, cultural icon, or folklore do you draw from? Is your story romantic, dramatic, or suspenseful? Is it contemplative with existential questions or light with comic flare? What is the theme of this book or movie? Does this story of your life infuse you with a sense of meaning and purpose?

Directing our awareness to these three planes expands our sense of self into three distinct domains. They are the three layers of self constructed by our psyche, each with its own distinct qualities, capable of mirroring, complementing, and regenerating each other. Having access to these three will enable you to see the dynamics and patterns formed by their relationship. Is there one layer of self that is more dominant than others? Is there a layer of self that is more absent in your awareness?

---

* In many traditional cultures, non-sexual touch (especially between members of the same sex) is an essential cohesive force that binds the collective experience. Our modern culture is becoming extremely touch-phobic to the point where non-sexual touch has become almost non-existent, one sign of the extent to which we have uprooted from our Dense Plane experience.

You may also experience the web of relations around you through these three planes. I invite you to draw out this web of relations as concentric rings.

Dense Plane

Here are your relations with people, places, and other living beings such as plants and animals with whom you share physical presence and somatic experience. In our formative years, this layer includes our birth family and the surroundings of our childhood. As an adult, it is your chosen family, intimate friends, neighbors and local communities. This layer of relations is the "soil" that supports our physical expression of life.

Middle Plane

Here are relations connected to your identity or professional interests. Your co-workers, bosses, subordinates, clients, customers, teachers, students, patrons, audience, (and don't forget, your competitors). This layer of the web also includes businesses, institutions, or any social organization that you either belong to or interact with in concrete ways. It also includes acquaintances and connections with whom you socialize in person.

Light Plane

Here are relations formed around your beliefs, purpose, interests, and whatever you see as meaningful in life. They might be impersonal and non-physical relations. They may include people with whom you share similar interests or hobbies. They may include public figures whose work has influenced you; celebrities or political figures who attract your attention, (in both positive and negative ways); and spiritual or cultural icons, (modern or historical), who influence your belief system, inspire purpose or meaning, and widen your perspectives of the world. This layer also includes various virtue communities that you interact with. Or it may include people with whom you share your intellectual, artistic or creative work.

Reflection

As you draw this web of relationships, what do you notice? Do the layers overlap or connect with each other? What does that tell you? Stand back and appreciate your web's uniqueness. No one else in the world shares this same web with you. It is your personal resource and asset. Some of the most valuable gifts are often hidden in the relations that have brought you the greatest challenge.

Now we have established the three planes as fundamental components of the architecture of the psyche. We will next explore how directing awareness to these three planes influences our actions, choices, and our very being.

I like to think of the relationship among the Light Plane, Dense Plane and Middle Plane as the relationship between the composer, instrument and performer.

The automated circuity on the Dense Plane is a precious instrument, a gift from Earth's billions of years of evolution. The infinite, expansive pattern which we might call soul is life's composer, containing a wellspring of possibilities waiting to be actualized. Our mind, both the linear rational and heart mind, is the performer that translates the composer's intention through her attunement and proficiency with

her instrument. The music of leadership on the evolutionary edge requires exquisite calibration, coordination, and attunement among all of these three planes.

In our modern culture, the ego self shaped by overuse of the linear, categorizing, rational mind is in a dangerously isolated, lonely, and misguided place. It is on one hand disembodied from the fertile soil of somatic awareness on the Dense Plane, and on the other hand cut off from the true possibility of a future sourced from soul awareness on the Light Plane. We need to recognize that the linear rational mind, which for most educated modern people is trained through the standard science-based educational system, has been developed in human civilization for a relatively short time compared to the much older faculties such as our sensory functions.

The ego self shaped by the linear rational mind is like a tender sprout that has just come out of the plastic container from a chamber of its greenhouse, ready to grow roots into a much deeper soil and learn to receive unfiltered natural light. Our culture is in a very vulnerable time of transition, hence the heightened sense of volatility, uncertainty, complexity, and ambiguity. This is the evolutionary challenge we are facing: reconnecting our linear rational mind, this tender shoot growing out of human evolution for the last 10,000 years, back into the whole system of the psyche. The architecture of the psyche presented here may help us meet this challenge.

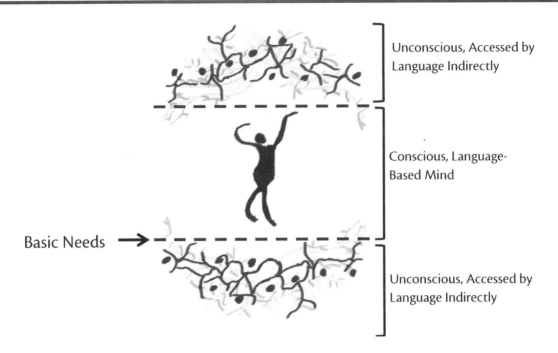

Unconscious, Accessed by Language Indirectly

Conscious, Language-Based Mind

Basic Needs →

Unconscious, Accessed by Language Indirectly

Since the majority of the intelligence locked in the Light and Dense Planes lies outside the access of language, the language-based Middle Plane mind has developed "interfaces" with its lower and upper planes. To reconnect the Middle Plane into the ecosystem, we need to develop more sensitive and robust interfaces. Now let us examine what these new interfaces are.

When some aspect of the automated circuitry on the Dense Plane needs to be programmed or rewired to connect with upper planes, usually it registers in our awareness as basic, unmet needs. These needs may include a fundamental sense of safety or belonging. They are often unconscious, and show up first as felt sensations of emotional pain. This pain points to a deeper source of primal life energy that wants to be refined and integrated with higher cognitive functions. It is the "fossil fuel" from biological evolution that can be harnessed as a source of creativity. A healthy and generative response to the pain is to open our sensory faculty to fully experience the sensations of pain while retaining a neutral and curious mental attitude. This way, one can let the richness of the somatic sensations seep through the vast "roots" of the Dense Plane and integrate with the higher levels of cognitive awareness.

However, our current culture usually does not adequately prepare us for this kind of skill. On the contrary, our culture conditions us NOT to feel the pain. It conditions us to find a quick fix for the pain and toughen up. As life energy surges up from below, and we respond by shutting it down from above, this conflict turns into reactivity.

Reactivity has two components. The first is a repetitive life pattern that presents us with similar challenges again and again. Examples may include falling into the same type of relational dysfunction, being stuck in a group where you feel left out or undervalued, or having a series of overly critical bosses. The other component is an emotional response disproportional to the outer form of these patterns, and reactive behaviors triggered by the emotions.

The repetitive pattern is a signal that the latent "raw energy" wants to be released from the Dense Plane. When we have not developed the capacity to harness it into creativity, we can be trapped by reactive behaviors such as defensiveness, blaming, victimizing, or cutting off from the people or situation. We stop being curious, open and vulnerable and become hardened to defend what we mentally see as right or wrong.

Cognitive and behavioral approaches that focus on gaining greater control over one's thought and behavioral patterns cannot address reactivity adequately. For example, if a person is trapped in a habitual lack of confidence triggered by a re-occurring professional challenge, she may use language and behavioral suggestions to reinforce her identity toward becoming more confident, strong, and competent. However, if she does not go "under the hood" into the interior somatic experience of the emotional reactions, the cognitive and behavioral approaches alone can only be a temporary fix.

Because it depends primarily on the logic and framework of the Middle Plane , focusing on cognitive thought and behavioral patterns alone does not effectively address the deeper cause of the reactivity. It cannot go under the hood

into the Dense Plane. As a result, the reactivity keeps popping up in more tenacious ways. One continues to crash into the shadow. Self-transformation feels like a never-ending chore. This is because the linear rational mind cannot control and dominate the primal life energies surging from the Dense Plane. Instead, with the knowledge of the three planes of the psyche as an ecosystem, we can develop a more robust and intelligent interface between the Middle and Dense Planes.

Imagine what a tree experiences as it grows. It needs to simultaneously reach up for more light and reach down into the soil to grow a deeper and wider root system. How much it grows upward depends on how deeply it is willing to reach down! To engage with the "raw energy" from our Dense Plane creatively, we need to consciously feel and absorb the energy, and build "pathways" to pass that energy to higher cognitive functions. We need to develop a conscious agency to harness the creative potential while keeping ourselves vulnerable and open. There are many psycho-somatic modalities that may help construct this interface. In our work, we primarily use Feelingwork for this purpose.

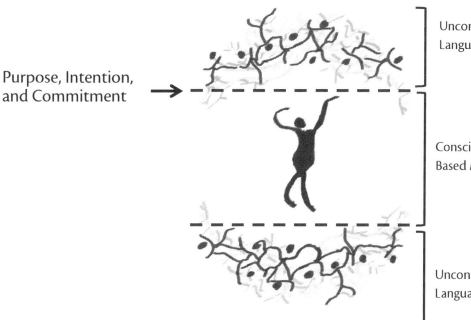

Purpose, Intention, and Commitment →

Unconscious, Accessed by Language Indirectly

Conscious, Language-Based Mind

Unconscious, Accessed by Language Indirectly

Let us turn our attention in the other direction. Pattern perception or soul awareness in the Light Plane pulls us through a longing for a future possibility different from our current experience. This longing is foremost an embodied experience before it is translated into words by the cognitive mind. As our Middle Plane mind translates this longing, we commonly refer to it as purpose, intention or commitment. These form the interface between the Middle and Light Planes.

These thoughts about the future are composed by linguistic elements and motifs shaped by our experience and knowledge of the past. For example, if someone lives their whole life on land and has never heard or seen any information about the ocean, an unconscious longing for the ocean will be constrained to linguistic elements and motifs of their land life. If someone is struggling with a lack of self-confidence, her cognitive picture of what it will look like when she becomes confident is limited by the thought and behavior patterns within her known domain. If she becomes too attached to those mental pictures, they can block her from accessing the greater sources of creativity hidden in the unknown parts of her Dense and Light Planes. The attachment masks these unknown parts with habitual thought patterns associated with the known domain.

For example, in the story I told in the prelude, my idea of reconnecting with the Taoist heritage of my culture was once limited to running a successful acupuncture clinic. At that time, nowhere in my cognitive mind could I conjure up the necessary elements that eventually emerged and enabled my work that has led to this book. Yet step by step, I sensed a different purpose spoken through patterns in the events around me and messages delivered by people in my life. Eventually my acupuncture clinic transcended its literal existence and became an archetypal symbol for the type of leadership I offer through this work.

The choice of running an acupuncture clinic, by itself, is a great one. Today whenever I visit the clinics of my acupuncturist colleagues, a beautiful sense of warmth and nostalgia arises to nourish me. However, it was just not the right choice for my soul, as my soul harbors an all-consuming desire to regenerate the Taoist knowledge tradition and explore what will happen if I marry the Western and Eastern intellectual systems through my work. A soul's desire connects us to the same frequencies of intentions in the collective psyche. It was when I said "yes" to my soul's desire that I activated a chain of synchronous events which have continued to bring me to the right opportunities, right challenges, right allies and resources.

Without purpose, intention, and commitment, one cannot organize actions and engagement effectively. Yet without being sufficiently grounded into the felt sense of longing, one runs the risk of mistaking thoughts about the future as the future itself. Only by actively experimenting with possibilities and improvising with the present can we create a future that is connected with our sensory experience. Without experimentation and improvisation, we may create a future that is trapped by the gravity of the past.

Many speculations about artificial intelligence (AI) are pointing to a future trapped by the gravity of the past. Artificial intelligence is an externalization of our own thinking process. It is rooted in a mechanistic, objectified, and materialistic understanding of humanity. It has not even begun to scratch the surface of the biological intelligence and soul awareness we have on the Dense and Light Planes. As computer scientist Donald Knuth puts it, "AI has by now succeeded in doing essentially everything that requires 'thinking' but has failed to do most of what people and animals do without thinking."

What people and animals do without thinking arises from modes of intelligence on the Dense and Light Planes. The fear and anxiety toward being replaced and out-competed by AI indicates that we collectively as a species are trapped by our own past. With these fears, we lose perspective on humanity's capacity to create a sustainable future. These technologies lead to an exciting aspect of the future, with immense potential for its own sake. Understanding and owning our Dense and Light Planes will open up unpredictable potentials to engage with technologies more consciously and wisely so that AI can complement human activity instead of replacing it.

As you can see, the linear rational mind has built a trap for itself by insisting on knowing everything and remaining in total control all the time. This insistence translates into ineffective interfaces with both the Dense Plane and the Light Plane.

This insistence played a positive role when the linear rational mind was the new player on the stage of evolution. Like any new agency in its nascent stage, the linear rational mind was vulnerable and insecure. It needed to affirm itself in order to sustain the momentum to develop. Throughout the history of modern science, the linear rational mind had to affirm itself by claiming itself to be the conqueror of the unknown.

Today it has reached a mature stage where the need to affirm itself is no longer intense, and it is wise enough to see the greater unknown. Modern physics has discovered that 95% of the energy and matter composing our physical universe is "dark energy" and "dark matter" that physicists cannot yet fit into their existing models of the universe.

In parallel, the field of psychology is also opening up to the idea that much more of who we are and what drives us lies outside the domain of cognitive thought and behavior, and is not included in our social identity and visible personality.

As we are now re-planting the linear rational mind back into the soil of our somatic experience so that it can receive the light from the Light Plane, we will re-open ourselves to embrace the unknown. Not just that portion of existence which we don't know, but that which we don't even know that we don't know!

The portion of the physical universe explainable by modern physics ~ 5%

Dark matter and energy, stuff we don't know ~ 95%

In this chapter, I have reviewed how our dominant culture and leadership has been primarily shaped by categorical thinking. The linear rational mind is a master organizer, labeling, sorting, and categorizing our experience of the natural world into the giant structures of scientific knowledge we have today. This is an amazing achievement. This knowledge has provided the infrastructure to support our modern way of living. And it is on the verge of giving birth to a new kind of intelligence on Earth, artificial general intelligence, or artificial super intelligence.*

As humanity is facing a new evolutionary threshold manifested in the many challenges displaying the qualities of volatility, uncertainty, complexity, and ambiguity, our rational mind needs to evolve beyond the master organizer. Here I propose that our rational mind needs to upgrade its interfaces with both the automated circuitry in the Dense Plane and the soul awareness on the Light Plane. With the upgraded interfaces, the rational mind can respond to the vibrational exchange that naturally happens between our Dense and Light Planes with more conscious and informed choices.

———

As a critical mass of people cultivate and work with the vibrational nature of their psyches, it is possible their cognitive minds will evolve beyond their current state and start to function like wireless devices that receive and transmit information directly with the collective psyche. This group of people could choose to consciously co-create conditions to maximize synchronous events, using their capacity as a new collective agency to organize social collaborations.

In the next chapter, I will present the two polar forces that enable the psyche to vibrate and function like a resonator. Before we finish this chapter, please explore how the three planes of awareness anchor your sense of past, present and future through the third exercise.

---

* The kind of AI devices we use in daily life such as Siri or self-driving cars are considered to be artificial narrow intelligence (ANI), or weak AI. They are designed to perform a single type of task, and their intelligence is quite low compared to the human brain. Artificial general intelligence and super-intelligence are the next stage of AI, where the AI will be able to perform any intellectual tasks that a human being can, with faster speed and stronger capacity and precision. Yet I'd like to point out that our capacities to feel, embody, and transmit Resonance, as well as to tap into synchronicity, have never been attempted by any existing or planned AI technology.

I invite you to experience how the three planes of awareness anchor your sense of past, present and future in a specific situation.

Every situation we experience is composed of elements and dynamics from these three planes. I invite you to focus your attention on an area of life where you feel the need for expansion, growth, or transformation. This may be where you feel some tension, blockage or simply a desire for thriving.

Next I invite you to bring your awareness into how these three planes operate by responding to the inquires outlined here.

Future

What wants/desires to happen? Can you hold it as an embodied sense of longing before translating it into words? When you translate it into words, what purpose, intention, or commitment come through? Do you hold the intention/commitment as an experiment with which you can engage through actions and further your learning? Or, do you hold it as a goal that <u>has to</u> be fulfilled as you imagine it now?

Present

What are you doing and not doing that fulfills your intention or commitment successfully? What are you doing and not doing that prevents you from fulfilling your intention and commitment? If you found incongruence in your actions, it is good news! You have located a pathway into an untapped potential.

We will follow this pathway and go down into the Dense Plane. Observing the parts of yourself that exhibit incongruence with our stated intention usually leads us to our reactive emotions. To explore this, ask yourself: If this intention/commitment never gets fulfilled, how would I feel? In what circumstance did this feeling first arise in my life? What needs were not met in that situation? Am I judging or criticizing myself for this incongruence? Nine out of ten times the most dominant reactive pattern we all carry is this judging and critical attitude toward our own vulnerability. Write down what you feel as you observe yourself judging yourself.

Future

Emerging
Present

Past

Past

Unconscious, unmet needs usually register as uncomfortable feelings such as a fear of failure, an insecurity about one's inherent self-worth, or pain from a loss. These reactive feeling states point to automated circuitry that needs to be updated and rewired to become the instrument for new possibilities sourced from the Light Plane.

Once you identify the feeling state associated with the reactivity, then you may begin to use Feelingwork to shift the automated circuitry from its reactive state to its more updated state. The experience is like riding an "elevator" located the bottom of the Dense Plane and rising into a higher realm that you may not have imagined before.

Note: These ideas may seem vague and abstract. I will illustrate how this works in Chap 6 that introduces Feelingwork. If you are interested, you may also jump there to read it first. For now, note that these reactive feeling states, as particular to us as individuals as they seem, are also our personal portal into the collective experience of the past. We inherit them from our parents and the social environment in which we develop. When we are doing this work, we are not just doing it within the private domain of our own psyche. We are connecting ourselves to the momentum, forces, and charges inherent in the collective psyche.

Chapter Three

The Tao of Wholeness:
Cyclic Flows of Yin and Yang

The Resonance Code is born of the marriage between Taoism and Western intellectual inquiry, its maternal and paternal sources. Like many other indigenous traditions, Taoism is an earth-based cosmology. It assumes that the psychic space that contains consciousness and the physical space that contains the natural world share a similar architectural design. Thus, all things we see "out there" — the sky, a tree by a river, a friend or an enemy, or even devices we have invented such as phones or TVs — reflect the structures and dynamics "in here," inside the psyche.

Learning from nature, the ancient Taoists perceived two complementary impulses in the psyche, called yin and yang. The polar tension and interplay between these two impulses drives the cyclic process of creating, destroying and re-creating. This cyclic process is called the Tao. To live in accordance with the Tao, a person would pay attention to the rhythms of the cycle, and the ebb and flow between yin and yang impulses. This involves coordinating one's actions and choices, like a tree balancing between growing up to reach the sunlight and growing down to absorb nutrients from the soil. Under this guiding

principle, Chinese medicine treats the human body by balancing and regulating the yin and yang of physiological processes.

The Resonance Code sees the psyche as a vibratory system oscillating between complementary impulses travelling up and down across the three planes of the psyche. These impulses are called the Enlightening (Yang) and Enlivening (Yin) pathways.

Abstract Knowledge
Symbolic Information

Embodied Experience
Somatic Information

The Enlightening pathway is the psyche's impulse to extract embodied, concrete, and lived experience into abstract and symbolic information/knowledge. It asks this question:

How do we externalize the instinctual and sensorial aspects of the psyche into knowledge and information to guide our actions and choices?

The Enlivening pathway is the psyche's impulse to enfold symbolic information and abstract knowledge into embodied, concrete, and lived experience.* It asks this question:

How do we embody symbolic information and abstract knowledge so that it may inform and influence the material (Middle) or somatic (Dense) experience?

---

* In learning theory, the Four Stages of Competence model describes the stages of learning as unconsciously incompetent, consciously incompetent, consciously competent and unconsciously competent. Enlivening brings us to a stage closely related to unconscious competence in which a skill has been mastered to the extent it can be performed without conscious thought. (However, the Four Stages of learning were presented in a linear fashion, which is fundamentally different than what is presented here.)

Imagine our psyche as an ecosystem. When being cared for properly, this ecosystem expresses wholeness that sustains an abundant flow of conscious awareness, creativity, and productivity. In its state of wholeness, it has vitality and resilience to respond creatively to challenges in its environment.

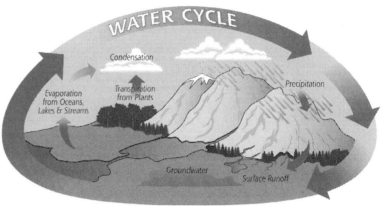

The ecosystem of nature maintains its sustainability and vitality through circulation. Basic elements essential for life processes such as water, oxygen, nitrogen, and carbon are cycled through soil, water, land, and air. They are consumed by plants and animals, and revitalized through oceans, forests, and diverse ecological systems. If we model our psyche after the natural ecosystem, how does our consciousness, either on the individual or the collective level, get circulated through the architecture of the psyche?

The circulatory flows of wholeness are schematically represented in the graph on the next page. The currents are held between two resource poles. The Dense Pole is the intelligence of biological evolution, connected to our psyche through the Dense Plane. The Light Pole, connected through the Light Plane, holds our capacity to imagine, intuit, and feel compassion for our fellow sentient beings, human or non-human. When the architecture of the psyche expresses wholeness, the impulses to enlighten and enliven form an ebb and flow between the Dense and Light Poles, circulating on all three planes like a double helix.

This double helix forms the inner core of the psyche, representing the terrain over which our conscious awareness travels. This terrain encompasses the three planes we reviewed in the last chapter. If you follow the Yang-Enlightening impulse, indicated as light blue, all the way to the top of the helix, you will see that this

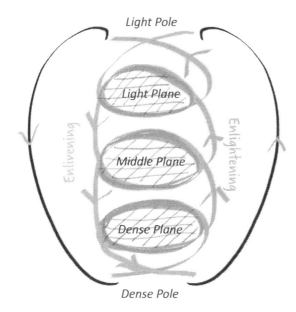

Light Pole

Light Plane

Enlivening

Enlightening

Middle Plane

Dense Plane

Dense Pole

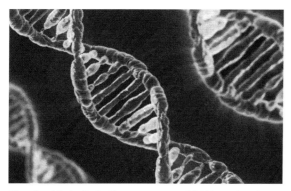

The double helix is the structure of DNA molecules, which contain the genetic information guiding our biological evolution.

Yang-Enlightening current connects with an outer downward flow. Likewise, if you follow the Yin-Enlivening impulse, the yellow line, all the way to the bottom of the helix, this Yin-Enlivening current connects with an outer upward flow. Why does the Yin-Yang flow reverse directions at the poles? And what do these outer currents represent?

This reversal reflects the cardinal principle of Taoism that yin and yang mutually transform into each other when they reach their respective peak expressions. This principle is expressed in the Taiji symbol. When the black and white flows reach their respective maximums, they give rise to their opposites, depicted as the black dot within  the white and white dot within the black. Guided by this principle, Taoists engage polarity through creating the conditions for each pole to reach peak expression, transforming into and fueling the regeneration of its opposite.

This yin-yang reversal connects conscious awareness, represented by the helical inner core of the torus, with the larger environment, indicated by the outer currents. The outer currents are the interface between conscious awareness and the surrounding environment. With the currents of wholeness, when we turn our awareness toward the environment, we perceive the Yin/Yang flowing not only in ourselves, but also in the environment around us. This perception is not a mental construct or doctrine. Instead it is a somatically felt experience, registered through our senses. The Taoists called this felt sensation qi, (also translated as chi).

With the sensation of qi, the ancient Taoists perceived yin and yang not only as fundamental impulses that sustain the vitality and ongoing evolution of the human body and psyche, but also as flows of similar nature sustaining the vitality and ongoing evolution of nature. Thus, human life is inseparable from the larger life of Earth, connected by the sensation of qi.

The perception of the Enlightening pathway in our environment has a huge implication. This means that the psyche, in its state of wholeness, perceives the natural environment expressing itself and demonstrating its evolutionary changes through observable symbols. In other words, nature is perceived as a larger, animated being with its own agency and will. This world view was shared by almost all earlier forms of human civilization all around the world.

Qigong, "the practice of qi," is an ancient Taoist psycho-somatic practice that strengthens the cyclic flows between one's body and the larger body of the natural and social environment. Today it has become popular worldwide. Tai chi is a more elaborate form of qigong.

Similarly, when the psyche, in its state of wholeness, turns awareness toward its social environment, it naturally perceives the larger social body such as the family, tribe, or country as a larger living being with its own agency and will. A leader who cultivates a larger and more intact sphere of her awareness naturally develops a larger and more robust surface area with her social environment. Her expanded awareness alone creates a wider scope of influence.

Disruption of Wholeness

As human civilizations have developed, this felt-sense perception of our environment as a larger life has gone obsolete, especially with the rise of rationalistic thinking along with scientific and technological enterprises. In the last three hundred years, modern civilization has primarily related with nature as a collection of material objects and resources to be taken and used. Seldom do we modern humans have the felt-sense, direct experience of nature as an animated being with whom we can communicate and consult personally. Even environmentalists seldom do that.

At the same time, we also relate with elements of our social environment as objects, machines actually. We see social systems as complex aggregates of conceptual categories our mind has constructed. We seldom experience our neighborhood, town, city, workplace or country as a larger being with which we can communicate in direct, intimate ways.

Humans today are living under the looming shadow of the global scale of environmental crisis, culminating as climate change. Climate, in Chinese, translates as the pattern of qi. Literally, climate change implies the disruption of the global pattern of qi.

The disruption of the global qi reflects the degree to which the wholeness of our collective psyche has been disrupted. Over the course of human history, we have constructed localized cultures with their norms, conventions and infra-structures to adapt to this fractured vision. Within it, each one of us builds life structures including identities, relationships, and careers to fit in. Each collective group forms around their partial interests and localized ideologies and beliefs. As modern communication and technology are weaving an all-encompassing, global web, these localized cultures have begun to violently crash into each other.

The world we live in today is replete with clashes: men versus women, indigenous versus modern, environmentalist versus corporate, political left versus right, global North versus South, conservative versus liberal, black versus white, immigrant versus native, scientific versus religious fundamentalist ... The list goes on and on. All of these contribute to the disruption of the global qi.

Re-weaving Wholeness

How do we re-weave wholeness? And more importantly, how do we relate to the disruption of wholeness? As a result of disruption, there is so much trauma, pain, and grief stored in the collective psyche. How do we metabolize them? And how do we re-establish channels to communicate with the larger beings of nature as well as our collective social body? What language do these larger beings speak? How do we translate their language into human languages? These are the central questions that have propelled the research and experimentation that my team and I have been conducting at Resonance Path Institute.

What I present here are not universal answers to these questions. These questions have to be answered by each individual for themselves. What I present is a new thought paradigm and methodology that will equip you for that task. And I will share with you what I have discovered as answers for myself. While qigong and tai chi are somatic exercises that strengthen the flow of qi in the body, centered around the Dense and Light Planes, the thought paradigm and methodology presented here is a "qigong" in the thought realm, centered around the Middle and Light Planes.

When I was a young girl, China had just begun the process of modernization. The Chinese people were caught in violent swirls of abandoning and even condemning the old traditions. All the old knowledge regarding qi was labeled as "toxic grass" and shunned with extreme fear and shame. Chinese medicine, whose practices are founded on the concept of qi, was regarded as a large "toxic grass". My paternal grandfather was a village Chinese medicine doctor. In a fit of fear about being condemned, his son, my uncle, threw all my grandfather's medical books, herbs and tools into a fire.

Qigong became a fringe practice, which made it vulnerable to the infestation of charlatans. This pushed true qigong practitioners underground, further and further away from public attention. Yet qi always finds a way to flow despite human attempts to block it. Even though my parents were among the first wave of scientists of the new China, my dad, probably influenced by his father, retained a strong interest in qigong. Intellectually, he could not fit qi into his pure rational and objective world view. But that did not stop him from taking me to learn qigong when I was 13.

I was a very sickly girl growing up. An extremely sensitive immune system put me in the hospital almost every month for an assortment of ailments. Learning qigong completely changed my physical constitution. The experience of self-healing was extremely empowering for me as a young girl. Even more importantly, having the experience of a current circulating through my body and the cosmos around me profoundly influenced how my mind works.

Following my parents' track, I dived deep into hard science. I came to the US to pursue a PhD in Molecular biology and a Masters in biostatistics. But because of my experience with qigong, somewhere in my being I had always preserved a space, my inner Earth, which I knew that the knowledge of modern science could not explain. That space was sacred to me, even though for a long time I had no words to describe or communicate that space to anyone else.

For almost my entire adult life, my nervous system had been grated by the painful tensions between the Eastern and Western thought paradigms. The one from the West is rational and scientific. It has taken a worldly authority that demanded my acceptance. Yet, I had never submitted my heart to it. My heart belonged to the one from the East. Despite my native people having chosen to burn the books and condemn the tradition, my heart

was connected to its mystery and essence through an ineffable bond. The tension between these polarities cut my heart like a knife blade.

The Tao brings polarities back into a whole. Even though for a long time my conscious mind did not know how to speak about the Tao, I am connected to it instinctively. I have been driven by an indomitable faith that somewhere in the universe is a larger framework where these two polar paradigms can both find home, together. In this home, they don't have to compete for authority or fight for priorities. They learn from each other's strengths, complement each other's vulnerabilities, and support each other's growth.

What I am about to present next comes from my life's journey following this instinct. I discovered that the architecture of the psyche, like our biological gender, has two complementary energetic patterns. While both are always present throughout time, they each played a dominant role influencing the thought paradigms that arose in the West and East. They take turns filling up the psyche with the currents of wholeness, and emptying it out into a new context. Through their eternal interplay, evolution expands into wider terrain with finer details.

Separation of Dense and Light Planes and the Emergence of the Linear Rational Mind

The energetic pattern that has dominated the Western thought paradigm originated as a drastic separation between the Dense and Light Planes. In this separation, the institutions of organized religion proclaimed a transcendent heaven beyond the earthly realm. This proclamation delineated a pathway to the Light Plane that is decoupled from the instinctual desires and sensory experience on the Dense Plane. Practices in those religions pulled believers away from sensory experience and instinctual drives as they sought to deny or transcend them.

This separation created a wide empty space in the psyche, beckoning for something new to emerge. Over the last several hundred years, the agency of linear rational thinking emerged, freeing itself from the dominant religious authorities. This culminated in the Age of Enlightenment, an intellectual and philosophical movement that dominated the world of ideas in Europe during the 18th century. This movement initiated a range of ideas centered on reasoning and logic as the primary source of authority and legitimacy and spawned ideals like liberty, progress, constitutional government, and separation of church and state. With reasoning and logic in the ascendant, scientific enterprise thrived without bowing to the authority of organized religion. This gave the linear rational mind the fullest freedom to develop. With this freedom, the agencies developed through the linear rational mind spread across the whole globe and thoroughly investigated nature through their materialist, scientific lens.

Disruption Offers Opportunities for Creativity

The combined forces of religious institutions in one direction and science in the other ruptured the circulatory flows between the Enlightening and Enlivening pathways. However, disruption also generates space and impetus for new surges of creativity. Evolution is a master of utilizing the opportunities generated by disruption to create something new.

In the wake of this disruption, Western culture has forged the most amazing gifts to humanity, individual freedom and sovereignty, along with the kinds of creativity they catalyzed. Modern technology has liberated people from the mind-numbing chores of manual labor. Modern medicine has greatly improved infant survival rates and reduced women's risk in child-birthing. These are only a few examples of the amazing gifts emerging from the disruption.

As the linear rational mind took leadership of human affairs, creativity and ingenuity burst into material abundance, driving a global movement toward progress and development. Perhaps more importantly, the linear rational mind enabled the birthing of a new universe, the universe of knowledge, information, and data, which are now easily accessible to billions of people everywhere on Earth. With modern technology, our ability to generate information has exploded like a big bang. In 2017 we generated 2.5 quintillion bytes of data every day, (quintillion = 10^{18}), and the rate is accelerating. By 2017 numbers, we generated 90% of the data in the world in the previous two years alone!

Through this amazing creativity, the technological hardware for connecting a global consciousness was put in place. A new neural network of the Earth, consisting of the individual human psyche as its nodal point, is rapidly emerging and growing.

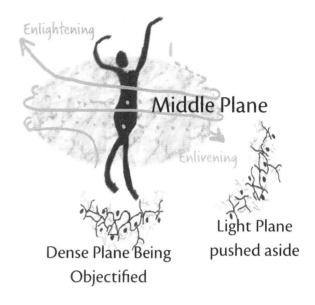

The energetic pathway that has dominated the Western thought paradigm:

- Decoupling between the Dense and Light Planes. Eventually, the Light Plane was pushed aside.

- The Middle Plane dominates and controls the Dense Plane by objectifying it as material substance.

- Energies of the Enlightening and Enlivening pathways are both directed into the expansion of the Middle Plane, leading to the development of the linear rational mind, individual ego, objective thinking, and scientific enterprise.

At the same time, the tremendous modern progress and development brought on by this energetic pathway are associated with immense costs to both humanity and ecological systems.

Cost One: Depletion of Dense Plane Aliveness

First, in this disruption, the linear mind takes control and dominates the Dense Plane. Our body, dissociated from the Light Plane, is primarily seen through the lens of the materialistic and reductionist tools of the linear rational mind. Without being connected to the Light Plane, the Dense Plane is no longer being sufficiently renewed by the Enlivening pathway.

While progress and development has led us to the peak of material abundance, on the Dense Plane collectively we are inhabiting a desolate wasteland. Signs of this include epidemic addiction rates, chilling loneliness and isolation, unfettered consumerism, increasing incidents of mass murders, and epidemic levels of anxiety and depression. Among these signs two are especially striking for me. First, more people commit suicide each year than those killed by natural disasters, wars and murder combined. Second, the December 2018 issue of Atlantic ran a cover story on the "sex recession." Despite the easing of taboos and the rise of hookup apps, Americans

are having less and less sex, especially among young people. These signs are telling us that the juicy aliveness that brings pleasure and enjoyment to human life seems to be sapped dry by our all-consuming drive toward progress.

Cost Two: Cutting Off from the Light Plane

The second cost is complementary to the first. While the Dense Plane is depleted, the psyche's capacity to rise above into the Light Plane is also compromised. Our grip on rational and intellectual thought is becoming so tight as to suffocate our imagination and spontaneity, which otherwise provide critical nutrients for the Light Plane. An important indicator of the integrity and well-being of the Light Plane is the sense of meaning and purpose in life. Psychologists assert that after our basic material needs for food, shelter and safety are met, more material abundance does not bring more meaning, purpose or happiness. In 2013, a paper published in Psychological Science analyzed the relationship between the sense of meaning and societal wealth in 132 countries. The researchers discovered that a sense of meaning in life is NEGATIVELY correlated with wealth. The people who have the greatest sense of meaning are concentrated in African countries with the lowest societal wealth such as Ethiopia, Sierra

Leone and Togo. Whereas people from some of the wealthiest places such as Japan, France and Hong Kong have the lowest scores for sense of meaning in life.

Cost Three: We Stop Feeling and Sensing Our Environment as a Subjective "I"

Through this trajectory of development, Western intellectuals developed the paradigm of objective thinking. In objective thinking, the observer is detached from the object of observation. Objectivity is a powerful methodology that allows scientists to learn vast amounts of knowledge about the materiality of nature. It also allows the development of an ego identity perceived through the linear rational mind. However, to perform objective thinking, one has to disrupt the currents of wholeness. When the cyclic flow of Yin-Yang currents is intact, the psyche naturally perceives itself embedded in the larger body of its environment. It perceives the world as a subjective "I" that includes itself. This is not the "I" as an individual ego with a self-identity defined by cultural values or titles. This is the "I" of the bigger life, either the natural world or the social body, of which a single human life is a part.

In the ancient forms of our human civilization, shamans, priests, and priestesses acted as an interface between human life and this larger "I". They were trained to allow this bigger "I" to move through their own body, speak through their own voice, and think through their own mind.

Later, due to the separation of the Dense and Light Planes, and the expansion of the Middle Plane, this intimate experience with the larger "I" was pushed into the unconscious. Subjectivity became confined to the isolated domain within an individual, often viewed as secondary attribute to objective thinking. The development of human agency has been primarily measured as the development from subjectivity to objectivity.

However, to feel and sense our environment as an animated larger being is the default setting of our nervous system. Disabling this part of ourselves is as traumatic as if one side of our body is paralyzed. The mounting environmental crisis is an outer manifestation of the inner trauma that has been intensifying inside our collective psyche.

Message from the Grief: Disruption Calls for a More Beautiful Wholeness

The disruption of the wholeness of the psyche and treating the body as a mechanical object to be dominated and controlled is causing great distress and pain for people in the West. With its energy focused in the material realm, Western civilization expanded throughout the world. The dominance and control asserted over the body was expressed as outer conquest and the eventual colonization of indigenous cultures and the Earth itself.

When China joined the West to adopt materialism and capitalism, the integrity of the collective psyche preserved through thousands of years of tradition was also ruptured. For decades, I grieved that trauma and loss. I roamed China as lands were torn open, rivers dammed and minerals dug up from the bowels of the mountains. Because my psyche preserved a basic level of integrity despite all the changes happening around me, I could still feel the larger body outside of me. I could feel the pain of the Earth as if these actions were done to my own body.

But I did not grieve just for self-pity. Grieving is a potent tool for the alchemical transformation of one's psyche. It was after surrendering myself to the transformational power of my grief that my psyche began to perceive a new message. I started to hear an invitation from evolution to rebirth a more beautiful wholeness on a larger scale.

As the consequences of disrupting wholeness are extremely painful, the tendency is to reject and even condemn the forces of disruption.

Influenced by this tendency, my heart harbored immense anger and resentment toward the forces of modernity. I adopted the mindset that modern progress was a mistake. However, to frame it that way is to assume that there is a "right" way we should have taken. But is there? What if evolution is an ongoing learning and experimenting process? How can anyone know which way is "better" when they are exploring an unknown terrain? Similarly, how can human evolution know the "right" ways to bring forth new human agencies before we actually try them?

If we accept evolution as a constant learning process, then we can always learn from our past lessons and chart a different course to minimize the cost and maximize the benefit. Now that we see what has been disrupted by the progress of modernity and the extent to which this disruption has traumatized humanity and nature, we can chart ourselves a new evolutionary journey. In this new journey, we need to learn how to heal ourselves back into wholeness. And perhaps even more importantly, we need to learn how to consciously interrupt the currents of wholeness to allow further development of new creative agencies, so that we can actively employ these new agencies toward weaving larger and more beautiful wholeness to nurture life.

I am not sharing this message to prevent you from going into your grief. The grief over mechanization, dominance, and control of our individual bodies, our collective body, and the Earth's body affects everyone on the planet, consciously or unconsciously. I share this message to encourage you to walk into your grief. In the model of Enlightening and Enlivening pathways on page 93, you can see how Enlivening the Dense Plane with grief can take the Enlivening pathway to the bottom near the biological pole. There, our awareness will have the opportunity to exit and join the Enlightening pathway on the outside. When that happens, our awareness expands beyond its original sphere and soars to the Light Plane as it rides the ascending currents outside one's awareness. You feel as if you are carried by a bigger life force. (Please refer to Chapter Six for details about Feelingwork.)

I invite you to follow your grief to descend down into the deeper chambers of your heart, so that you may find the exit out of the limited sphere of ego self and ride evolution's upward wind to soar.

Now I would like to describe the energetic pattern that has dominated the Eastern thought paradigm. In the East and within indigenous cultures embracing Earth-based cosmology throughout the world, prior to encounters with Western civilization the severing of the Light and Dense Planes had not occurred as drastically as in the West. As a result, the integrity of the circulation back and forth between the Enlightening and Enlivening pathways had been maintained relatively intact.

In the tradition of Taoism or Zen Buddhism, for example, spiritual development is tightly coupled with embodiment training. In many disciplines, embodiment practice is the most important, far more so than intellectual understanding. In Eastern traditional culture, the body was never viewed in mechanistic way. It was viewed as a holistic expression of the energy and dynamics of the Light Plane. That is why the notion of qi is the most important concept in Chinese medicine. Even among more scholarly traditions, a classically-trained Chinese intellectual usually was devoted to an embodied art such as music, painting, martial arts or calligraphy, so he could intentionally create an ebb and flow between embodiment experience and intellectual development.

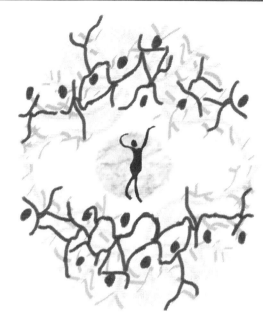

The energetic pathway that has dominated Eastern thought paradigm
- *The overall architecture remains intact*
- *A weak Middle Plane*

Since the '60s, many practices of Eastern spirituality have been introduced into the West, spawning the New Age movement. Yet without accessing this fundamental architecture of the psyche, many New Age practices grafted the surface layer of behavioral or cognitive patterns of Eastern or indigenous practices and philosophies onto a Western psyche. That union has infused some wonderful new life forces into these age-old practices. However, because of the lack of structural integration in the psyche, the changes brought out by New Age movements have tended to be disengaged from the linear rational mind on the Middle Plane and sensorial/somatic experience on the Dense Plane.

The New Age has begun to pave the way toward an integration between the Eastern and Western mind. However, it has not touched the deeper core of the teachings in the East, especially in the profound transformation of the Dense Plane psyche. An example is the earlier discussion of the importance of embodying and embracing grief. We have a long way to go to understand what it is like to cultivate a global consciousness that integrates its Eastern and Western hemispheres.

Shown on the right is the schematic drawing of the key features of Eastern enlightenment. I'd like to draw your attention to its gift as well as its vulnerability. Its gift lies in the integrity of the structure that supports a sustainable circulation between the Enlightening and Enlivening pathways. This circulation is comprised of flows both through the inner core and outside surface.

The outer flows give rise to our psyche's ability to sense energy and consciousness beyond the human being's. This is a feature of the psyche

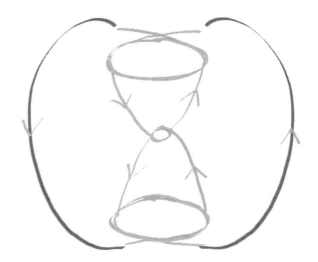

Cyclic flows of consciousness when the architecture is whole and intact. With this intact structure, the psyche perceives nature as an animated, conscious being.

Notice the shape of the inner core is an hourglass, a tool to measure time. Perhaps this reflects a shared, intuitive knowledge that the architecture of the psyche serves as the time-keeper of evolution.

characterizing all indigenous cultures around the world including the West before organized religion. With the architectural integrity of the psyche being intact, our indigenous ancestors had a very different sensory experience of the world.

They experienced nature as an animated Inter-Being, inside of which humans live.

Their sensory experience extended into the animal and plant kingdom, the ecosystems and non-human worlds around them. And nature was for them not just made of material things, but replete with unknown forces beyond the comprehension of their minds. (These forces are still beyond the comprehension of a modern mind informed by the most sophisticated scientific knowledge!)

A modern person steeped in the developed world is conditioned to consider this way of sensing to be "primitive" or "unscientific." Yet, from the perspective of the indigenous psyche, this modern person suffers from atrophied sensory capacities with which he perceives the world as a mechanical place made with cold and inanimate objects. Cultural ecologist David Abram has written extensively about the experience of indigenous culture. In an article published on the online magazine *Emergence*, he wrote:

"The members of such [indigenous] cultures seemed to respond to their surroundings as though all things were alive and (at least potentially) aware. Further, from this animistic perspective, it seemed that all things were felt to be expressive; all things had the power of meaningful speech (although, of course, very few of them spoke in words).

The Tibetans have maintained an intimate relationship with the mountains as animated, live beings. This is a pilgrimage site I visited where the Tibetans taught me how to awaken my sensory channels to communicate with Earth as a living being.

"The conventional interpretation of such ways of encountering the world, among social scientists, has held that traditional, "tribal" persons are confusedly projecting human attributes—such as life and consciousness—into nonhuman and ostensibly inanimate phenomena. I wish to argue, however, that <u>animistic perception is utterly normal for the human organism, a kind of default setting for our species;</u> that in the absence of intervening technologies, the human senses spontaneously encounter the sensorial surroundings as a field of sensitive and sentient powers."

While this energetic pathway of the East has preserved the architectural integrity of the psyche, it is associated with its own costs. It has a weak Middle Plane, which has several extremely painful impacts.

First, the kind of reasoning, critical thinking, and intellectual processes that support the Middle Plane is not as robust. Therefore, the sovereignty and creativity of an individual is bound to be muffled by the weight of authority and tradition. Also, material existence in these cultures can be more easily devastated by destructive forces of nature, such as drought and flooding.

Lastly, without a stable Middle Plane, the architecture of this psyche cannot be scaled and standardized easily. The traditional knowledge of Taoism and Chinese medicine is notoriously difficult to teach. Most of this knowledge stayed in the subjective realm, passing down lineages over generations through oral traditions, making systemization of knowledge nearly impossible. Due to its difficulty to standardize, this kind of knowledge is easily corrupted, misunderstood, and misinterpreted once the lineage is broken. Thus its replicability and applicability has been weak and unreliable. In contrast, the strength of Western thinking lies in its ability to objectify, standardize and systematize knowledge.

In my experience living in the West, I have encountered Western people idealizing Eastern spirituality or indigenous culture. (This goes the other way too; the Chinese also idealize the gifts from the West.) Eastern spirituality, when taken out of the soil of its cultural context, fills in the blank spot of the Western psyche. It provides a dose of comfort to relieve the stresses incurred through the disruption of the Western psyche. That is why in the West, Buddhist or Taoist retreat centers are often set in beautiful, serene resorts, visited by well-to-do, often white people when they are on vacation. There is nothing wrong with that. I have participated and benefited immensely from it. However, my heart always knew that

In Chinese culture, the lotus has long been used as a metaphor for wisdom and knowledge. The lotus lives bonded with a thick layer of putrid mud at the bottom, yet its flower is ethereal and its essence fragrant. It reminds us that beauty and life arise out of death, destruction, and decomposition.

this is Eastern spirituality being preserved as a fossil sample, displayed beautifully behind a glass window in a museum. I want to apply the knowledge and test it out in the messiness of the real world. How can we apply the teachings of the Eastern traditions in business, intimacy, or politics?

Both glorifying and denigrating the other prevent us from perceiving the organically emerging nature of wholeness. Eastern spirituality is a part of its native cultural ecosystem. In its long history, it also participated in the authoritative suppression of individuals, subjugation of women, and inhibition of the development of critical thinking. In its existing form, it inevitably carries the imprints of all those shadows.

When we do not open our hearts to be in touch with life's vulnerability, when knowledge is no longer being planted firmly in the murky ambiguity of life and nourished by the humus composted from the grief and sorrow, then knowledge ceases to be a live stream of water and life stops regenerating itself. Life is both joy and pain, glorious triumph and sorrowful loss. There is no way to avoid this paradox and uncertainty. It is through embracing and accepting both life's gifts and vulnerabilities that we will be invited into the playground of wholeness.

I want to highlight another contrast between these two pathways of the psyche. In the picture on the left, the figure in the middle, symbolizing self-identity (ego) shaped through the intellectual and rational mind, takes the center of attention. In contrast, on the right, the little figure at the center is almost like a fetus, contained within a viscous, primordial, ocean womb of inter-connectivity. The difference between these two patterns is expressed in two dominant cultural paradigms called I-Culture and We-Culture.

I-Culture, primarily active in the more modern, developed countries in North America and Western Europe, is centered around individual identity connected through shared values constructed by rationality and intellect. The ways of life, belief systems, and collective agreements such as rules, customs, and laws in

I-Culture countries privilege and protect individual sovereignty and agency over group identity and agency.

We-Culture, primarily active in more traditional countries in Asia, Africa, and South America, is centered around group identity constructed through nonrational or trans-rational means such as story, archetype, and myth, (Light Plane activities). In We-Culture life, a felt sense of belonging is often expressed through non-verbal means such as physical presence, touch, and shared rituals and customs, (Dense Plane awareness). In We-Culture countries, the privilege is given to protecting and maintaining the integrity of group identity and agency much more than individual sovereignty and agency.

In We-Culture, a self is not experienced as a fixed object distinct from all others, but as a unique set of relationships woven around and through the self. One self is still distinct from the next, but in We-Culture the source of this uniqueness lies in the surrounding web of relationships.

This Chinese poem may illustrate what it is like to belong to We-Culture. "*When he stops breathing, he does not die. When his body gets buried or cremated, he still does not die. But when no one thinks about him anymore, no heart misses him and no soul entwines with his soul, he then is truly dead."*

In I-Culture, products of Middle Plane agencies such as rules, contracts, laws, and codes play an important role in cohering the collective. Whereas in We-Culture, the collective is more cohered through shared somatic experience, myth, and stories, woven by Dense and Light Plane faculties.

Throughout human history, I-Culture and We-Culture largely developed within their own environments without substantial interaction until the late 19th century. This was particularly true with China. Before the 19th century, China was almost completely sealed off from the West. Today, I-Culture and We-Culture are in close contact, powerfully changing and influencing each other. Our work places and neighborhoods are becoming increasingly international. If we imagine the humans of the Earth as one mind, with the I-Culture and We-Culture modes of awareness being like the left and right hemispheres of the brain, the integration of both is critical for us to develop competency in our increasingly inter-connected global culture.

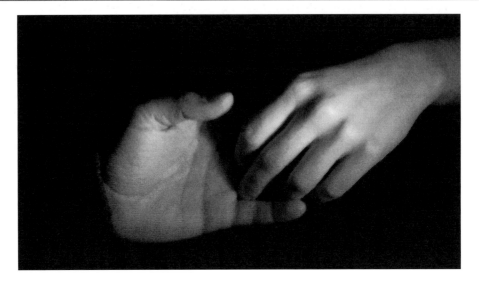

I have outlined two energetic pathways that have influenced the Western and Eastern thought paradigms. These two pathways are like the masculine and feminine modes of the psyche.* The process of evolution employs the feminine psyche to preserve an original order of wholeness. It employs the masculine psyche to disrupt the original order, initiating an impetus to create a new human agency. It is the creative interplay between these two modes that moves us toward greater and renewed expressions of wholeness. (See graphs on the next spread.)

I have also synthesized the dominant features of the Western and Eastern thought pathways to illustrate the architectural differences between them. This is not to say the Western psyche is masculine and Eastern is feminine! Every person's

_____

* Here I use the terms feminine and masculine to refer to energetic patterns of the psyche. They are used to refer to Light Plane subtle patterns. I use the terms male and female to describe the differences in reproductive systems. They refer to Dense Plane embodiment. In this scheme, we may think of man and woman as social identities that we may choose for ourselves. They are Middle Plane phenomena.

psyche, whether Eastern or Western, modern or indigenous, can oscillate between these two modes. The distinction between them depends on where we place our attention, whether we are discussing a global pattern, a social movement, or an individual person.

As we lay out the architectural structure of the feminine and masculine modes of the psyche, we may gain a new perspective in the evolutionary process human civilizations have gone through. Single-celled organisms appeared on Earth 3.5 billion years ago. It took evolution another 2.3 billion years to figure out sexual reproduction, which is now automated in our physiology. I propose that evolution is asking us to reenact the meta-patterns associated with sexual reproduction on the conscious level, enabling a creative, resonant interplay between the two modes in our social life. Embracing both modes and their interplay will give us tools and agency to heal ourselves and to consciously participate in evolving toward wholeness.

Feminine   Masculine

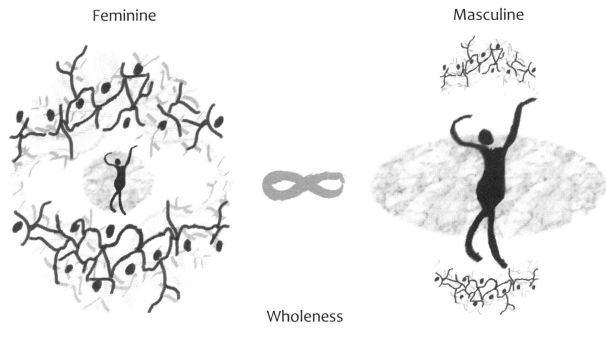

Wholeness

Feminine   *Masculine*

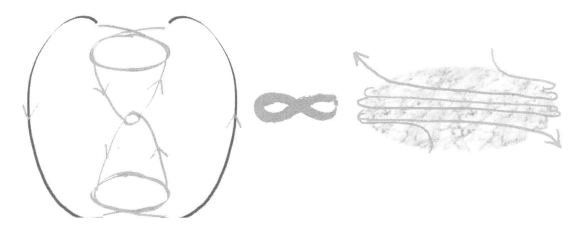

Renewed Wholeness

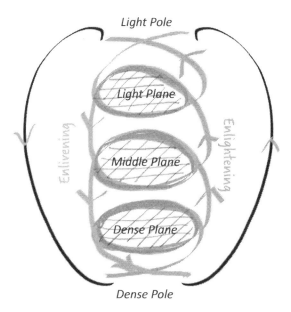

There are two major cognitive traps that prevent us from this resonant interplay. The first cognitive trap is thinking in binary and absolute terms, a habit formed through mechanical, objective thinking. The two modes of the psyche are relative qualities, not a concrete expression. In the pictures I drew on the previous pages, I drew the two modes in their most extreme forms to illustrate my point. However, it is not hard to imagine that there is a whole spectrum of shapes in between these two extremes. The shapes in the middle will be naturally ambiguous and relative. This means the distinctions of feminine and masculine are only meaningful in a specific context. For example, my body has a female physiology, which does not change in any context. In contrast, my psyche may express a more feminine or masculine quality depending on with whom I am speaking, in what activity I am engaging, and what time of the day it is!

In contrast, our linear rational mind tends to think in absolute terms, often insensitive to the context, by assigning values such as right or wrong, true or false. Paradoxically, if we look more closely, those places where we hold a tight grip on a binary, good-and-bad distinctions are often associated with strong emotional charges. In other words, underneath the rigidly binary categorizations are deep, non-rational currents. To overcome this trap, our heart needs to open to those non-rational undercurrents and transform them. Then our mind can be more supple and flexible, capable of making distinctions in ways that are sensitive and congruent with the specifics of the context.

The second trap lies in our deeply ingrained pattern of only inhabiting one mode of the psyche at a given time. We are conditioned to fear and resist the tension and ambiguity inherent in inhabiting both modes. In our social upbringing, as men and women we are conditioned to cultivate only one mode and actively inhibit the other. Boys are encouraged to be bold, strong, pursuing freedom and individual power, and they are punished for being sensitive and empathetic. Girls are encouraged to be nurturing, sensuous, sensitive, and to seek bonding and belonging. They are shunned when displaying strength and self-will. As a result, we have this deeply ingrained belief that developing one quality means diminishing the other. Often our experience in life corroborates our belief. For example, men who intentionally cultivate sensitivity and

empathy may suppress their natural expression of strong masculinity. Conversely, a woman who is powerful and strong, especially in the corporate environment, often loses her feminine softness. This phenomenon reflects the ingrained unconscious belief as well as ancestral or collective habits associated with the rupture of our psyche.

The reason we experience this imbalanced competition between the poles is because we are fairly good at changing our behavioral or cognitive patterns, but we lack tools and pathways to genuinely transform the underlying psychic structures. The behavioral traits of strength and will exhibited by a woman, or sensitivity and empathy exhibited by a man, may not come from an authentic expression of an integrated psyche. Changing cognitive and behavioral patterns only without getting in touch with the underlying psychic structure is similar to improving fitness by editing our photos instead of exercising our bodies. Its effects often feel awkward and inauthentic.

To work with this trap, we need to cultivate perception and agency to work with our instincts, feelings, senses, imagination, intuition, and pattern and energy perception. In other words, we need to be committed to being whole, and not settle for anything less than wholeness, while loving, embracing, and even enjoying our imperfection and vulnerability along the way!

After I ended my career as a scientist, my longing for wholeness led me to become an acupuncturist. I was very happy to stop using my intellect as my primary tool. When the development of The Resonance Code started to intensify and I was called to re-engage my intellect, I resisted. Caught in my own mental trap, I feared the potential rupture to the integrity of my psyche, and held on dearly. However, through practicing The Resonance Code, I experienced that engaging my intellect actually amplified my healing and embodiment practices. In turn, through my healing I sensed that my feminine mode actually invited me to dive deeper into my masculine. This gave me the confidence to expand my capacity to use the linear rational mind as a creative tool.

I did again experience the painful rupture of the original integrity of my psyche. At the same time, my feminine ability to heal and restore myself amplified. My creative work became an ongoing, cyclic process of disrupting myself and becoming whole again. With Resonance, the more strongly I disrupted myself, the more nourishing and healing the wholeness became. I was rewarded with a creative process effervescent with emergence, adventure, spontaneity, and discovery.

I also experienced this resonant interplay in inter-personal relationships and discourse. In the process of stewarding the birthing of this work, I've been collaborating with many people where this resonant interplay is a key ingredient. My masculine expression draws out the feminine expression in my collaborators and vice versa. We appreciate the life-giving pleasure of this resonant interplay as well as the potency of its alchemical power within and among ourselves. It strengthens our commitment to bring its fully enlivened potential into the world.

Wholeness thrives on the resonant interplay of the feminine and masculine. In this dynamic, cultivating one mode will eventually lead to an amplification of the other mode, resulting in a positive feedback loop. The three key principles that enable resonant interplay are:

- *Cultivate the awareness of wholeness.*
- *Embrace vulnerability in ourselves and others.*
- *Facilitate emergence through spontaneous play.*

In the next few pages I'll visit each of these three principles to illustrate how they work together.

Resonant interplay generates a positive feedback loop!

Cultivate the awareness of wholeness.

Wholeness is an attribute of a larger life process, the Inter-Being of Earth in which humanity takes part. It is the current that has sustained evolution on Earth for billions of years. The current of wholeness is right here and now, always present, just like the electromagnetic field surrounding the Earth. Humans have lived millions of years without conscious knowledge of this electromagnetic field, (although new evidence suggests our ancestors could have used an intuitive awareness of the earth's magnetic field in navigation). Without the right instrument or perception, we normally are not aware of the electromagnetic forces infusing our physical space. Likewise, we live within the currents of wholeness yet can remain unconscious of it. Learning how to attune our awareness can develop our inner senses as instruments to perceive the current of wholeness.

In Chapter Five, I will begin to describe the practice of The Resonance Code through which one may train this subtle perception. The 64 hexagrams of I-Ching describe 64 patterns of how the currents of wholeness flows through the larger systems of life around us. The Resonance Code establishes a vocabulary and syntax that one

"The binding force of wholeness is not right or wrong but love & compassion"

can use to translate these patterns into common language. In native Chinese cosmology, forces governing the rise and fall, union and division of human society are similar to those that govern nature's climate patterns. Thus this larger life, this Inter-Being, also includes the rise and fall, union and division of human society, including the most destructive forces.

Embrace vulnerability in ourselves and others.

On the surface, this principle might appear to negate the first one. If we can perceive wholeness, why would we acknowledge, let alone embrace, our imperfections and vulnerability? However, the binding force of wholeness is not right and wrong or good and bad, but love and compassion. When given time, wholeness can always regenerate, so it can never be harmed. Therefore in the eyes of wholeness, nothing could be absolutely wrong or bad. Instead of judging, wholeness is always curious: how can this be woven in? With creativity, everything can be recycled and repurposed in wholeness, even the darkest, least desirable, or worst parts of ourselves. If we expand our heart wide enough, we can hear the painful outcry for wholeness even within the most horrific destruction or the most abhorrent violence.

A supercomputer-generated model of flow patterns in Earth's liquid core.

This does not mean that wholeness tolerates violence and injustice. Discerning right and wrong and protecting ourselves and others from harm is necessary and crucial, *as the first step*. If we want true transformation to happen, though, once we protect ourselves from harm, we need to suspend judgment and engage with the alchemical transformation through diving deep into our own vulnerability and imperfection.

In my own journey, Feelingwork offers an essential tool to dive into the dark chambers of my inner vulnerability. Through Feelingwork I encountered many aspects of my deepest self that I would rather not have seen, much less shown to anyone. Yet I clearly saw how these aspects, because they had been pushed deep into my unconscious, created dysfunctional patterns in my life, especially in my intimate relations with men. My partner Joe was the first person who showed me an unshakable faith in the "worst" parts of my humanity. In his embrace, I learned how to embrace the "darkness" in both myself and him. Eventually, through transforming these vulnerabilities, I found new sources of power and strength to fuel the resonant interplay between the masculine and feminine in myself and with others.

In my client work, I have repeatedly encountered these "outcasts" that have been living in people's unconscious. They may take forms of forbidden lust, laziness, addiction, vengefulness, a sadistic impulse, tyrannical anger, or unbearable shame. These traits and qualities have been long rejected or devalued in people's upbringing. Often people discover these forces as a surprise. On the outside, a person may have an extremely successful career or live a respectable life, yet inside there can be a deep-seated sense of failure and unworthiness. Experiencing these "outcasts" in their unconsious, they realize the life and identity they have built has all along been preventing them from getting in touch with the painful feelings associated with these vulnerabilities. The surface life can only protect them from the vulnerability temporarily, though, because these "outcasts" contain powerful life forces. They demand to be integrated back into wholeness!

As leaders committed to continuous self-transformation, diving into vulnerability and imperfection is essential for establishing Resonance. Working with our own inner darkness strengthens our muscles to develop wider capacity for compassion. That compassion catalyzes a greater degree of wholeness and Resonance. For details of using Feelingwork as a tool to explore our vulnerability, please refer to Chapter Six and *TheFeelingMind.com*.

Facilitate emergence through spontaneous play.

With the first two principles, the virility of the masculine and fertility of the feminine are ready to play with each other and generate Resonance. Our psyche is ready to give birth to the child, the emerging present. The resonant interplay resembles our experience of sexual reproduction in that we participate with our whole selves and relinquish control over the outcome. That tension activates the fullest, most authentic contact with the bigger currents of wholeness surrounding and coursing through us. Spontaneous play enables a fluid and adaptive response to the uncertainty and complexity of emergence, sourced from the whole person. It requires a mastery to oscillate between powerfully executing our own will and flexibly surrendering to the bigger will of life.

In my leadership development journey, I have spent a long time awakening the neurological patterns for spontaneity in my body through improvisational play and dance. Eventually my somatic patterning of spontaneity started to broaden into other realms, influencing my intellectual work and my ability to lead and facilitate. My mind began to think in ways I could never imagine before. It was then my creative process began to flourish.

People who have not experienced improvisation may judge it as trivial. On the contrary, improvisation requires just as much, if not more disciplined practice to systematically remove the conditioned patterns built into our body and reprogram new ones. A more precise term for improvisation is actually instantaneous composition. When people improvise together, they both compose and execute while coordinating with one another. It draws on a synthesis of many dimensions of our cognitive capacities and automatic reflexes. Waking up neurological patterns for spontaneity in leadership is a primary focus of the work done at Resonance Path Institute. We're planning in-depth discussions of this topic for later volumes of the book.

I envision conscious evolution toward wholeness through resonant interplay as the emerging phase of humanity's developmental journey. This suggests some deep healing needs to happen for us to enter this phase. When the feminine and masculine modes are not directed by the resonant interplay, they can be trapped in their wounded states. Both men and women can inhabit wounded masculine and feminine. In fact the wounded modes of the psyche are often intertwined and inter-locked within one person. In turn, healing one mode can restore the other.

The Wounded Masculine

In working with myself and clients, I have found three major blocks in the masculine mode of psyche that prevent people from opening to the resonant interplay. The first is the deeply ingrained conditioning that sees the body as a machine whose primary function is to maintain a robust physiology. Evolution toward wholeness asks us to see our body as a highly sophisticated and sensitive instrument that we cultivate to amplify the frequencies from the Light Plane. This is particularly relevant to leaders. Our bodies, including our instinctual and sensory processes, are the instruments to embody what we are advocating. Our somatic presence, as well as every minute, unconscious gesture, tone of voice, and facial expression will transmit information to the people around us. Skills to work with the intelligence of our bodies as instruments are a big part of leadership development.

The second block is the habit of controlling our bodily functions through directives issued from analytical thinking. We want to command our body to serve our ego's will and intention instead of surrendering to its inherent intelligence. This reflects on the dominant paradigm of Western medicine that treats disease as a problem to be fixed, or an enemy to fight, as in the message to fight wars on cancer. In contrast, holistic medicine sees disease as our body's way to send important information from the Dense Plane to our conscious mind. Illness becomes a valuable window of opportunity to integrate the ego self within the ecosystem of the psyche.

The third block is an intolerance for chaos, uncertainty, and ambiguity. These dynamics are actually the feminine psyche's way of flirting with the masculine. Conditioned to see the world through a right and wrong binary lens and categorize things through labeling, the wounded masculine wants to force chaos into order, uncertainty into certainty, and ambiguity into clarity. That kills any chance for interplay and instead fosters distrust and animosity.

The Wounded Feminine

On the feminine side, there are complementary blocks. One of these is a profound distrust of and separation from the true power of feminine creativity. With feminine creativity suppressed by the worst part of patriarchy, most of us only know what feminine power should look like within the framework of a patriarchal social structure. Feminine power tends to be associated with roles assigned to women to serve the patriarchy, such as healing, nourishing, bonding, and uniting. While these are all important functions, we often remain blind to the most potent feminine creative power. Through the physiological template of our monthly cycle, our feminine psyche is naturally attuned to the temporal rhythm of resonant interplay. Men can develop that awareness too through training their feminine mode and paying attention to their partner's cycles. Few women and men are taught that. Instead, women are conditioned to think of our monthly cycle as a shameful nuisance. In truth, a woman's body is a natural gift which maintains an internal space, an "emptiness," nourished by stillness, through which form is birthed into the world. If we look at this on the most physical and concrete level, sexual intercourse is an intrusion into the female's body. When the creative interplay between the feminine and masculine modes has not fully matured, this intrusion can be invasive and traumatic. The creativity of the feminine lies in its powerful ability to transform this intrusion into the act of birthing life. A woman can consciously develop her higher cognitive functions by drawing on her body's somatic knowledge, but few women in our modern era have access to body-centered insight or even know what is possible.

The second block in the feminine psyche is associated with the deep sense of victimhood and violation as a result of being subjugated by the worst of the patriarchal power. Because women's physiology is naturally more attuned to the Enlivening pathway, we are more sensitive to the pain associated with the internal colonization of our bodies. On the collective level, the part of us that identifies with the Earth's body also naturally resonates with the grief of Earth's body being colonized. Without a tool to metabolize that grief, it becomes too much for us to bear. We can turn resentful and angry toward the masculine. We are also conditioned to compete with the masculine for power in ways reflecting our wounded inner masculine. We become argumentative, judgmental, and aggressive. I have personally experienced all of these in my journey of growth and I am eternally grateful for all the people, men and women, who did not judge me but held a compassionate space for me. I learned that relying on the tools made by the wounded masculine does not liberate our feminine creativity. If we want to experience our wholeness, we have to awaken our full potential by diving more deeply into ourselves.

In my own journey, the grief associated with the victimhood of my feminine provided me a great opportunity to learn how to heal by diving deeper into the bottom layer of my psyche. In metabolizing this grief, the feminine aspect of my psyche opened herself up and "mated" with my inner masculine. As I embraced and embodied the resonant interplay, Resonance led me to meet my co-creative partners Joe Shirley and Joseph Friedman and many others who empowered and supported me.

The line that divides feminine and masculine crosses everyone's psyche. As long as we do not accept that we are wholeness incarnated as sexual beings, as long as the feminine in men and masculine in women are still dormant, as long as we are still closed off to resonant interplay, we will always be plagued by this divide. This is what evokes my deepest compassion and commitment to be of service to the awakening of wholeness in humanity.

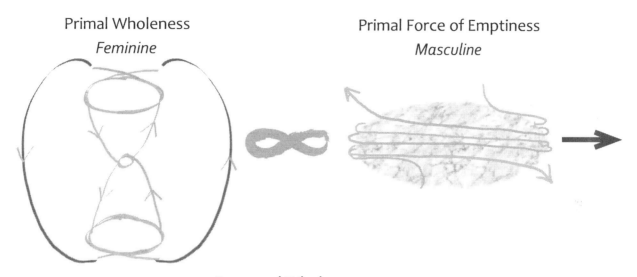

Primal Wholeness
Feminine

Primal Force of Emptiness
Masculine

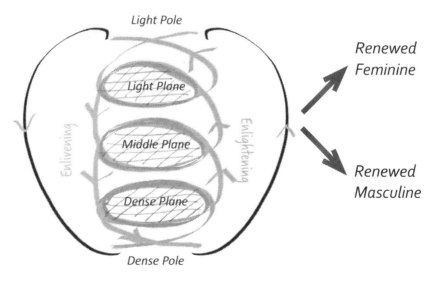

Renewed Wholeness

Renewed
Feminine

Renewed
Masculine

Let us take another look at the resonant interplay between the feminine and masculine as expressed in the energetic circuitry shown on the previous page. The resonant interplay between feminine and masculine is the engine that propels the evolution of wholeness.

The primal feminine represents an original state of wholeness, whereas the Dense and Light Planes are tightly connected to support the circulatory flows through both the inner core and outer surface. It is the web of life experiencing itself as a cosmic, subjective "I". The primal masculine represents the force of emptiness, which separates the Dense and Light Planes. In human civilization, what emerges is the powerful faculty of the linear rational mind, along with its scientific methodology based on objective, analytical thinking. Each of these modes anchors a host of world views, philosophies, cultural practices, and knowledge lineages. They are the left and right hemispheres of our collective brain.

When these two modes engage in resonant interplay, they give birth to a renewed wholeness. This renewed wholeness provides a new next context in which feminine and masculine find more innovative ways to differentiate from each other, refine their expressions, and join together to co-create again. In their renewed forms, the feminine and masculine each find stronger expressions of themselves, as well as more intelligent, passionate, and compassionate ways to interface with their opposite. This is the essence of the Tao, the dance between polar opposites, an inhale and exhale breathing life into evolution.

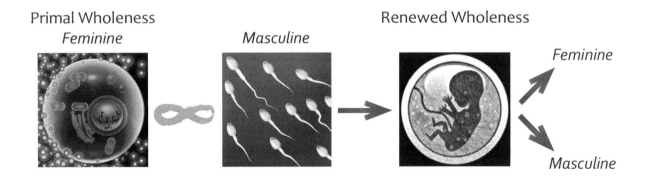

Primal Wholeness
Feminine   *Masculine*

Renewed Wholeness

Feminine

Masculine

Parallel with Biological Evolution

We may appreciate the evolutionary principle guiding this dance between feminine and masculine by drawing an analogy with the biology of the egg cell and sperm cell.

Size and Shape: The egg and sperm are two types of cell with polarized differences. The egg cell is the largest human cell, visible to the naked eye. She is almost perfectly round, therefore has the largest volume to surface ratio. A large part of her volume is the fluid cytoplasm. Sperm cells, in contrast, are the smallest human cells. They are no more than a nucleus with a small amount of cytoplasm, some mitochondria to supply energy to the cell, and a long tail. They have hardly any cellular content and are the straightest cells.

This difference is parallel with the polarity of the holistic paradigm and the linear paradigm in the human mind. This polarity is not just an accident. Its energetic blueprint is embodied in our physiology. This polarity is the basis of life.

Mobility: Externally, the egg cell is inactive. After her release, she is passively moved by the fluid flow in the oviduct. On the contrary, the sperm cells are externally active and mobile, using their tails to swim against the stream of fluid in the oviduct. Internally, the picture flips. The egg cell is internally active because of her fluid content. Whereas the sperm cells are largely nucleus, therefore internally rigid, structured, and immobile.

This difference parallels cultural manifestations of the feminine and masculine psyche. The feminine is intrinsically more adept at internal agency and internal movements, whereas the masculine tends to exhibit more active agency in external movement and propulsion. The active internal, agency of feminine is coupled with an external stillness. The active, external agency of masculine is coupled with an internal rigidity.

Metabolism and Relation with the Environment: An egg cell is active in her metabolism, releasing and absorbing substances from outside. She is open to the environment. Sperm cells are passive in their metabolism. They do not absorb or release substances, and there is no exchange with the environment. The open and vulnerable state of the egg cell is polar to the closed and robust state of the sperm cells.

This difference highlights the contrast between vulnerability and strength. Being open to the environment renders the egg cell vulnerable. Being closed to the environment makes the sperm strong. Again, it is between the egg cell's vulnerability and the robustness of sperm that conception happens and life blossoms. In the conscious evolution of our psyche, we need to embrace and develop both.

Number: Conception requires one egg cell and about 100 million sperm. A man with less than 20-40 million sperm in an ejaculation is barren. Such great numbers are necessary because most sperm do not reach the ovum. The ovum is alone and the sperm are with millions. One sperm cell is nothing, one ovum determines everything. One is polar to millions. One comprises everything, it is all there is, whereas the millions of sperm cells are infinitive, having no importance on their own.

This points to a very important distinction between the feminine and masculine psyches. The feminine psyche is concerned with quality. More is meaningless to fertility. The quality and degree of wholeness of that one single egg determines everything. The masculine psyche is concerned with quantity. A larger number indicates more robust virility. Our current scientific paradigm relies heavily on quantitative methodology. It is predominantly masculine-oriented. This masculine orientation widely influences our education, policy making, investigation, and formation of public opinion. Much less attention is paid to qualitative research and qualitative experiments. If science and our culture are to develop further to embrace wholeness, we must evolve beyond this one-sided obsession with quantity and start to educate ourselves about how to think in qualitative ways.

Development: All the egg cells a woman will ever have are produced well before her birth in a huge number. Each is called a primordial ovum. From the very beginning, primordial ova continue to die off. At birth there are about two million primordial ova. At the onset of puberty about 40,000 ova are left. Then every four weeks a number of them begin a process of maturation. Of these, only one, sometimes two or three, matures. The rest die. At menopause, no egg cells are left. In men, a very different process is going on. The first sperm cells are formed in puberty. Then the production goes on and on and never stops, hundreds per second, millions each day. Sperm cells are constantly being newly produced.

Egg cells are old cells. For primordial egg cells, life is a continuous process of dying. Sperm cells are newly formed and are young. The maturation process of the egg cell is an expiring process. It stops. The formation of the sperm is a vital process, it never stops.

This difference is in parallel with two distinct relationships with time in human culture. In more ancient traditional cultures, there was a sense that the glorious peak of humanity happened in the distant past. Humans' tasks in the present moment were to slow down the decline of this glory. From this more feminine perspective, human development is a process where the primordial life energy continues to decline.

In contrast, for modern culture, the peak of development and progress is held to be in the future. Humanity's task in the present moment is to race and accelerate toward that glorious future. From this more masculine perspective, human development is a process of progress, growth and continuous production.

Both of these perspectives are correct. And neither is complete. Life emerges in the present moment between the interplay of both. When we can see both of these modes, won't we appreciate the brilliance of evolution? When we develop the flexibility to move between these two polar modes of the psyche, we will have a choice to accelerate or slow down in the present moment, enjoying the thrilling adventure, riding the waves of the emerging present.

	Egg cell	Sperm
Size and shape	Large and round	Small and straight
Mobility	Externally still; internally mobile	Externally mobile; internally still
Open or closed to its environment	Open to its environment	Closed to its environment
Number	One	Many millions
Development	Declining of primordial eggs	Proliferation of sperm cells

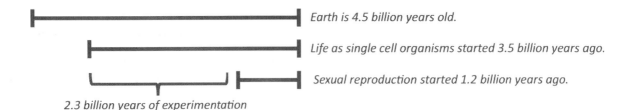

Earth is 4.5 billion years old.

Life as single cell organisms started 3.5 billion years ago.

Sexual reproduction started 1.2 billion years ago.

2.3 billion years of experimentation

Conception of a New Human Civilization

In appearance and processes egg and sperm are mutually antagonistic. In the process of maturation, these two types of cells go to extremes in their individuality. Their development and maturation show increasing divergence, a process of polarization. When they are mature, egg and sperm can come together and resolve the polarity in conception, so that a new human being can be born. All 200 other human cell types lie between the two extremes. If they cannot resolve the polarity, there is no conception. There is only death.

I imagine that the feminine and masculine psyches of our civilization are at such critical junction of conception. As a collective species and as individuals, we are all facing such a challenge: how to resolve the polarity inherent in our feminine and masculine psyches? What do you think? Can we give birth to a new human civilization? Imagine all the evolutionary experiments that took place and failed during the 2.3 billion years before sexual reproduction matured on Earth. How many times did evolution have to start all over again? How many rounds of destruction? Yet, evolution persisted and succeeded. With sexual reproduction, biological life has a whole repertoire of strategies to preserve, exchange genetic information, and invent new evolutionary strategies. Life is able to thrive on Earth.

Now we are at this evolutionary frontier, poised to bring the resolution of this polarity through our psyche. I-Ching contains vital information that guides this grand experiment. It has recorded 64 patterns out of which the primordial feminine and masculine interact and give rise to the renewed feminine and renewed masculine. The Resonance Code decodes these patterns into modern English language. Incidentally, The Resonance Code reveals that the structure in the hexagrams is same as the structure in the 64 genetic codons of biological evolution. We will explore that in Chapter Five.

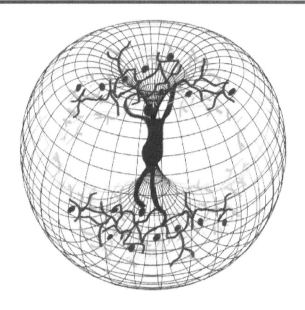

Scientists have also suggested that the entire universe may be shaped like a torus. American inventor Itzhak Bentov in a book called <u>A Brief Tour of Higher Consciousness</u> presents the idea that all reality including consciousness itself can be modeled with the toroidal structure. His diagrams show galaxies as being toroidal forms with a "white hole" putting out energy on one side while a "black hole" on the opposite side takes it back in. The inventor of the Bell Helicopter and other major innovations, Arthur Young, also explores the function of the torus as a model of primary cosmology in his work <u>The Reflexive Universe</u>. The toroidal structure is also becoming important in the field of particle physics and in designing gravitational environmental habitats.

In this chapter we have reviewed the yin-yang flows, the Enlightening and Enlivening pathways, and the circulatory pattern that sustains wholeness. We have seen how the psyche may expand and contract, resulting in a spectrum of shapes, giving rise to the feminine and masculine modes. The circulatory patterns formed by the Enlightening and Enlivening pathways give rise to a toroidal structure. In many spiritual traditions, the torus has long been associated as the geometry of consciousness itself.

Perhaps our psyche does hold the key to a new source of creativity locked in the 95% of the universe that science has just begun to discover. I believe that unlocking this creativity requires a much wider collaboration among natural science, social science, and above all, our own dedicated practice to develop our awareness as a vehicle to explore the infinite universe within our own psyche.

Do This

Exercise 4: Self-Introduction in I-Culture (Masculine) and We-Culture (Feminine) Modes

This is a simple exercise through which you may experience your sense of self in two modes of awareness. You will do a self-introduction in two ways. If you can do this with a partner, that's great. If not, imagine yourself with a partner in a workshop as you do the exercise. If you're doing this by yourself, you may wish to write out your introductions.

I-Culture (Masculine) Mode

Introduce yourself to someone by describing your profession, skills, affiliation, and title. You may also tell your partner about your strengths, interests, and some aspects of your personality that make you unique.

We-Culture (Feminine) Mode

Introduce yourself to someone by describing a relationship that matters to you in a personal way. Focus on describing the history and dynamic of this relationship instead of talking about yourself. It is through listening to you speak about the relationship that your partner will infer a lot of information about who you are.

Reflection

After these two methods of self-introduction, reflect on how their differences felt to you. You may want to journal about your observations first and before reading further about my report of other people's experience.

This exercise was used in a series of cultural competency trainings my co-worker Marci McReynolds and I conducted. Most people reported very different experiences using these two modes. Most of the time immigrants from Asia, Africa and South Americans immediately felt at home in the We-Culture mode. That was the self that they were more familiar with growing up. They were more at ease not having to present a self-identity separating and distinguishing themselves from others as is expected in a predominantly I-Culture society.

Some Americans, having been socially programmed in the I-Culture, felt lost in the We-Culture mode, as American society focuses largely on the individual. But that is not always the case. Women tend to feel more at ease in We-Culture mode than men. Once an American man who grew up in a farming area of the Midwest came up to me and said the We-Culture mode of self was the culture he grew up in. When he came to the city, he had to learn to put the We-Culture self behind just like an immigrant.

There were also people who could fluidly go into either mode. They would report being in touch with different aspects, or aware of a polar tension in their personality. The nature of the tension is unique to each person. For example, one person reported feeling strong and confident in I-Culture/Masculine mode, and feeling vulnerable and naive in We-Culture/Feminine mode. Another person reported feeling playful and cheerful in I-Culture/Masculine mode, and guarded and cautious in We-Culture/Feminine mode.

If you discovered a polar tension through this exercise, I encourage you to inquire how these different aspects of your personality relate with one another. Do you keep them in different domains of life? Or does one generate and relate with another? Are there situations where you experience both of them?

From the perspective of an observer, I distinctly notice the difference in the quality of attention when people are in these two modes. In I-Culture mode, people were active, outgoing, fast, and formal in their talking. When they go into We-Culture mode, the room switches into a more contemplative mood. People talk a lot slower, as they seem to be going deeper into themselves. At the same time, their partners are usually more engaged and the conversations are more intimate. Often the listeners report that they learned so much more about their partner in We-Culture mode even though they didn't talk much about themselves at all.

This exercise can be extended to many different aspects in life. Look at simple, material objects for example. For any item you select with your attention, you may choose to focus on its intrinsic qualities, or to notice instead how it is in relationship with the environment around it. If you wish to explore the We-Culture mode further, give full rein to your imagination and construct a story that relates this object to any (or every) other object in the room.

Do excercise 4 then explore thru constellation.

LT - Consider food & eating.
I culture - thinks of food in terms of its value to the individual in eating

We Culture - thinks of the web of multidimensional inter species relationships that participate in the growing & sharing of food.

Chapter Four

The Four Subtle Energies

In previous chapters, I introduced the architecture of the psyche and reviewed how this architecture may enable a circulatory flow of awareness within the psyche. When this circulatory flow is sustained, the ecosystem of the psyche is healthy, vibrant and whole.

Before humans circumnavigated the Earth, our maps of Earth's geography were partial. Our ability to navigate was limited. Likewise, when we do not have maps of the psyche as a whole, our ability to move our awareness within the terrain of the psyche is also limited.

In the next two chapters, I will take you on a tour of the torus, introducing the main features of the terrain of the psyche. These features are not some abstract elements in an esoteric realm. They are right within ourselves, reachable through simply shining the light of our awareness into the dimmer corners of our psyche.

Having a high resolution map of the psyche also has very practical implications. It will reshape the lens through which we experience the relations around us. My wish is that with this new lens, you may start to perceive how inter-connected we are with one another, including those with whom

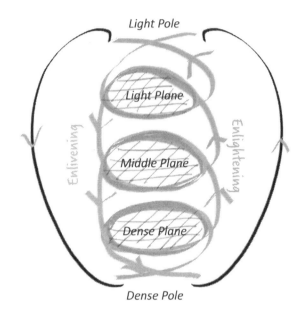

you are not close or those with whom you have a challenging relationship. As a leader, the more accurately you can perceive the inter-connectivity around you, and the more you embody wholeness yourself, the more resources and agency you will have available for activating the potential of the system you lead.

To describe a concrete object that occupies physical space, we usually refer to its three dimensions of width, depth and height. To describe this imaginary space of the psyche, I borrow the same coordinate system. In the previous chapter, the two psychic impulses, the Enlightening and Enlivening pathways, are forces that give rise to the *height* of the psyche. In this chapter, I introduce the psychic impulses that give rise to the *width* and *depth* of the psyche.

At the beginning of Chapter Three, I described how the ancient Taoists intuited a pair of complementary forces, the Yin and Yang currents. Their interaction and inter-penetration are crucial to sustain life as a holistic system. The Yin and Yang impulses along the height dimension are the Enlightening and Enlivening pathways. Two more pairs of complementary forces define the dimensions of width and depth. With these three pairs of complementary forces, The Resonance Code expands the ancient Taoist idea of Yin and Yang into a three-dimensional map.

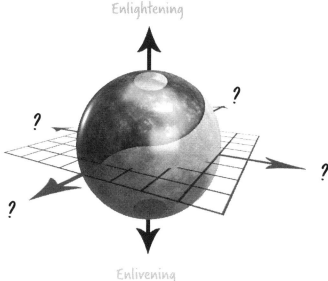

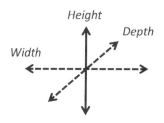

Let us dig a little further into the dimensions of width and depth. The depth axis, functioning as individual awareness, and the width axis, functioning as environmental awareness, anchor two drastically different world views. Through the depth axis, the psyche experiences the self as a body, ego, or subtle pattern of soul. Through the width axis, the psyche experiences the sense of self as the environmental context itself — the natural landscape, social group that inhabits the landscape, or life principles adopted by the group.

The collective modes of I-Culture and We-Culture prioritize the depth and width axes respectively, giving rise to very different sets of cultural values and ideologies. The I-Culture mode gives priority to depth, the individual awareness. In turn it primarily treats the environment as an object separated from the self. The environment is seen as a thing without agency, passively subjected to the will and actions of the individual. The We-Culture mode gives more priority to the width, the environmental awareness, and anchors the sense of self as a relationship between the individual and its environment. It is not that people from a We-Culture are less egoistic. Instead, they identify themselves with specific geographical settings, social groups, and life principles. In this configuration of the psyche, these environmental contexts are considered as entities with their own agency too!

In *The Geography of Thought: How Asians and Westerners Think Differently... and Why*, social psychologist Richard Nisbett explored this in detail.* He wrote, "*to the Westerner, it makes sense to speak of a person as having attributes that are independent of circumstances or particular personal relations. This self — this bounded, impermeable free agent — can move from group to group and setting to setting without significant alteration. But for the Easterner, the person is connected, fluid, and conditional. As philosopher Donald Munro put it, East Asians understand themselves 'in terms of their relation to the whole, such as the family, society, Tao Principle, or Pure Consciousness.'*"

---

* *In modern times, many Asian countries have started to adopt an I-Culture value system due to Western influences, especially in metropolitan areas. The traditional We-Culture becomes more hidden and unconscious.*

In the framework of The Resonance Code, a full development of both the width and depth of the psyche are necessary to evolve toward wholeness. To develop them, we first need to become aware of how our social and historical conditioning, as well as our individual predispositions, have concertedly shaped and influenced us.

In the next section we will begin to review the width and depth dimensions further by focusing through the lens of the Middle Plane. On the Middle Plane, the depth axis is the linear rational mind which perceives the world as objects and categories. When it applies this perceptual lens onto its sense of self, it perceives itself as an individual ego. The width axis is the heart mind, consisting of thought patterns arising in our emotion experience. Through the heart mind, the ego self perceives its relationship with its specific environment. This environment is the socio-cultural context around the ego.

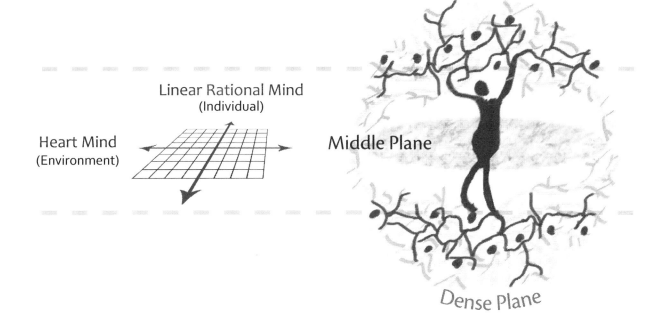

Linear Rational Mind
(Individual)

Heart Mind
(Environment)

Light Plane

Middle Plane

Dense Plane

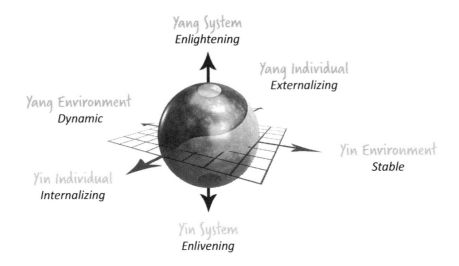

Yang System
Enlightening

Yang Individual
Externalizing

Yang Environment
Dynamic

Yin Environment
Stable

Yin Individual
Internalizing

Yin System
Enlivening

Let's take a look at how the Yin and Yang pathways are expressed on the depth and width axes of the Middle Plane. On the depth axis, where the psyche experiences itself as an ego, the complementary impulses are expressed as externalizing and expressive (Yang), or internalizing and receptive (Yin). In its Yang-externalizing mode, the psyche as an ego self is outgoing, extroverted, and active in projecting itself to the outside environment. In its Yin-internalizing mode, the ego self is directed inward, introverted, digesting and integrating the information from outside.

On the width axis, where the psyche experiences itself in the context of its environment, it can either attune to the stable aspect of the environment (Yin), or the dynamic aspect of the environment (Yang). For those of us who have been acculturated in an I-Culture paradigm and conditioned to relate with the environment as an agent-less object, accessing the balanced Yin-Yang pathways on the width dimension requires a few drastic shifts of our mental framework.

First, we need to grow accustomed to the idea that the agency which controls and directs our life does not lie only within our individual self as we currently experience it. Nor does it lie exclusively in an outside authority. The agency that directs and controls the events and flows of our life is held in the relationship between the individual and the individual's environment. To be in alignment with the Tao of wholeness, we need to develop the fluidity to take control with our own self-agency and simultaneously give control back to the agency of our environment. We need to develop a sense of rhythm to regulate how our psyche can go between taking and giving control in a manner similar to breathing.

Second, since the I-Culture psyche primarily sees the environment as an object, it attributes the quality of the environment it perceives, such as steady or changing, as a quality exclusively of the nature of the environment unrelated to the psyche itself. Here I invite you to take on a new framework. Rather than thinking that there is an intrinsic, absolute quality of the environment, separate from the individual, consider that what we perceive is a function of how we direct our awareness on the width dimension of the psyche. To direct our attention in this way means we always have the potential to choose to focus on either the steady or changing aspect of the environment. It is relatively easy to see we have

this choice in our relationship with the physical environment. For example, as I walk down the busiest street of Seattle downtown, my awareness can be pulled toward the dynamic aspect, such as the busy traffic, crowds and noises. Yet I have the choice to attune my awareness to the stillness and persistence of the buildings, the trees, or the sky above. It would be quite unsafe if I completely tune out the moving and changing aspect of the environment and get lost in the tranquility of the trees and sky. I would be run over! But it would be equally disorienting to attune only to the frenetic motion. Wholeness in our awareness means maintaining a fluid state of attention that moves freely from tranquility to responsiveness regarding the activities around us.

It is harder to see this option in a chaotic and changing socio-cultural environment. This is exactly the plight we are in right now. As I discussed in the Introduction chapter, our current socio-cultural environment can be characterized as VUCA (volatility, uncertainty, complexity and ambiguity). Many rapid changes and unstable factors influence our collective existence. Within this framework, the first thing we need to shift is the thinking that the VUCA we perceive is an outside quality. Instead, I invite you to adopt a hypothesis that the VUCA we perceive outside mirrors the scope and limitation of our awareness, especially along the width axis of the psyche, the dimension in which we perceive the environment.

If our psyche is whole and our awareness free to expand, then we can rest in the security and solidity provided by the stable quality of our environmental awareness. We can then inquire into what new learning opportunity is presented by the volatility, uncertainty, complexity and ambiguity we perceive in the environment. This is like walking down the busy street of downtown, centered yet remaining alert and responsive to the changing environment. In this state of awareness, we can discern the right course of action to navigate the challenges presented by VUCA.

As we learn to pay attention to our environment as a larger being with its own agency, and as we learn to perceive both its dynamic and stable aspects, we will acquire a surprising new agency of our own. We will experience that just through tuning to different aspects of the environment, our very attention can have a subtle, yet powerful impact on the environment itself. It is as if the environment as a being can "hear" us through the quality of attention we pay it. Just like human beings, it tends to settle when it is being heard, and it reciprocates in response to what is brought into its presence. The effect of our attention on the natural environment might ordinarily be too subtle to perceive. However, it is relatively easy to experience this in a social environment. When a skilled meeting facilitator convenes a group, the width of their psyche is very active in attuning to the emotional energies in the space. Through their own embodied presence, they may calm the volatility of the emotional energy and create a stable container to hold the social environment. Meanwhile, they remain open and alert to discern the dynamics of what wants to shift, so they can facilitate that shift through their embodied presence. If you have been in the presence of such facilitators, you may experience how your own emotional energy is influenced by their artful use of their own awareness.

One cannot gain the perspective of wholeness by restricting one's awareness just to the Middle Plane. We also need to expand our awareness to the Dense and Light Planes and understand how consciousness flows and cycles through the whole architecture. At the end of this chapter, I will extend this discussion to the Dense and Light Planes. For now, let us deepen the understanding of how the Yin-Yang forces on the depth and width of the psyche work on the Middle Plane.

Because the essential pathways along each of the dimensions of the psyche are comprised of Yin and Yang, complementary forces, we can represent them using a binary code.

Yang pathway: solid line ⸺

Yin pathway: broken line ⸺ ⸺

In the next chapter, we will use this code to assemble a language that describes the energy state of the psyche as a whole system. For now, we will begin to construct our language by looking more closely at the four subtle energies in the Middle Plane, using our binary code to represent the interactions between the width/environment and depth/individual dimensions of the plane.

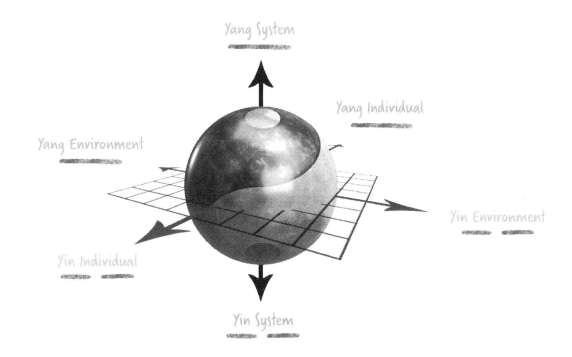

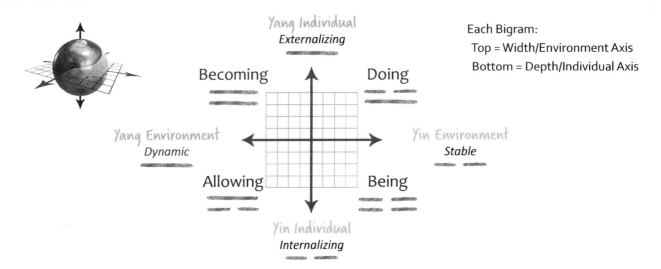

The depth and width of the psyche interact with each other to give rise to four subtle energies: Being, Doing, Becoming, and Allowing. These subtle energies take on their characteristic qualities depending on where we focus our awareness within the architecture of the psyche. You can see them on the diagram above as the interactions between the respective Yin/Yang polarities on each of the axes, width/environment and depth/individual. Doing and Allowing form one set of polar opposite subtle energies, while Being and Becoming form the other. In the diagram, the four subtle energies are identified as bigrams, drawing from our Yin/Yang code.

Doing: The depth aspect (individual awareness) is its Yang mode, externalizing and expressive. Width (environmental awareness) is Yin, attuning to the stable aspect of the environment. When your ego self awareness is anchored in Doing, your externalized expression of self is supported by the still and steady elements of the environment. You perform from a place of knowing, strategizing, planning, and executing using rational approaches. This is the mode for productivity. Through this mode of awareness, you forge self-discipline, will, and drive. This is where you practice the art of control.

Allowing: Depth (individual awareness) is Yin, internalizing and receptive. Width (environmental awareness) is Yang, attuning to the dynamic aspects of the environment. This is exactly the opposite of Doing. The skills of Allowing are seldom taught by modern, Western education. Yet this was the primary mode of awareness fostered by traditional Eastern education before encountering the West. When your awareness is drawn toward Allowing, you are attuning to the movements and changes of the environment, and actively using them to inform your internalizing process.

Martial arts such as tai chi or aikido demonstrate Allowing energy in the somatic realm. A tai chi or aikido master rarely strikes first. Even in a battle, they rest their bodies in a relaxed and alert state. They stay keenly attuned to their opponent's movements, moving and responding accordingly. The purpose of their movement is not to conquer their opponent. Instead, the martial artist's awareness perceives herself and her opponent's body as a whole system. The principle guiding their movements is using their opponent's energy to establish a new equilibrium within the context of the whole system. In the realm of ego, Allowing energy actively lets go of the known and consciously surrenders to the guidance of the unknown. In doing so, one can "compost" one's expired ego, or habitual way of thinking and acting, becoming more fluid and resilient. In this sense, Allowing is regenerative.

Cultivating Allowing helps one to be at ease with being vulnerable and authentic. A leader who is able to lead from his own vulnerability and authenticity is most effective in inspiring other people to change.

Being: Depth (individual awareness) is Yin, internalizing and receptive. Width (environmental awareness) is Yin, attuning to the stable aspect of the environment. When your awareness rests in Being, you rest in the part of you that simply exists, taking no effort to present itself, holding space. Similar to the presence of the Earth, Being just is. Commonly people associate Being with being static. It is not. The entire solar system, including the Earth, moves through the cosmic background at about 370 miles per second. We perceive the rock and mountain as static because they move at the same speed with the Earth. Being is synchronized movement, which sets a reference of stillness for our awareness. But remember, this reference of stillness is movement itself in a larger context.

Becoming: Depth (individual awareness) is Yang, externalizing and expressive. Width (environmental awareness) is Yang, attuning to the dynamic aspect of the environment. In the Becoming mode, the forces of the unknown are actively moving and manifesting. Usually this is a time where a new element, energy, or strategy is being introduced into the system. As a result, some old conditions, containers, or boundaries are being broken, and new ones being installed. When your awareness is pulled toward Becoming, you are participating in the kind of morphogenesis where a caterpillar transforms into butterfly. On this journey, you might experience the agonizing moment of not knowing what awaits next, and the ecstasy of being ushered into something totally magical and unexpected. It is the polar opposite of Being.

Circumnavigation of the Psyche

Let us stand back and look at these four energies as a whole. Even though I present the four energies as a flat surface, remember the full architecture of the psyche occupies a torus with a spherical outside. When we refer to a map of physical space, we understand it as a two-dimensional rendition of a three-dimensional, spherical space. If we travel far enough in one direction, eventually we will come back to the original spot. Similarly, even though these four energies are full of tension and opposition with one another, together they make a whole, just like the four cardinal directions of the landscape.

In wholeness, the opposites mutually generate one another. When one's awareness travels far enough into Being, the transformative process of Becoming naturally happens. Similarly, when one practices Allowing, a more powerful way of Doing will emerge. However, what we experience more often in our social life is tension and sometimes prejudice among the four energies. That is because our ability to move our awareness in the space of the psyche, especially as a collective, is as primitive as our tribal ancestors' ability to explore the landscape of the planet. There was a time when circumnavigating the globe required an incredibly arduous journey, taking many generations to complete. Now, anyone can complete it within a couple of days. Similarly, the psychic space is immense, with many mysteries. We are only at the beginning of this new journey. It will take many generations and collective efforts to circumnavigate. We will require higher-resolution maps, more innovative means to traverse the terrain, and a leap of faith to believe that we are whole.

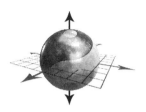

Becoming

- Resetting conditions and container
- Reaching into the unknown
- Opening to new elements, energy or algorithms

Doing

- Linear process
- Cultivation of control, will and discipline
- Productive activities through known, rational approaches

Yang Individual
Externalizing

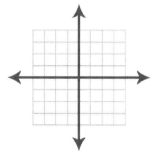

Yang Environment
Dynamic

Yin Environment
Stable

Yin Individual
Internalizing

- Holistic, organic process
- Cultivation of fluidity, vulnerability, and resilience
- Controlled letting go of the known and surrendering to the unknown

- Holding conditions and container
- Resting in what is present
- Effortless in being present and holding the space, like Earth that just is

Allowing

Being

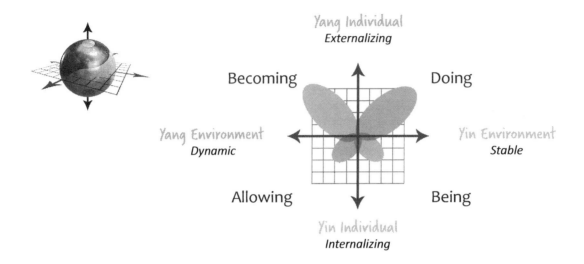

Yang Individual
Externalizing

Becoming   Doing

Yang Environment   Yin Environment
Dynamic   *Stable*

Allowing   Being

Yin Individual
Internalizing

In our modern, developed culture, Doing and Becoming, driven by a Yang individual awareness, tend to receive more attention than Being and Allowing. This often results in an inflation of Doing/Becoming, leading to excessive Doing or obsessive Becoming. Inflation of Doing is Doing stuck in a stagnant place, resulting in a culture that over-privileges material productivity. Most work places are set up to emphasize Doing, leading to an unwholesome work environment. Becoming, when ungrounded in Being, can lead to an obsession in unwholesome transformational processes, which exhausts one's resources. On the organizational level, this can manifests as a rush to implement new management styles or ideas without a foundation based on what the organization needs as a whole. On the personal level, this may manifest as an obsession with trendy "transformational" techniques without fully digesting them, and a persistent dissatisfaction no matter how much change is achieved. Eventually one becomes fatigued and shuts down to true transformation.

One big blind spot contributing to this pattern is a lack of understanding of Being/Allowing. Being is often mistaken for passivity or even laziness.

Allowing is often mistaken for ineffectiveness or may be perceived as self-sabotage. When we do not actively cultivate the skills of Being and Allowing, the latent potential for Being/Allowing often has nowhere to go but to express itself as passivity, laziness and withholding patterns.

Being and Allowing both possess a more feminine quality driven by the impulse to enliven, expressed as processes of receiving, digesting, and internalizing. Healthy versions of these create an attractive, inward pulling energy. We all have the experience of being drawn to or nourished by someone's sheer presence, for example. Many Eastern spiritual traditions teach the arts of Being and Allowing through mindfulness practices. Yet relying on these practices is far from sufficient. There is much to be learned in exploring how to expand our awareness of Being and Allowing in order to integrate them with Doing/Becoming in work environments and communications.

As a woman, I find cultivating the awareness of Being/Allowing and its integration with Doing/Becoming particularly crucial for female leaders. The subjugation of Being/Allowing is so severe in our culture that women are operating with the belief that to excel and succeed, we need to expand our capacity for Doing/Becoming while inhibiting Being/Allowing. This belief compromises our inherent feminine strength, perpetuating a power imbalance between genders.

The natural fluctuation between Yin and Yang impulses on all three dimensions generates a sustainable source of power. When our awareness is stuck in any of these modes, the circulation of energy in our psyche will be blocked.

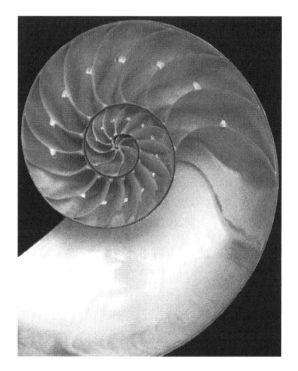

With this map of the four subtle energies, we see that when our attention becomes fixated on Becoming, we can lock ourselves into unchanging Being. We keep going through the same cycles over and over, without any real growth. Similarly, when our attention is fixated on Doing, we tend to get caught flat-footed, unprepared for things that are going on around and within us. We eventually will be forced into Allowing as we become overpowered by circumstances and forces that weren't part of our Doing plan. In other words, our striving for Becoming prevents us from changing. Our striving for Doing forces us to give up control and fall into the Allowing subtle energy we have ignored. With that, we can understand the elusive passage #22 from the Taoist classic *Tao Te Ching*.

> *If you want to become whole, first let yourself be partial.*
>
> *If you want to become straight, first let yourself be crooked.*
>
> *If you want to become full, first let yourself be empty.*
>
> *If you want to be reborn, first let yourself die.*
>
> *If you want to be given everything, first give everything up.*

This passage speaks about a wisdom that is exactly opposite of our normal thinking. It is teaching the "you," the psyche that is contracted inside a bounded, fixed and individual self, to be in intimate contact with a fluid and more expansive self of wholeness.

To translate this into the map of the four energies, we might say, if you want to gain a greater control, allow yourself to first be receptive to the wills and agencies from the environment. If you want to experience a deeper transformation, start by embodying what wants to be embodied, even those parts your ego mind rejects. Try going deep into the opposite of what you want most. The more you want something, the more you might choose to experience its opposite, *first*. In doing so, you will be creating a field of momentum by which you will be catapulted toward the direction you want, not by your own individual will and strength, but through the power and grace of wholeness. This is the dance of the Tao.

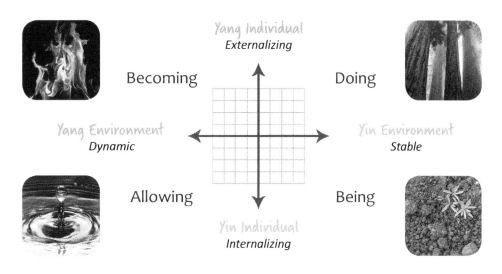

These four energies are closely associated with the Five Phases framework in the native Chinese cosmology. It is applied to everything from astronomical movements to interactions of internal organs, from successions of political and social changes to geographical features. The translation of Five Elements is due to a false analogy with the Western four elements theory. Unlike the four elements of the West, this Chinese cosmology framework is not concerned with substance or essence. It is concerned with the phases of cosmic process and change that govern the creation, destruction, and regeneration of both natural and social events. This framework was an ancient understanding of evolution as a meta-process that expresses itself through both biological and social organisms.

The Five Phases are usually translated as water, wood, fire, mineral, and soil. However, this translation easily misleads English speakers who think of them as names for concrete objects. In fact, the ancient Chinese language used these words as metaphors to refer to specific phases in the arc of evolution.

The four subtle energies of The Resonance Code correspond to four of the five phases. Doing energy is associated with the wood phase, as wood is an embodiment of linear, productive growth. Allowing is associated with the water phase as water symbolizes nature's fluidity, resilience and ability to regenerate itself. Being is associated with the soil phase as soil is the quintessential symbol for nature's ability to hold space and set conditions for evolution. Becoming is associated with the fire phase. Here fire should be understood in its broadest sense as a symbol for a source of energy.

The phase that is missing here is mineral. Minerals are beautiful manifestations of the geometrical structures of chemical compositions. The phase that mineral symbolizes is the process of crystallization. In The Resonance Code, this phase is implicitly held by the toroidal structure, the geometry that holds the architecture of the psyche. A torus can be thought of as a "mother source" of many of the geometric forms with which we are familiar. They include circles, squares, triangles as well as more complex forms such as dodecahedrons.

Without this kind of knowledge, it is easy to see why our human psyche has become separated from nature, thinking that it is fundamentally different from what it perceives outside. Having this connection between the elemental phases of nature and the fundamental energies of our psyche invites our psyche to weave back into the wholeness of the entire ecosystem. Now, as we stand by an ocean, we may recognize the same currents of Allowing inside ourselves. As we gaze in awe at the display of energy during a thunderstorm, we may use that to tap into the surges of Becoming in ourselves. When we walk in a forest, we may let the trees inspire the linear growth of our Doing. When we touch the soil, we may tap into the rhythm of our own Being, the intelligence of biological evolution, synchronized and orchestrated to support our conscious awareness. When we are mesmerized by the beauty of a crystal, we can feel its Resonance with the wholeness of our own psyche.

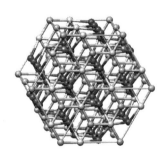

Bastnäsite crystal and the geometrical structure of its chemical composition

As we understand how this inflation of Doing and obsession with productivity has shaped our collective psyche, it is natural to see how the issues we are facing in the outer ecosystem mirror the imbalances and stuckness inside our psyche. The depletion of topsoil in our ecosystem correlates with how the Being energy of our psyche is neglected. We give so much attention to doing, performing, and producing, yet much less to practicing and refining the art of Being. When we are in Being mode, we tend to compartmentalize it. We think of Being as a time for meditation in a beautiful resort. But how to apply Being energy in leadership, in a boardroom, or in negotiations for a business contract? Further, the increased carbon level in our atmosphere is also directly related to the imbalance of excessive production in our modern civilization. However, if our approaches to addressing environmental issues are still run by the habitual patterns of Doing, although our intention is to bring balance and sustainability back to the outer ecosystem, we continue to unconsciously deposit "carbon" into the collective psychic space.

Activist Burn out.

The pollution of our waterways and the overwhelming amount of garbage in the ocean correlates with how we have neglected and misunderstood the Allowing energy of the psyche. Without the active composting of our ego and identity, the "water" in our psyche has become a garbage collector of all the "waste products" generated by an ego disconnected from the rest of the psychic ecosystem.

Finally, energy is a critical key to a sustainable economy. Many of the issues we face have to do with an economy heavily reliant on fossil fuel as the main energy source. To transition into the next phase of human evolution, introduction of new energy sources is critical. Throughout human evolution, every time a new energy source is introduced, it also catalyzes a new way of living, and thus new ways of thinking and seeing the world. The technology to transition our civilization out of fossil fuel has long existed. Making the transition would require many industries dependent on fossil fuel to transform, allowing new industries to emerge. That requires a level of Becoming for which our collective psyche has not prepared.

We are at a point of evolution where we have to realize that what propels our civilization in evolving further is no longer outer technology that allows us to manipulate natural resources with greater control and power. Instead:

The opportunity for our greater evolution is the inner technology that allows us to navigate the psyche as a whole with greater ease and control.

Inside the terrain of the human psyche are massive "mountains," structures of belief shaped by cultural habits shaped over thousands of years. There are vast "oceans," emotional imprints of joy and sorrow from the collective journeys of our ancestors, passed down through epigenetics. There is the inner Earth, our raw experience of life that lies beyond existing language constructs. All of these "landscape features" are within each human's psyche, accessible simply by attuning our awareness to them.

Following this line of thinking, I envision in the future we humans will realize our own psyche is our most important energy source containing the seeds for all possibilities in the emerging present. In that future, we cannot simply apply outer technology without considering the impact on the inner landscape. By engaging wholeness in our inner landscape, we can make conscious, holistic choices about what we do with outer technology. It will be through a deeper connection with the inner technology that humanity will truly launch into a new era of progress.

Becoming

- Innovation
- Bringing forth new energy, knowledge and technology.

Allowing

- Regenerative process
- Replenishing energy in non-linear fashion

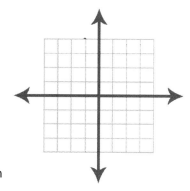

Doing

- Productive process
- Productivity measured in linear ways

Being

- Embodiment
- Strengthening existing energy, knowledge, and technology

In summary, the four energies point to four phases of change required for a living system to thrive and evolve in a sustainable way. The intelligence of a system is hinged on the concerted, timely coordination among all four phases.

Becoming: The system searches for and experiments with new ways to capture energies sustaining the system. In social evolution, it leads to innovation of new knowledge or new technology.

Doing: The system looks for ways to utilize the new energy and express it as concrete forms and products. In social evolution, the new knowledge takes a mature form. Technology leads to a wide variety of products. The productivity of the system can be measured in linear ways.

Being: The system experiences itself as the forms and products that express the energy. Through experiencing itself, the system provides the container and reference point for all other phases.

Allowing: The system deconstructs the more sophisticated and refined forms into simpler and more primal forms. In doing so, it regenerates and replenishes the overall energy state of the system. The regeneration of energy is a non-linear process.

Depth is the channel through which the psyche perceives itself as a unit. On the Dense Plane, the depth axis represents the instinct, the channel of perception where the psyche perceives itself as an individual body. Width is the channel through which the psyche relates with its environment. On the Dense Plane, the width axis represents our five senses that allow the body to receive information from its physical surroundings: sight, sound, smell, taste and kinesthetic vibrations.

In our Dense Plane experience as a body and interacting with the world through the five senses, human cultures have established relatively universal, shared common ground. We can relate to our instinctual desires for food, water, shelter, and companionship. We also share a relatively common understanding of our sensory experience of the physical environment.

The Light Plane is the plane of a more ephemeral existence, one which humanity largely acknowledges exists, yet describes in many different ways. Differences in culture, belief and ways of life affect how each person perceives the Light Plane. This makes it difficult to communicate perceptions and experience across different cultures. Yet it has never stopped us from experimenting and trying new ways.

On the Light plane, the depth axis is a channel through which the psyche perceives itself as an individual subtle pattern, which is also referred to as soul awareness in this book. The width axis is what I call the energetic perception, the channel through which this individual soul perceives itself in relationship to other souls.

In our culture, usually a great deal of our attention is given to the three depth channels. For example, modern psychology is very much is concerned with how the ego may emerge from the raw instincts. Spiritual traditions are concerned with how a soul may emerge from an ego self. (In many indigenous cultures, a lot of attention is also given to how a Dense Plane body may emerge from a Light Plane soul. The Tibetans, for example, are well known for their knowledge of reincarnation. However, in the disruption of the wholeness of the psyche, this knowledge is prohibited in the framework of modern science.)

In comparison, the width channels — our senses, heart mind, and how we perceive energy — usually receive less attention. Often they are

Energy
(Energetic
Aspect of
Emotion)

 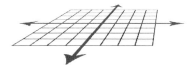

Soul/Subtle Pattern

Heart Mind
(Cognitive
Aspect of
Emotion)

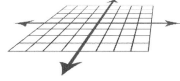

Ego / Linear Rational Mind

Senses
(Physiological
Aspect of
Emotion)

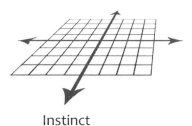

Instinct

Light Plane

Middle Plane

Dense Plane

considered secondary to the channels on the depth axis. The width of the psyche, senses, heart mind, and energy all have to do with our emotional or feeling experience. I will illustrate with a personal example.

When I witnessed the devastating consequences to the ecosystems in China brought forth by a hunger for wealth and progress, I went through powerful waves of grief. In my grief I experienced soreness in my tear glands, fuzzy vision, a heaviness in my body, and muffled sound around me. That information came from the channel of senses, the width axis on the Dense Plane.

There were also thought patterns and memories associated with this grief. There was a part of the Yangtze River that held a very precious childhood memory. That part of the river is now submerged under the water due to the construction of Three Gorges Dam. This controversial engineering project not only destroyed ecosystems but also valuable archaeological sites while displacing 1.2 million people from their homeland and traditional livelihood. The thought patterns and psychological constructs that surfaced in my experiences of grief came from my heart mind, the width axis on the Middle Plane.

The Qutang Gorge, shown above, was flooded by the Three Gorges Dam, shown left.

Energetic perception is probably the most elusive and least understood channel. In my example of grief, when I expand my awareness and start to perceive the universal, transpersonal patterns behind my very personal experience of grief, my awareness is in the energetic realm. This energetic perception is not an intellectual understanding, although intellectual understanding can greatly enhance the quality of this perception. The energetic perception is a felt sensation and lived experience of self as an embodied, transpersonal archetype.

Because energetic perception is a human experience that does not yet have a solid language base to it, I will not elaborate here. Instead I invite you to experiment with it using the information I have provided so far, and form your own opinion about it. During the courses and trainings we offer at our Institute, we explore energetic perception in the context of experiential learning.

In professions that deal with deep, interpersonal or even transpersonal experiences such as holistic healing, coaching, and counseling, energetic perception is becoming a key ingredient. In my experience in these fields, I often hear professionals using this concept. Yet our understanding of how energy is related with other constructs such as ego, instincts, emotion, and soul varies drastically. Until we have a standard way to conceptualize and talk about these phenomena, we cannot build upon collective knowledge and experience.

Overwhelmed by Six Channels of Information?

By now you might be thinking: this is complicated. How am I going to understand this? Don't worry.

> *You do not need to understand this in order to engage with the work.*

Through the research and experimentation at the Resonance Code Research Lab, we have come up with practices and processes that provide a whole-person engagement. The intellectual mind will catch up once you acquire experience through your embodied awareness, heart, and soul. In fact, not-understanding at the beginning is a blessing. It provides the most fresh, open mind to engage with experience, which is critical in laying the foundation of this work.

On the Middle Plane, the four energies together maintain the innovation, production and regeneration of rational knowledge. Through the Middle Plane, the psyche experiences itself as an ego-self, an abstraction of the linear rational mind.

On the Dense Plane, the psyche experiences itself as an individual body, a product of biological evolution. The four energies together maintain the innovation, production and regeneration of automated circuitry. Automated circuitry, as discussed in detail in Chapter Two, constantly records and stores our lived experience as preferences, habits, and implicit assumptions. Many of these operate below the threshold of cognition.

Learning theory outlines a Four Stages of Competence model for the acquisition of this automated knowledge. In the first stage, we don't know we are incompetent at a particular skill (unconscious incompetence). Next, we become aware of our incompetence (conscious incompetence). This awareness motivates us to learn while we are consciously acquiring the skill (conscious competence). Finally, we fully integrate the learning, which then becomes "stored" as an automatic skill. This last stage, unconscious competence, involves automating newly acquired neurological patterns into circuitry on the Dense Plane.

In learning motor skills such as walking, running, and riding bicycles, the learning usually reaches the final stage. We perform these tasks needing little conscious effort. Yet, skills that require coordination of all six channels of the psyche, such as self knowledge and self control, are much harder to reach the final stage of unconscious competence. To bring these skills to the final stage requires knowledge of the psyche as a whole.

Now let us examine how the Yin-Yang pathways express on the Dense Plane and what the four energies look like.

Being: Depth (individual as a body) is Yin, internal and receptive. Width (sensing of the environment) is Yin, attuning to the stable and predictable aspects of the environment. In Being, the psyche experiences the synchronized aspects of biological processes. In its experiencing, it provides the context for all other phases.

Doing: Depth (individual as a body) is Yang, externalizing and expressive. Width (sensing of the environment) is Yin, attuning to the stable and predictable aspects of the environment. In Doing, the psyche constructs more sophisticated and complex forms of automated circuitry.

Becoming: Depth (individual as a body) is Yang, xternalizing and expressive. Width (sensing of the environment) is Yang, attuning to the dynamic and unpredictable aspects of the environment. In Becoming, the psyche transcends its primal instincts and automated circuitry, searching for new pathways to access its somatic energy.

Allowing: Depth (individual as a body) is Yin, internalizing and receptive. Width (sensing the environment) is Yang, attuning to the dynamic and unpredictable aspects of the environment. In Allowing, the psyche deconstructs higher, more sophisticated forms of automated circuitry and returns them to simpler and more primal circuitry.

Exercise 5:
Experiencing Dense Plane Energies

Practice tuning into these four energies on the Dense Plane through these activities. See if you can consciously experience the awareness pathways.

Being: When you are resting on the couch after a meal, register the sensation of your body digesting and internalizing. Experience your sensory channels attuning to the still and stable aspect of the environment. The time before we fall asleep is also a good time to experience Being energy.

Doing: This can be when you are engaging a repetitive and semi-automatic physical action that requires skills that you are still learning and perfecting. The conscious, repetitive actions automate it. The automation needs a stable environment.

Becoming: This can be a time when you are taking a physical adventure such as biking down a steep trail you are unfamiliar with. Your body is actively moving. And the environment contains unknown and uncertain factors. Your body learns new pathways to respond to the changing environment through these activities.

Allowing: In modern days, it is not a common practice to experience the more primal parts of ourselves. Yet, it can be profoundly healing and regenerative, so I've extended this portion of the exercise to support you in exploring this energy.

Consider a moment when you were captured by the beauty of sunset on the beach. For a brief moment, you feel as if your body merges with the ocean waves reflecting the golden lights. You experience yourself as the essence of nature. It could be a moment when you encounter a large wild animal in a remote mountain. In that moment, the protections around the ego identity fall away. That encounter may evoke your primal instincts that are normally submerged under the streams of thought of modern life. Or it could be as you are watching a football game in a stadium with a wild crowd. At the height of the game, the controlled and civilized modern self-identity dissolves and you experience yourself as a primal warrior with instinctual desires, roaring along with the surging energy of the crowd.

Whenever we have a felt sensation as if our own embodied existence is no longer limited to our skin, but extending to a larger body, that is the working of Allowing energy. We experience a more primal, undifferentiated self. In that regard, sexual intimacy and pregnancy offer windows of opportunity for us to be swept up by the currents of Allowing.

In modern society, there is a lot of inhibition and shame associated with this primal existence. This resistance often interferes with a healthy expression of Allowing energy. Motivated by the desire to experience Allowing on the Dense Plane, people sometimes enact the ritual of medicine plant

ingestion or shamanic journeys. These practices used to be embedded in native, indigenous cultural environments where there was an intimate, day-to-day relationship with more primal life forces. When modern people practice these rituals out of a reaction against the intense inhibition programmed in the unconscious, their psyche might be vulnerable to quite disruptive forces.

As the Middle Plane is concerned with intellectual process and its products, and the Dense Plane is concerned with somatic processes and automated circuitry, the Light Plane is concerned with subtle energetic processes and patterns.

The subtle energy pattern, or soul awareness, is reflected in the templates of life we adopt such as world views and beliefs. It is also reflected in the mythology and lore about our origins, the meaning of life, and future possibilities. It shows up in the movies and stories that touch us, games that capture our attention, and fantasies that stimulate our imagination.

The subtle energy pattern, especially our world views and belief system, orients our awareness toward what is possible and where are the limits; what needs to be prioritized and what needs to wait. It leads us to what our soul most yearns to experience. This is the musical score that directs how we play our awareness on the instrument of the psyche.

Who are the people with whom you share similar kinds of beliefs and world views? What are the forces that have shaped your templates of life? How is your template of life evolving and changing? Before the modern era, those people with whom we shared our Dense Plane, embodied experience, such as our family, tribe, or people with the same ethnic origin, were usually also those with whom we shared our Light Plane world views. Thus the subtle energy pattern that anchors our world views is a life force with a much, much longer life-span than our individual lives.

Through the rise of the information age and prevalence of globalization of all kinds, we have now gained a tremendous ability to choose, experiment with, and reinvent our belief systems. We can encounter and adopt beliefs that are different, sometimes even drastically apart from those with which we grew up. We can beome deeply intimate through marriage and other relations with the subtle energy patterns of widely divergent cultures. As our workplaces and neighborhoods become more and more diverse, this kind of influence, challenge, and cross-pollination takes on a constant presence.

While this shift has catalyzed cross-pollination of different belief systems, giving rise to a much richer pool of templates for life, it has also resulted in traumatic fractures between the Light and Dense Planes, where family and traditions have been torn apart; relations and intimacies withered. Healing these wounds and channeling them into collaborative creation is a new evolutionary threshold to cross, one carrying great potential. The subtle energy pattern of the Light Plane is a potent creative force. The direction to which it orients our attention through faith, sense of purpose, or riveted interests has the power to create a reality.

As with any power, using it wisely requires specialized knowledge and dedicated practice. This subtle energy pattern, our soul awareness, is like a subtle "body" of ours, each with its own unique dispositions, quirks, and gifts. It is a legacy we inherit from our ancestors, as well as the seed of potential that connects us to humanity's future. We need to approach it as carefully and respectfully as we approach our physical body.

Being: Depth (individual as a subtle pattern) is Yin, internalizing and receptive. Width (energetic awareness) is Yin, attuning to the stable and predictable aspects of the environment. In Being, the psyche experiences the receptive aspect of soul. The beliefs and world views are stable. In its stability, the soul provides the context for all other phases.

For most of the people who adopt a fixed and unchanging world view, they are enacting Being energy unconsciously. Their souls serve to stabilize the energetic environment. However, without consciously choosing to enact this energy, they can get stuck in the Being phase. In today's world, the clashes between belief systems and world views are ever-present in our daily life. It is because many souls are waking up from this unconscious Being phase.

Becoming: Depth (individual as a subtle pattern) is Yang, externalizing and expressive. Width (energetic awareness) is Yang, attuning to the dynamic and unpredictable aspects of the environment. In Becoming, the psyche searches for more abstract, subtler patterns that reflect the deeper truth of the universe.

Some of the archetypal expressions of Becoming are devoted yogis, philosophers, and genius scientists. They are on a continuous quest to search for finer knowledge. They can get unconsciously stuck in Becoming too. In the stuck mode, they can be disembodied and ungrounded. Their knowledge can turn rigid and dogmatic.

Doing: Depth (individual as a subtle pattern) is Yang, externalizing and expressive. Width (energetic awareness) is Yin, attuning to the stable and predictable aspects of the environment. In Doing, the psyche constructs patterns to represent subtler and more universal energies.

The architectural drawings and maps presented in this book are products of Doing energy on the Light Plane. They present the flow of subtle energies, equivalent of qi, in a living system. All four energies on all three planes are involved in producing these drawings. But the Doing on the Light Plane played a significant leadership role here.

Allowing: Depth (individual as a subtle pattern) is Yin, internalizing and receptive. Width (energetic awareness) is Yang, attuning to the dynamic and unpredictable aspects of the environment. In Allowing, the psyche deconstructs the subtle patterns and renders them on the Middle Plane. For example, the intellectual discussions and rationalizations presented in this book result from applying Allowing onto the architecture drawings. Through Allowing, the subtler pattern expands into denser realms. Its expansion into the denser planes leads to more practical application as well as testing and refining the Light Plane architecture.

Changing the Subtle Patterns
of Beliefs and World Views

In earlier forms of human society, individual agency was limited compared to today's world. The pressures of survival required us to collectively band together and subscribe to a shared template of life. We inherit these templates from our tribal, familial, or spiritual lineages, products of millennia of evolution, and experience great psychological resistance even to the point of taboo against questioning these templates.

For example, one of the most universal beliefs is that life is a battle for survival. Imprinted by this template, we are automatically driven by the urge to win and fear of losing, especially between one "tribal" group and another. This template has historically ensured our survival. But in today's world, it becomes a hindrance to creativity and collaboration, which in fact undermines our chance to survive as a species when facing global issues such as climate change.

This template is not wrong. It has served a great purpose for humanity and will continue to play an important role. However, always prioritizing this template as the cardinal principle is inadequate for humans to evolve further. We need new beliefs to play win-win, non-zero-sum games and to support the flourishing of co-creative, co-evolving, and collaborative relations.

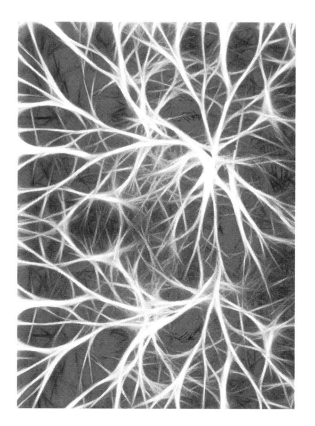

awareness. In order to change these patterns, we need to develop skills to go "under the hood" and rewire our dense plane circuitry.

Second, we need to be very mindful of the intrinsic immune pathways associated with the old belief systems, and understand the complex circuitries that protect their integrity. As I have just discussed, judging beliefs as wrong and changing them by brute force is not only ineffective, but can be counter-productive.

The Resonance Code presents a new strategy. Instead of judging a belief as right or wrong, we consciously steward its natural dissolving and reincarnation with a sensitivity to timing in the context of the whole psyche.

as in a. Constellation

The architecture of the psyche presents a deeper and more wholesome web of connections so that we can enroll the energetic patterns of old beliefs into new games. As we play in the new games, new automated circuity will rewire on the Dense Plane. New instincts will arise. New sensory pathways will be wired. New thought patterns associated with the energetic pathways will naturally emerge on the Middle Plane. Gradually, new belief patterns with their new life forces will take root, grow, and thrive.

Changing these old belief patterns is as complex as performing neurosurgery. Changing beliefs through linguistic and cognitive processes on the Middle Plane is usually insufficient, for two reasons. First, these beliefs are rooted in lived experience, intricately woven with automated circuitry on the Dense Plane, operating outside the scope of our linguistic and cognitive

This table summarizes all three pairs of Yin-Yang pathways.

	Yang	Yin
Height	Enlightening	Enlivening
Depth	Externalizing	Internalizing
Width	Dynamic	Stable

As the vertical axis and horizontal plane come together, they form into double spirals, shown below.

Double Spiral

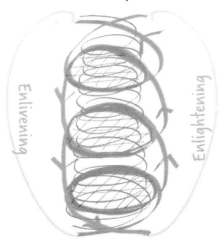

Doing and Becoming generate momentum for an ascending spiral. Within this spiral, somatically felt experience is extracted into the intellectual realm in the Middle Plane. Intellectual knowledge is further extracted into subtle patterns of the Light Plane. This process generates finer and more universal knowledge. When the ascending spiral reaches the top, it exits the core and reverses into a descending current in a larger context. (This reversal is explained in Chapter Three.) This teaches us that when knowledge reaches its finest level, it naturally wants to experience itself as life.

Allowing and Being generate the descending spiral. With the descending spiral, subtle patterns constructed by abstract symbols can embody and develop into denser realms. Light Plane patterns embody as intellectual products; intellectual processes as material products; biological processes as the larger ecosystem of life. As the larger ecosystem experiences itself, it provides the container for evolutionary process. Similarly, at the bottom of the core, the spiral exits the core and reverses into an ascending current in a larger context. This teaches us that a pathway to reach for higher and more refined knowledge is to dive deeper into the more felt experience of life.

If we see the development of computer technology as an externalization of humanity's evolution process, then we can see the echo of this architecture in computer network systems.

The mechanisms that allow a computer to operate as a stand-alone unit correspond to the depth dimension. The majority of modern computers have the capacity to connect themselves to a network environment, sending and receiving information to and from each other. These mechanisms correspond to the width dimension.

As for the height of the computer system, upward along this axis delineates the development from human intelligence to technology. This

Height: From human intelligence to technology and back

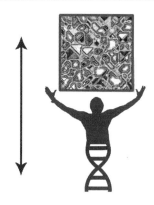

corresponds to the Enlightening pathway. How we learn and deepen our experience as human beings with the aid of technology corresponds to the Enlivening pathway. Computer technologies are products of the Enlightening impulses. We make them to serve us, enliven our lives, and possibly teach us things we would have never learned. We do not need to fear or reject them as long as we have access to our own wholeness.

Width: Connection with computer network

Depth: Information processing between hardware and software

In this chapter, I have taken you inside the architecture of the psyche, introducing its depth and width dimensions. Depth has to do with perceiving the self as an individual unit (a body, ego, or soul/archetypal pattern). Through the width dimension, an individual senses the environment in which she is immersed.

In this model, the psyche has a total of six channels of information processing. Each channel is shaped by the Yin and Yang pathways. The Yang pathway moves the individual self to externalize and express itself, and to attune to the dynamic aspects of the environment. In essence, the Yang pathway moves us to develop new agency and knowledge. The Yin pathway moves the psyche to internalize and be receptive, and to attune to the stable aspects of the environment. In essence, the Yin pathway expands our capacity for new experience and engagement.

When we learn to direct our awareness guided by knowledge of this architecture, our psyche becomes a resonator that vibrates along these six channels. Each of these six channels underpins a constellation of experience, knowledge, and values unique to the universe within each

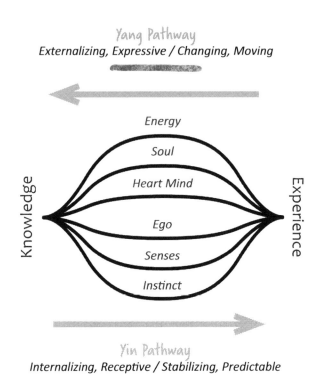

individual's psyche. It is the composite pattern of these six channels that gives rise to the tapestry of our ongoing learning and life experience.

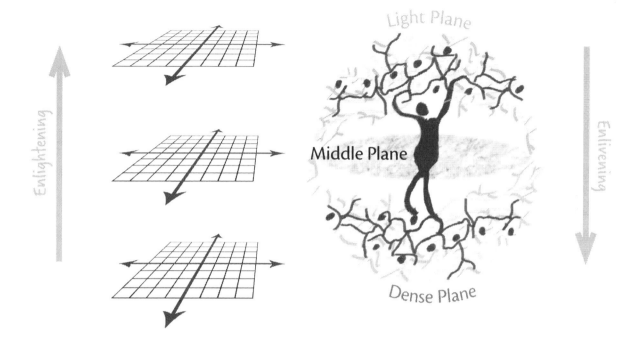

Imagine making decisions and choices through operating this complex system as a whole. What happens in a situation where your linear rational mind tells you something is right, yet your intuition says no? What about a situation where your heart is open and receptive to a vision, yet you find yourself energetically non-committal?

Are you emotionally drawn to a relationship yet your soul is moving to the other direction? No scripted or formulaic answer can address the complexity of these questions. Answering these questions is both an art and science; an art that requires dedicated and embodied practice, and a science of continuous inner inquiry.

Chapter Five

64 Hexagrams:

The Language of Evolution

In this chapter I describe how the knowledge presented so far assembles into a new language and a communication system. With this language and communication system, we can employ our psyche as a resonating device to directly communicate with the energy of the larger life forces in both our natural and social environments. I call these larger life forces the Inter-Being.

You may ask, "What for? Why do I want to communicate with this Inter-Being?" It's a good question. So please take a moment to ask yourself the following questions:

Are you willing to take a leap of faith? Are you willing to believe that no matter how much volatility, uncertainty, and crisis appear to disrupt human civilization, there is a larger life force of Inter-Being evolving toward wholeness? That there is a nascent order being birthed even though the nature of this order may remain unknown to your conscious mind at this moment?

If the answer is yes, then learning this language will enable you to become a conscious participant in collaborating with the larger life forces of the Inter-Being, so that you can be the compassionate and inspiring leader facilitating your family, community, or organization to find creative ways to respond to the challenges of our time.

This Inter-Being can be simultaneously the greatest teacher challenging and stretching you to the furthest reach that you dare not to dream, while being the most loving and nurturing caregiver, providing you with the nourishment and healing you need in the most personal way.

First let us review the channels of communication within the three planes of the psyche.

Verbal and Written Language

Our verbal and written interaction in daily life, books, media, and professional communications is primarily a language of the Middle Plane. When our language expresses through rational and logical reasoning, it comes through the channel of the linear rational mind. When it expresses emotional contents, such as in fictional writing, it comes through the channel of the heart mind.

Verbal and written language can also be used to bridge and connect with the Dense and Light Planes. When fiction writers evoke a strong sensory experience or arouse instinctual desires, they use language to interact with the Dense Plane. When poets weave image, imagination and ethereal beauty with words, they build a portal to access the Light Plane.

Communications Within the Dense Plane

Dense Plane channels express the intelligence of biological evolution. Its language includes raw sensations, feelings and instinctual impulses. The language of the Dense Plane has been spoken for

millions of years and connects us to the wholeness of life as it has evolved on Earth. To communicate with the body effectively, our mind needs to develop the sensibility to respect the body's intelligence and interpret its messages in its logic, instead of forcing our rational logic onto it. For example, if our linear rational mind is obsessed with Doing energy and forces that onto the body, the body may "fight" back as disease symptoms and force us into Allowing.

Modern Western medicine has conditioned the rational mind to treat our bodies as passive, mechanical objects, subject to the intentions and interests of the ego self. We were taught to analyze, quantify, and test all aspects of our bodily functions. Our mind is usually not prepared to communicate with the Dense Plane effectively.

Language of the Light Plane

The Language of the Light Plane is the most abstract. Its purest form is mathematical symbols and geometric shapes. However, Light Plane language by itself is lifeless. It needs to be rendered into the Dense and Middle Planes to be appreciated and understood. Contact with the Light Plane often inspires the most beautiful expressions of Middle or Dense Planes such as poetry, prose, or dance and music.

The language I soon will describe is a language of the Light Plane. With this language we can train our psyche to perceive the energetic connections between the dynamics of the inner and outer worlds. Embedded in those patterns is a higher form of logic and mathematical abstraction that penetrates deeper into the underlying principles of the universe. I want to emphasize that at the core of this Light Plane language is a commitment to the three planes of the psyche as a system of wholeness. The authority of the system lies in the relationships among the three instead of being centralized to any one of them.

In the last chapter, I demonstrated how the four subtle energies can be coded as bigrams, where the Yin and Yang impulses are represented as solid or broken lines. To represent the energetic qualities of the psyche as a system, we take one bigram from each plane and assemble them into a hexagram. The example below illustrates such a hexagram. (A more detailed explanation of this specific hexagram will be presented in a few pages.) Since there are 4 energies on each plane, there are 64 possible hexagrams (4x4x4 = 64). These hexagrams inform us about our relationship with the Inter-Being as a set of coordinates.

At this moment, you probably will find it hard to interpret these coordinates into language and

meaning to speak to your Middle Plane. That is totally understandable. Just as learning a foreign language involves rewiring neurological pathways and developing fine motor controls of the larynx, tongue, and facial muscles, learning the language of the hexagrams requires rewiring cognitive pathways and reprogramming automatic circuitry. It will take time to develop such skills.

At the same time, this is also different than learning a foreign language. You will still use English as a tool. But with practice, you will learn to derive new meanings and make sense of these hexagrams based on your own lived experience and experimentation.

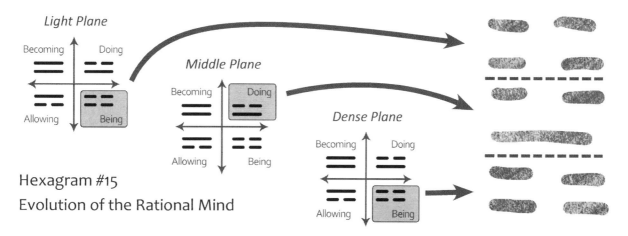

Hexagram #15
Evolution of the Rational Mind

The book of I-Ching is widely known in the Western world. However, the hexagrams as a mathematical abstraction are rarely understood. The hexagrams are codes, each composed of a set of six binary digits. These codes represent the principles by which intelligent living systems adapt to their environment through evolving toward wholeness. As mathematical symbols, hexagrams hold universal meaning across cultures. Each hexagram represents an evolutionary lesson that the psyche needs to learn by coordinating and integrating the soul, mind, and body.

The ancient Chinese started to experiment with the hexagrams as early as 7,000 years ago, around the same time when the earliest forms of written language arose. For thousands of years, people in ancient China, from philosophers to politicians, from Taoist sages to Confucian scholars, from ordinary people to emperors, contributed their experience and lessons into the experiential database of I Ching. This database forms the DNA of Chinese culture.

Nourished by the wisdom transmitted through these hexagrams, ancient Chinese culture was

Hexagrams: A Six-Digit Binary Code System
Each hexagram consists of six lines. Each line is a
binary symbol, either solid ▬▬ or broken ▬ ▬

able to sustain its vitality and resilience for thousands of years, integrating diverse streams of cultural systems along the way, rebirthing itself time and time again through periods of destruction. Through these hexagrams, we can connect to one of the most ancient wisdom systems on Earth.

About 2,000 years ago, Chinese intellectuals started to compile texts that are now called I-Ching, or the Book of Change. I-Ching is an intellectual abstraction based on about five thousand years' history working with the hexagrams. Today, the I Ching text has been widely translated into non-Chinese languages. However, few translated versions touch upon the origin of the binary coding and the structure of the hexagrams. The translated versions are far from adequate in delivering the core knowledge contained within the hexagrams for two reasons.

First, the original text is imprinted with the limitations of the cultural and social conditions of ancient China. For example, the ancient Chinese social structures prescribed very fixed roles based on one's gender, family origin, age, and other social attributes. This greatly limited individual creativity. Another limitation is privileging collective interests far above the individual's sovereignty and agency. My personal experience of growing up in China taught me that this was just as hurtful as privileging the individual interest far above the collective's. Eventually the collective interest gets severely compromised after all.

Second, without knowledge of the architecture of the psyche, reading the translated texts is like interacting with software without the knowledge of computer coding language. One can only be an end user. In order to be an engineer who can develop new apps, one needs to learn the underlying code.

If hexagrams are like the numerical coordinates of a GPS device, the I Ching texts are like maps that show the roads, highways, towns, and cities, as well as the mountains, rivers, and oceans surrounding human civilization. If we were navigating the physical terrain, we would not rely on a map made thousands of years ago, would we? However, if that is the only map we have, then we have to rely on it to draw new ones.

No matter how much the maps change, the mathematical coordinates of a place do not change. Where my home is in Seattle used to be a fishing village of the Duwamish people for thousands of years. Now it is the hustling and bustling industrial part of downtown Seattle next to the multi-cultural scene of the International District. The map of this place changed dramatically within two hundred years. Yet its geographical coordinates, 47.6 degrees North and 122.3 degrees West, have remained the same. These coordinates thread through all the changes happening on this land through the indigenous life and history of the Duwamish people and the modern life that is unfolding. It connects this place with all other places on Earth in a timeless relationship.

As modern education biases toward linear rational thinking and objectification of the world, one of the impacts is that the coordinate number becomes a dead, mechanical, measuring device. In cultures that have maintained the original order of wholeness, number is part of the language spoken by the Inter-Being. Numbers are enlivened with character and personality. They do not just transmit quantitative information, but also invite the feeling, sensing and imaginative faculties on the Dense and Light Planes.

The challenges we face today ask us to learn how to navigate the terrain of the psyche and renew wholeness as a collective. To do that, we need leaders as new map-makers to launch expeditions into our individual and collective psyches. For any map-making technology, the most important first step is to orient toward the cardinal directions and establish a coordinate system. That is why the bulk of this book focuses on constructing the coordinate system by updating the meaning of the width, depth, and height dimensions of the psyche in modern English.

Evolution presses us to be more individual and more inter-connected at the same time. The ancient I-Ching text is a compilation of collective work done over many generations, primarily within China. Today after thousands of years of human evolution, we have new opportunities to evolve this treasure of Earth's wisdom. With the coordinate system now translated into English, the collective effort can be worldwide, encompassing diverse cultures. It is possible for each individual to compile a personalized Book of Change, annotating the hexagrams, the coordinates, based on their personal experience of relating and experimenting with the Inter-Being. Then I Ching will no longer be one version of text, but a database of personalized information, organized by a shared coordinate system that translates lived experience into personal and collective maps of evolutionary progress.

The Resonance Code Research Lab pioneered this effort of compiling a new database using The Resonance Code as a shared platform. We are at the beginning of this exciting journey. We hope you will join us!

Resonance Code Research Lab

The Resonance Code reveals an underlying structure shared between the hexagrams and the language of biological evolution, the DNA code. DNA is a long chain of large molecules packed tightly within the nucleus of the cell. This long chain is composed of four kinds of nucleotide acids, called A, C, G, and T. These acids combine in groups of three to create 64 DNA codons, (four possible acids for each of three positions = 4x4x4=64). In parallel, The Resonance Code organizes hexagrams as a permutation of four energies over three positions, giving rise to 64 hexagrams.

The DNA codons instruct cells how to assemble proteins important for cellular functions. The simple set of 64 codons underlies all of the infinitely rich and vastly complex life forms. This demonstrates that the complexity of life is an emergent process supported by a small set of core principles. This juxtaposition of simplicity and complexity is also the essence of Taoism. The core teaching of Taoism is that the most universal Tao is also the simplest.* If we see our social organisms

as living systems, then the hexagrams represent a set of energetic patterns around which their emergent processes organize themselves.

As DNA is the evolutionary code written with Dense Plane material, the nucleotide acids, the Hexagrams can be viewed as the evolutionary code written with Light Plane material, the energetic states of the psyche. As knowledge of DNA enables biologists to learn and experiment with biological evolution, knowledge of the hexagrams enables leaders to be intentional participants in consciousness and social evolution.

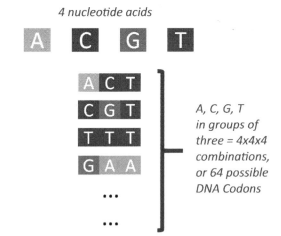

4 nucleotide acids

A, C, G, T in groups of three = 4x4x4 combinations, or 64 possible DNA Codons

---

* Simple does not mean easy. While the abstract patterns of hexagrams are quite simple, translating the patterns into culturally relevant meanings and embodying these patterns as actions and ways of life is much, much harder.

Next, I will present a few examples of how to make meaning out of the hexagrams using The Resonance Code. First, though, here is a great way to relate with the hexagrams.

Imagine the three planes of the psyche as an ensemble of three musicians. They come together either to play pre-written songs or improvise in the moment. They are all virtuosos, capable of playing the lead or accompaniment. Whatever they do, they need to make some agreements about the songs they choose to play, the musical scale and mood they all tune into, and who is taking the lead in what song. With these agreements, the musicians have the maximum freedom to self-organize their musical expression while participating in the organic co-creation of a brilliant performance.

Applying this metaphor now to the hexagrams, with any given song, each of the three musicians, (planes), expresses through one of four styles, (subtle energies). As all three musicians rotate through all four styles, together they will play in 64 (4x4x4) different combinations, giving rise to 64 distinct songs, (patterns of the psyche). In the database of The Resonance Code, every

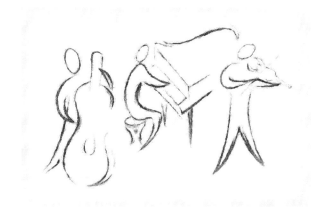

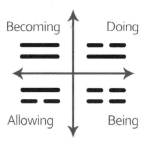

hexagram is such a song. It sets up a frame around which the Dense, Middle, and Light Planes organize themselves. Each of the 64 hexagrams provides a lesson through which we may learn how to coordinate the three planes for the fullest expression of resonant interplay.

Now let's take a look at a few "song" examples!

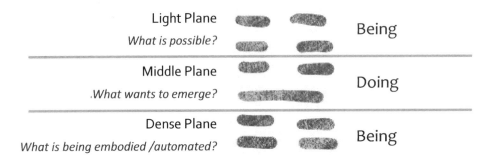

Light Plane
What is possible?
Being

Middle Plane
.What wants to emerge?
Doing

Dense Plane
What is being embodied /automated?
Being

This hexagram signifies either the nascent or mature stages of the rational mind. In this hexagram, the Middle Plane expresses Doing energy while the Dense and Light Planes express Being energy. With the Dense and Light both expressing Being, the psyche carries a strong feminine quality.

In this energetic pattern of the psyche, the channel of the linear rational mind is the only one that expresses Yang, the externalizing impulse. The other channels are Yin, internalizing and receptive. This means that here, the knowledge extracted by the linear rational mind is fully integrated with one's instinct, senses, emotions, soul, and energy, simultaneously feeding them and being supported by them.

This pattern can be either at the nascent or the matured stage of the evolution of the linear rational mind. At its nascent stage, the linear rational mind, like a burgeoning new life, is held within the womb of the Dense and Light Planes. In its maturation, the linear rational mind returns to the embrace of the Dense and Light Planes, both serving them and being served by them.

In the classic I-Ching text, this hexagram is named Humbleness. The linear rational mind in this hexagram is in intimate connection with the somatic intelligence (Dense Plane) and the human imagination and intuition (Light Plane). It embraces the intelligence outside the realm of rational knowledge. Therefore, humbleness is a natural expression of the openness of a mind, and its wisdom and courage to say "I don't know." It is no wonder that many I-Ching scholars, including both the Confucians and Lao Tzu, treasured this hexagram as the most special one of the whole I-Ching. Humbleness is a highly valued personality trait and most cultivated in the Eastern intellectual tradition. In recognizing the power of the rational mind, the Taoist sages pay special attention to cultivate the yin, receptive quality of the heart, body, and soul, ensuring the power of intellect is not used toward flaunting its superiority, but to promote the well-being of the whole.

This hexagram teaches that to liberate the true potential of one's linear rational mind, a person needs to grow a strong root through developing their heart and soul and cultivating the soil of instinctual desire. In the context of wholeness, the linear rational mind can be most aligned with its evolutionary purpose, becoming the most potent tool for higher knowledge.

To learn this lesson, one may inquire:

- How do I hold my instincts and senses as a container for the development of my linear rational mind? (Being in Dense Plane)

- How do I bear witness to the belief patterns that I am adopting? (Being in Light Plane)

- How can I employ the knowledge of my rational mind to deepen my embodied experience of life? (Doing in Middle Plane)

When I opened the Resonance Code Research Lab and invited my collaborators to join, I did a "reading" to ask the Inter-Being to advise me how to lead this collaborative effort. (A reading is a trans-rational method one uses to communicate with the Inter-Being. I will explain what a reading is and how to do a reading later in this chapter.)

It was poignant for me that this hexagram came to me as the answer. Due to the surge in development of the linear rational mind, the part of us that communicates with the Inter-Being has become compromised. Now, as we reawaken this part of ourselves, the Inter-Being sends a message inviting us to consciously take part in the further evolution of our linear rational mind, bringing it to its maturation. The Inter-Being encourages us to integrate the linear rational mind back into the ecosystem of the psyche and reweave the cyclic flows of wholeness.

Light Plane *What is possible?*	▬▬▬ ▬▬▬	**Becoming**
Middle Plane *What wants to emerge?*	▬ ▬ ▬▬▬	**Doing**
Dense Plane *What is being embodied /automated?*	▬ ▬ ▬▬▬	**Becoming**

This hexagram presents a lesson where the psyche is storing potential for transformation on the Dense and Light Plane. It invites one to cultivate the stabilizing function (Yin) of one's Heart Mind.

Here the Doing energy on the Middle Plane is in a context different than Hexagram 15. Here the Dense and Light Planes are both in the transformative phase of Becoming. What is being produced from the Middle Plane enables the transformation of what is possible on the Light Plane and what is being embodied and automated on the Dense Plane.

The reason that this hexagram is called Accumulating Potential is because the templates on the Light Plane and automated circuitry on the Dense Plane are not yet in a state of stability to yield a great harvest. Therefore, even though this is a great time to practice the agency of Doing, it is not a time to expect fruition.

The I-Ching text presents the following metaphor for this lesson. A storm gathers clouds over the sky, yet no rain comes down. Wind blows across the sky, restraining the clouds, the rising breath of the productive energy, making them grow denser.

In this hexagram, the Heart Mind is the only channel of the psyche that is in Yin mode, stabilizing the emotional energies through integrating multiple perspectives. This Yin line holds the five Yang lines in check.

The image associated with Hexagram 9 Accumulating Potential: A storm gathers clouds over the sky, yet no rain comes down.

One may conduct these inquires for this lesson:

- How do I widen the Yin mode of the Heart Mind to integrate multiple perspectives?

- How do I integrate these perspectives into a new model of reality? What skills am I practicing and what potential am I accumulating?

- This is also a time to practice Doing without being attached to the outcome. If you find what you get out of your Doing is different than you intended, then ask, What beliefs need to be transformed? What automated circuitry in the Dense Plane needs to be reprogrammed?

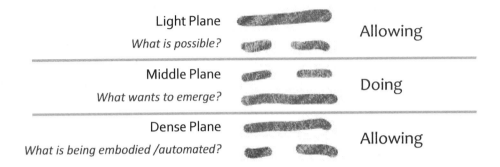

Light Plane		Allowing
What is possible?		
Middle Plane		Doing
What wants to emerge?		
Dense Plane		Allowing
What is being embodied /automated?		

This hexagram teaches how the healing potential of the unknown often manifests itself in forms of toxicity. In this hexagram, the Middle Plane is again expressing Doing energy. However, this Doing is embedded in an energetic pattern very different than Hexagrams 15 and 9. Here the Dense and Light Planes are both expressing Allowing energy, the polar opposite of Doing. This indicates the Doing energy of the ego self has reached a limit and is being redirected by forces coming from the Dense and Light Planes.

The I-Ching text paints a very vivid image for this hexagram: a bowl of spoiled food where worms are breeding. In ancient dwellings, there was no refrigeration. Left-over food naturally spoiled in warm temperatures. Here, the worms should also be understood in a greater context.

They represent the microorganisms involved in the decaying process. This image symbolizes excessive drive and will associated with over-production, the Doing energy of an ego self that is disconnected with the rest of the psyche.

At the same time, the intelligence of the Dense and Light Planes is releasing a tremendous source of healing. The regenerative power in the Allowing energy is working on restoring the imbalance caused by over-active Doing upon the Dense Plane. The nature of this healing source is likely to be unknown to the rational, ego mind. In fact the source of healing may evoke repulsion as "worms" do to a rational mind conditioned by sanitation-obsessed modern medicine. But sometimes, what the mind finds repulsive is the most potent source of hidden healing.

This hexagram has a tremendous teaching. It illustrates the profound polarities that the psyche can harbor. The toxicity of repulsive decaying matter and the life-giving source of healing are often simultaneously present. Therefore holding fast to categorical thinking based on binary labeling is ineffective in releasing the creative potential held within the complexity of the psyche. Experiencing the teaching of this hexagram helps one's mind naturally shift out of the mechanical binary mode and start to adopt a more holistic mindset.

Toxicity is always an aspect of medicine. Many medicinal substances exist as "toxins" in the natural world. This principle applies to the psyche too. What aspects of the psyche do you fear, reject, feel ashamed of, repulsed by, or regard as "toxins?" The "toxin" might point to an unknown source of healing. One client received this hexagram in a reading when she was working with an addiction problem. She felt ashamed about this addiction and held a lot of judgment toward it. Her rational mind tried to rectify her addictive behaviors. This was not very effective.

I pointed out to her that under the surface of any addictive behavior there is an unmet need. Instead of being obsessed about stopping the addiction,

I helped her to inquire into her Light and Dense Planes with this question. What are the true nutrients that will "feed" her unmet needs?

Through Feelingwork, she was able to get in touch with the felt-sense of the pain associated with the hidden unmet needs. Allowing herself to feel the sensation of the pain, bringing awareness to it without resisting or judging it helped her transform it into a self-healing energy. She also realized this pain of unmet needs was inherited from a family lineage. Its force is bigger than her individual ego self. As she learns to transform this pain into a healing source, she can also invite the ancestral source of this pain to shift through her efforts as well. As she consciously invites collaborative forces larger than her individual ego self to participate in healing, the automated circuitry on her Dense Plane gets reprogrammed.

For support learning this lesson, one may apply the following inquiry:

- What is my mind rejecting, fearing, or judging as toxic? What are the underlying unmet needs?

- How can I transform the pain associated with the unmet needs into a source of healing?

The Images of I-Ching

In the book of I-Ching, all hexagrams are associated with a particular image to give form to the subtle energetic patterns. As I-Ching is a language primarily describing Light Plane patterns, the image is important to stimulate imagination and intuition through the associative capacities of the mind.

It is important to be mindful of the social context surrounding the images. For example, the image associated with Hexagram 18 is "worms," microorganisms infesting spoiled food. To a modern mind, this picture may evoke a repulsive response. However, Chinese culture has a rich tradition, in fact, a love affair with fermented food. Every region of China develops their own unique ways to ferment rice, beans, vegetables, and meat products. Some fermented foods are considered medicinal. I can only imagine that this knowledge about how to work with microorganisms came from a curious and experimental attitude when the early ancestors observed their food being spoiled.

Knowledge about fermentation comes from experimenting with microorganisms that spoil food.

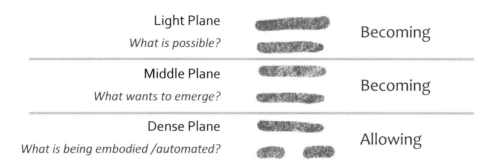

Light Plane		Becoming
What is possible?		
Middle Plane		Becoming
What wants to emerge?		
Dense Plane		Allowing
What is being embodied /automated?		

This hexagram has only one Yin line situated at the bottom with five Yang lines above it. It represents the deepest drive to enfold knowledge that has been accumulated on Middle and Light Planes into one's basic instinct on the Dense Plane. Our most basic instincts concern matters such as birth, death, mating, and the incarnation of subtle energy into somatically concrete felt experience.*

The I-Ching text paints a picture of a woman who is a seductive temptress, attracting five men to compete for her. This is a situation full of contention and struggle, which eventually leads to a chaotic breakdown. The commentaries associated with this text are most controversial, ranging from a harsh criticism of the temptress to a celebration of the most powerful feminine energy.

The controversy around this hexagram reflects the evolutionary context in which I Ching was written. At that time, humanity faced the challenge of overly-abundant Yin-Enlivening surges and needed to develop the Yang-Enlightening impulse. This was necessary to allow human civilization to evolve by lifting knowledge out of the chaotic sea of somatic experience.

---

* I want to make a distinction between incarnation and reincarnation. Incarnation points to the process of embodying subtle energy into somatic experience. It is a constant process between individual and Inter-Being, with or without our conscious awareness. Reincarnation is associated with the death of an individual and returning to life in another form. Presumably, if one lives an entire life cultivating an awareness of the cyclic exchange between individual self and the Inter-Being, reincarnation can be a possible choice.

Today, we live in a different time facing a different evolutionary challenge. Our challenge has shifted into how to regenerate our lived experience out of the infinite sea of knowledge. We are living in a time of a dire shortage of high quality, enlivened experience. The overly abundant knowledge about external material reality does not help us to feel content and fulfilled about our embodied experience of living or being intimate with another human being. We yearn for the most direct, somatic experience of life force at the most instinctual level. The reverse conditions are now true and the Yang-Enlightening impulses are over-abundant, calling for Yin-Enlivening surges.

This hexagram highlights our most instinctual drive to internalize and experience through our body. In modern culture that presses us to externalize and produce, it is not easy for us to be in touch with this drive. The channels through which we become aware of this drive are usually carnal or physical desire, sometimes behind the tightly shut door of inhibition and taboo.

In the previous phase of human evolution, we have collectively, through conscious or unconscious choices, developed an assortment of psychological taboos toward this Yin impulse in its strongest, most carnal expression. The I-Ching text referred to this particular expression of Yin-Enlivening impulse as "evil" or "dark." The original texts advised people not to fear this "evil" but instead restrain it properly. Unfortunately the word "evil" often evokes fearful reactions. To compound things, in English the word "evil" often gets mingled with the Christian connotation which is very different from its meaning in native Chinese culture.

It is true that each creative power has inherent risks. The power of our most carnal desire can lead or has led humans to many unwanted outcomes. But the power in fire and in electricity contains similar potential. Any form of power needs to be treated with care. The more power there is, the more knowledge, skills, and care are required to use that power wisely.

Here are questions to expand the meaning of this hexagram when it appears in a reading.

- How do you consciously use your intellectual knowledge, heart knowledge, and soul knowledge to renew your deepest instinctual drive?

- What is your strongest physical desire that has been shut behind the door of inhibition or taboo?

Let us turn our attention to this question: in what manner do we "speak" with the Inter-Being? How do we know which evolution lesson are we learning at any given moment, especially when we are disoriented in situations of VUCA — volatility, uncertainty, complexity and ambiguity?

As I reviewed in Chapter Three, we are always embedded within the currents of wholeness belonging to a larger life. Our human existence is part of this larger life. The currents of wholeness infuse every moment of our life like the electromagnetic forces infusing the space. But we may not be conscious of them, especially in moments of VUCA. How do we cultivate an awareness that allows us to communicate with this larger life? How do we interpret the communications in ways that support our own well-being and thriving, as well as our public and professional activities?

Resonating with the Inter-Being is a natural function of the psyche.

I now introduce a framework to relate with the vibrational nature of the psyche. You can test this framework through an exercise at the end of this chapter. In this framework, we consider there is an informational field associated with the Inter-Being. Our psyche naturally resonates with the informational field of the Inter-Being, much like our cell phones that receive cellular signals. This exchange of information is constant, often without our conscious knowing. The content of our psyche, thoughts, emotions, sensations, instincts, or subtle perceptions are not completely sealed off as an exclusively private domain. In the background, there is a constant stream of information exchange with the Inter-Being.

Modern people are unaware of this constant stream of exchanges. This is particularly true in social environments dominated by the I-Culture paradigm. The I-Culture paradigm holds a powerful belief that the individual psyche is separated from the Inter-Being's psyche. I-Culture teaches that as individuals we should have total control and power over the activities of our mind. It is as if our psyche is a cell phone with a powerful receptivity, yet the operating system installed on the cell phone has not developed mechanisms to render the cellular signals into meaningful messages.

Resonating with the Inter-Being has always been a natural function of the human psyche. In earlier civilizations, our ancestors used this function to communicate with the Inter-Being of Mother Nature, for example, to support agrarian and hunting activities. Resonating with the Inter-Being also occurred between individuals and the social body, but was limited to the scope of family, clan, and tribe.

This is why indigenous cultures often have very different ethics and justice systems. If someone commits a horrible crime, people do not ask the individual to take the full blame. Instead, this individual's behavior signaled that some aspect of the tribal Inter-Being is out of order. Everyone takes responsibility in participating in that aspect. Therefore, the whole tribe would come together to figure out what went out of order, performing healing collectively and restoring things to order.

Modern culture with its strong emphasis on individuality over collective identity muted the information exchange between the individual psyche and the collective psyche. Muting this information exchange disrupts the natural sense of belonging that is one of the strongest needs we have. Today, human connections have become fragile, superficial and conditional. In a study done at UCLA, psychologists tracked the lives of 30 dual-earner parents. They found that on average they spent very little time with one another. Most of their talks were about errands and to-do-lists. Today many couples rely on texting or email to resolve a fight or send love notes to each other when they feel distant. When marriages are maintained with brief written communications on electronic devices, we can see how isolated from each other we have become. The intimate moments of connection through physical presence, touch, play, and interaction that support both the Light and Dense Planes are lost.

The human psyche's function as a resonator is fully activated when we are born. It is a natural ability formed in the womb. Our very first somatic sensation of life is being embedded in another life form, our blood flowing with our mother's, flesh and bones attached to her womb. The fetus's psyche needs to be intricately attuned to the mother's to successfully develop through the pregnancy. This form of attunement persists for a long time in a baby's psyche after the birth, until the baby starts to acquire language ability and develop cognitive faculties on the Middle Plane.

If this baby grows up in an industrialized, modern culture, it is likely that he will experience a disruptive separation of the Dense and Light Planes, an over-privileging in the development of the Middle Plane, and an objectification of and domination over the Dense Plane. Through the disruption, the information exchange with the Inter-Being will become muted. It is not correct to consider this a mistake of modern civilization. Muting this channel of our psyche set the conditions to maximize the development of the individual ego and the linear rational mind. However, we have reached a point where the cost of continuing to mute this channel is bigger than the benefit we are reaping.

Evolution constantly explores and experiments with new directions. There is no "right" way to proceed in a new direction. The linear rational mind is a priceless gift crystallized out of our collective human journey. All we can do is learn from the lessons of past experimentation so we can make new choices for the future. And there will always be newer lessons to learn. As always, every disruption presents a new opportunity. We now have the exciting opportunity to reweave wholeness, amplifying resonance to resonate with the global Inter-Being. This had not been possible in earlier human civilizations. The wars between tribes and clans were often violent. It was much harder to experience the Inter-Being on the global scale that we do today.

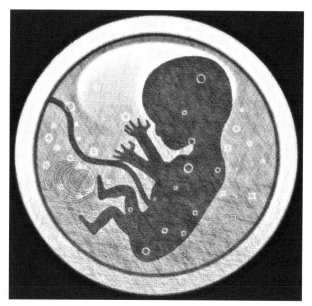

In Tao Te Ching, Lao Tzu expressed his aspiration for the evolutionary journey of one's soul in an ardent question, "[Toward the end of life] can I develop a soft and fluid quality in my [differentiated] mind, body, and soul so that I might return to the state of a fetus, the state of being one with the cosmos?"

I now invite you to shift into a new model of the psyche. In this model, your psyche, instead of being sealed off as a private domain, is a unique nodal point in an inter-connected, informational web, like your cell phone with its unique phone number. With the right methods and consistent practice, your psyche will be able to exchange information with the Inter-Being with precision and accuracy.

I invite you test this model through experience. At the end of this chapter, I present a process called Fieldtuning for this purpose. In Fieldtuning, your linear rational mind is asked to step off from its habitual leader role, and step into a new role as a follower, following the leads of the faculties on the Dense and Light Planes. The experience of Fieldtuning can be very healing as our psyche yearns for this shift.

I have facilitated Fieldtuning in many different settings with a diverse range of people, many of whom were quite intellectual and used to rational thinking. Often, when I describe the process of Fieldtuning, there is some resistance as this model of the psyche is so against the deeply ingrained beliefs of the linear rational mind. Yet again and again, I have watched people's resistance melt once they step into the field of the Inter-Being. Even the most resistant people often access the signals from the Inter-Being with little difficulty.

Communicating with the Inter-Being requires a rigorous methodology.

Accessing the signals from the Inter-Being is the easy part. What is more challenging is how to parse the signals into meanings that are pragmatic and safe to both our personal lives and public work. Twenty years ago when I lived in China, the wired telephone was not even a household item yet. Back then, families living in an entire neighborhood shared one telephone. This phone was the communication device for hundreds of people. Often, an elder would be the messenger of the neighborhood, relaying messages to different households.

In today's world, while our external communication is well developed, the internal communication technology is extremely poor. Those of us who use our psyches this way naturally function as a "messenger", a "central router" for a whole section of humanity that has not consciously developed this capacity. This simultaneously grants us a large responsibility and immense power. There is inherent risk in doing this without the proper skills, as one's psyche can be overwhelmed by the flood of information.

If you consciously develop this capacity of the psyche, paradoxically, the safest and the most personally satisfying way to use this power is put yourself completely at service to humanity. That is why I encourage you to stand up as a leader, even if no one grants you that title. As leaders, we need to develop specialized knowledge and skills to process this information so we can use it responsibly. Moreover, our job is to build a culture that encourages more people to develop a personal relationship with the Inter-Being.

Healthy inter-connectivity relies on clear boundaries. As physically connected as a fetus is with its mother, their immune systems set clear boundaries between the two. Without these boundaries, the baby has no chance to develop full term before being absorbed by the mother. Or conversely, the mother's well-being would be threatened by the aggressively developing baby. In conscious evolution, we become both more individuated and more connected. And we become aware of the temporal rhythm that regulates the individuation and connectivity. To develop these skills, we need to treat the communication with the Inter-Being with a kind of rigor, discipline, and critical mind similar to how a scientist treats her subjects of study.

When I was a graduate student at the University of Iowa, I was operating a state-of-art microscope that allowed me to insert an electrode into a single neuron to record electric currents of microamps flowing through the cell membranes. I spent a third of my time caring for and calibrating the instrument, making sure it was operating properly. Otherwise, I could not rely on the data I collected with my microscope at all. Likewise, our psyche is a sensitive instrument that requires constant care, calibration and refinement.

The Inter-Being is a living being with extremely complex dynamics beyond our knowledge. Just think how often your phone runs updates to sync up with the "web." Likewise, our psyche also needs to be "synced up" with the Inter-Being.

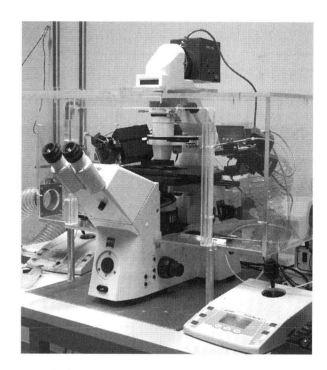

A patch-clamp microscope like the one I used as a PhD student. Working with the psyche requires as much rigor as working with sensitive scientific instruments.

The knowledge and skills presented here point to a new form of human potential burgeoning on the stage of evolution. We are given such an exciting opportunity to harness this potential and apply it consciously toward restoring the wellbeing of our planet and human life.

To become an effective resonator with the Inter-Being requires an ongoing practice. Next I will introduce the most basic practice with The Resonance Code: casting a reading. Casting a reading using The Resonance Code is like using a compass to navigate a physical terrain. To understand this, I invite you to consider these hypotheses:

1. Just like Earth's electromagnetic field has two opposite poles, the field of Inter-Being also vibrates between two most fundamental drives of psyche, Enlightening, the drive to extract experience into knowledge, and Enlivening, the drive to enfold knowledge into experience.

2. Our evolution unfolds in the context of the field of the Inter-Being. The particular lesson we are experiencing at any given moment can be seen as a "time coordinate" of our evolution. The hexagrams are the time coordinates.

3. When we are traveling through the physical landscape, with the right map and a compass, we will be able to tell our physical coordinates. Likewise, when we navigate the terrain of evolution, we will be able to tell our time coordinate with the right maps and compass. So far I have extensively described the maps. Next I will introduce the "compass."

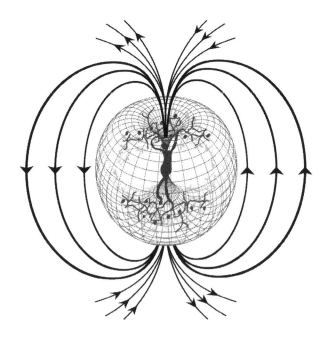

Similar to the Earth's magnetic field surrounding us wherever we are, the currents of wholeness from the Inter-Being infuse every moment. Despite that, in our daily lives, our awareness is mostly influenced by other factors. These factors range from deeply ingrained patterns of the past to mental projections of the future, from personal goals to the energies of the collective unconscious, from deep needs to primal impulses. These forces are the "friction" that prevent our awareness from freely responding to the Inter-Being and accurately discerning our "coordinates."

However, when we consciously observe a random process, such as tossing a coin and observing which side is up, our awareness is most friction-free. Which side of the coin will turn up is not dictated by any particular force in our awareness. Thus, observation of a random event becomes our "needle" in the compass, which reflects the evolution lesson that the whole of ourselves most yearns to learn and experience.

If we consider the hypotheses stated above, we may begin to construct a "compass" in the navigation of conscious evolution. Then we will be able to test these hypotheses.

The magnetic needle in a high-quality orienteering compass floats in liquid so that it can rotate freely inside the housing with minimal friction. Therefore, it can respond to the magnetic field with sufficient sensitivity and accuracy.

At this point, you might be wondering — how could a random process be so meaningful? Most science education teaches us that random process is meaningless. This reflects the current developmental stage of our science education, which is primarily based on the masculine mode of the psyche and largely disconnected from the feminine. Its perception of reality is limited.

I invite you to do this following experiment. First take a look at the pattern A. It's hard to make sense of it and it probably looks somewhat random. Now take a look at pattern B. B is actually a computer-generated artwork with a clear spiral pattern. Pattern A, which looks more random, is a small inset of pattern B, a much more ordered pattern. This small experiment tells us that what we perceive as random with our everyday perception can possibly be a part of a larger, complex, and ordered pattern that our mind does not yet recognize.

The patterns and dynamics of the Inter-Being are beyond what our minds can currently comprehend. For us to attempt to understand it with the rational mind is like a fish living in a tidal pool trying to understand the ecosystem of the ocean. Yet not understanding does not stop us from engaging and experimenting with it. Readings using The Resonance Code provide an empirical interface through which we can begin interacting consciously with the Inter-Being.

A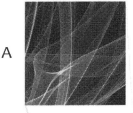

B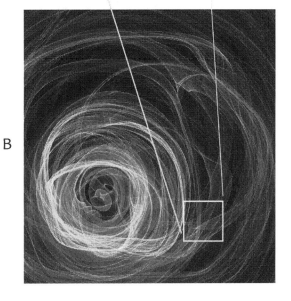

each world, there is Buddha and non-Buddha." Physicist Mae Wan Ho in an interview with philosopher Tam Hunt summarized this sublime interrelatedness as "a universal simultaneity in which no space-time separation exists." These ideas underlie the phenomenon of synchronicity, where events of no apparent causal relationship co-arise in meaningful ways. Carl Jung wrote about this phenomenon extensively.

If we accept this model of the world, then information relevant to our evolutionary process is fractally present within a random process. Yet random processes do not speak in human language. They speak through numbers and patterns. How do we decode this information into something meaningful? How do we calibrate and refine the decoding system?

The Resonance Code decodes the patterns from a random process into meaningful guidance for one's conscious evolution. The Resonance Code is designed to maximize one's individual agency to generate meaning tailored to individual experience. This is in contrast to the classic I Ching where meanings were mostly prescribed by a small number of ancient sages.

Teachings from Eastern mystical traditions and findings in quantum physics converge on a similar model of the world. In this model, every point in time and space is a fractal representation of all other points in time and space. This teaching infuses Chinese traditional culture and I absorbed it from many sources. For example, the Buddhist Avatamsaka Sutra says, (my translation), "Inside one speck of dust, there are many worlds. Inside

Now I will take you through the practice to generating a reading from a random process.

With maps and a compass, a traveler orients himself in relation to the physical landscape. When we choose to be a conscious participant in our evolution, a reading allows us to orient ourselves in relation to the evolutionary field of the Inter-Being. Remember, the largest portion of this field lies in the domain of the unknown.

When we use a compass to navigate through a landscape, we first locate our current coordinates on a map. Then we locate the coordinates of the next destination. The relationship between the current coordinate and the next gives us a general sense of how to prepare for the trip ahead.

Similarly, in navigating evolution, the reading will usually generate two hexagrams, thus two time coordinates. The primary hexagram points to the current time coordinate and a secondary hexagram as the most likely next time coordinate. With the information provided with each hexagram, we may "plot" a route that supports the evolutionary lesson to be learned and integrated.

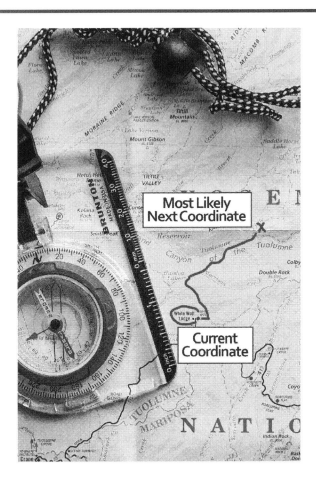

It is important to note that the reading is not a prediction or forecast of the future, just like a plotted route on a map does not ensure a sailor will cross oceans; nor does it predict what we will encounter in our journey. Just like a compass reading to a traveler, a reading simply orients us in relation to the terrain of conscious evolution.

Historically, allured by its "magic power," people attempted to use the hexagram readings to predict or try to control the future, or to avoid facing difficulty or making choices on their own. That is not how we engage with this practice. A traveler will never get to any place if he is obsessed with playing with the compass. Likewise, if we do not commit ourselves to the process of conscious evolution, doing readings is useless at best, and detrimental at worst.

For exploring an unknown territory, it is wise to use a tool to orient ourselves, so that we can maximize learning and avoid being trapped in habit patterns and circular cycles while making more refined choices about risk-taking.

Exploring the unknown is inherent with uncertainty and ambiguity. Sometimes we need to follow our gut instinct and try something that has never been tried before. At other times we need to flex the muscles of our analytical power and take methodical steps. Sometimes we need to remain still while being receptive to what happens around us. At other times, we need to go all out and push for what we stand for. A reading helps an individual committed to conscious evolution practice finer discernment about energies and influences within herself and in relationship with the Inter-Being. This leads to more integrated, resonant choices.

To prepare for a reading, we align multiple dimensions of our awareness to include more of ourselves in the inquiry. The more we prepare ourselves in this step, the more coherent a signal the reading will produce.

Begin by drawing your attention to an area of your life where you feel some tension or blockage, or where you feel a desire for thriving. Conduct an inquiry to organize your awareness on the three planes as indicated on the right.

Future

Emerging Present

Past

Light Plane/Future

What is my mental abstraction of what wants to happen? Is it a commitment, a goal or a felt sense of longing? Am I holding the mental abstraction as an experiment, or a goal to attend? Whether an experiment or a goal, is it a conscious choice?

Middle Plane/Present

What are my actions that align with my intention or commitment? What are my actions or non-actions that seem to contradict or distract my intention and commitment? What are the unmet needs underlying the actions or non-actions that are not aligned with my intention and commitment?

Dense Plane/Past

How am I experiencing those unmet needs as feelings, sensations and somatic experiences? Can I feel them deeply without judging or forcing them to be different? (You may engage with the Feelingwork practice provided in Chapter Six to release some of the reactive configurations.)

Here, I introduce the coin method to cast a reading. After you have done the preparatory inquiry, take three coins and identify the head (H) and tail (T) sides. The head side represents the Yang and tail side, Yin.

First let us get familiar with how to toss the coins to generate a hexagram line. Find a clear and empty surface where you can toss all three coins at once without interference by other objects. Toss the coins in the air a few times and record the head-tail patterns. You will discover that there are four possible patterns. HHH, HHT, HTT, and TTT. Each pattern carries two key bits of information: whether it indicates a Yin or Yang line, and whether the line changes or not.

HHH and TTT, with all three coins showing the same side, indicate Yang and Yin lines respectively. They also indicate that these are changing lines, meaning the line changes from Yang to Yin, or Yin to Yang in creating the reading's primary and secondary hexagrams.

This is a crucial point. In Chapter Three, I presented how in Taoist philosophy, when yin and yang develop to their respective maximal expression, they naturally transform into their opposites. This idea is reflected by the changing lines. These changing lines point to the dimension of the psyche that has reached its peak, ready to turn.

The remaining two possible patterns indicate unchanging lines. HHT, two heads and a tail, represents an unchanging Yin line, indicating a Yin energy that is in its developing mode. HTT, two tails and a head, represents an unchanging Yang line, indicating a Yang energy that is in its developing mode.

These four patterns are summarized below.

Coins	Line	Changing To	Line Name
H H H	▬▬◯▬▬	▬▬ ▬▬	Changing Yang
H H T	▬▬ ▬▬	No Change	Yin
H T T	▬▬▬▬▬	No Change	Yang
T T T	▬▬✕▬▬	▬▬▬▬▬	Changing Yin

Note: there are many methods for casting a reading. I also present a rice method in Appendix I. Try both to see which one feels right for you.

After reviewing this table, now you are ready to generate a hexagram. Relax into a meditative mood. Connect with the intentions you identified in your preparatory inquiry. Toss the three coins to generate a pattern. Record the pattern, (HHH, HHT, HTT, TTT). Look up the corresponding line in the table. The first toss produces the bottom line of the hexagram. Draw the line to the left, leaving room for your second hexagram on the right, making sure to indicate whether it is a changing line as indicated in the table. Toss five more times to generate and draw the next five lines, from bottom to top, making the last toss as the top line. Now go through to generate your secondary hexagram to the right, duplicating unchanging lines and flipping changing lines from Yin to Yang or Yang to Yin. You should wind up with two six-line hexagrams like the pair shown in the example on the next page.

A reading presents the potential naturally inherent in a situation. To use an unusual analogy, this is a bit like forecasting the rise and fall of the stock market. Based on this forecast, the investors will make choices about buying or selling. Likewise, with this energetic forecast, an evolutionary traveler can more consciously choose how to invest in her Being, Doing, Allowing, and Becoming energies on each of the three planes.

In Volume 2 of The Resonance Code, I will be providing detailed guidance for each of the 64 hexagrams. For now, you may look them up along with the classic texts associated with them in any I Ching book. My personal favorites are the translations by Wilhelm and Huang. Keep in mind, though, that these texts were written in another age, and even with the modern translations you might find it challenging to extract meaning for your own life. The Resonance Code is reaching back to the origins of this wisdom to revive its relevance to our lives today. If you would like to engage your readings within the Resonance Code framework, I invite you to get involved with the next phase of our Research Lab. See the end of the book and the Resonance Path Institute website (www.resonancepath.com) for details.

In the meantime, try these online resources:

1. To look up which hexagram corresponds to your pattern of six lines: https://en.wikipedia.org/wiki/Hexagram_(I_Ching)

2. The Wilhelm translation for each hexagram: https://ichingfortune.com/hexagrams.php

3. A more modern site whose interpretations I appreciate, by Kari Hohne: https://cafeausoul.com/iching/hexagram-detail-pages

Here we review a Resonance Code reading done by Jake, who gave permission to share his journey. Jake has worked in the organizational consulting industry for two decades. Recently he sensed an aching longing for another way of working that was more intuitive and aligned with his whole self. But he did not know what that would look like. Jake began with a preparatory inquiry similar to what I presented a few pages ago.

Preparatory Inquiry

Light Plane: When inquiring about what wants to happen, Jake became aware of a strong urge for a more authentic self-expression. This urge was accentuated by a heightened awareness of his mortality. He anticipated regret as he considered reaching the end of his life without figuring out his unique and authentic expression. He also reflected on how his physical energy felt depleted with the current mode of working and longed for a work-life balance that was more spacious. "Productivity and spaciousness is a polarity that I have been struggling with for 20 years," he reflected.

Middle Plane: Whenever Jake tried to "figure this out" by strategizing schemes and mapping out actions and plans, it never worked. He realized this process of transitioning into a new phase of work needed to come from an emerging process. To facilitate emergence, he needed to carve some space out from his currently very full schedule.

Dense Plane: When Jake thought about the potential to carve out space, he felt a surge of anxiety. With reflection, he realized that his deeply-held sense of identity was being threatened.

Casting the Reading

Jake then cast a reading, receiving the primary hexagram of #44, Renewing Deep Instinct, and the secondary hexagram of #1, Pure Potential.

Hexagram 44: Renewing Deep Instinct		Hexagram 1: Pure Potential
6th: H T T		
5th: H T T		
4th: H T T	→	
3rd: H T T		
2nd: H T T		
1st: T T T	X	

The general description of Hexagram 44 is on page 193. Jake strongly resonated with the theme of Renewing Deep Instinct. He realized that with his decades of work of facilitating transformation in others and himself, he rarely gave priority to his own deepest instinct. He inquired about what his instincts wanted. His instincts guided him to resume a creative writing project for which he never seemed to find time. This writing was inspired by his decades of experience working with human relationships and dynamics. However, as there was not a visible connection to his professional identity, he had never been able to justify giving it priority.

To Jake, this request from his instinct looked impossible at first. He was right in the middle of work with a client. What would he say to his client? He did not want to make up an excuse to cover things up as that was not aligned with his values of integrity and transparency. At the same time, when he imagined telling his client what he truly wanted to do, he was afraid of not being taken seriously, and not being respected anymore.

When we inquired further into this fear, he realized this fear of not being taken seriously was an internal fear that he had projected onto his clients. How his clients would respond to him was actually unknown. It would largely depend on how Jake presented himself. If he did not resolve this internal conflict, he would come across to his clients as being incongruent and inauthentic.

With that insight, I helped Jake to turn his attention to his internal conflict. I took him through a scenario in which he imagined what would happen if he did lose the self-identity he built with his life energy for four decades. He experienced an immense fear. Using Feelingwork, he was able to somatically experience this fear and invite it to reveal its deeper intention. To his surprise, after being fully experienced, this fear transformed into a sense of freedom and ease. With this sense of freedom and ease, Jake found himself having the following thoughts, "This instinctual drive deserves to be given a chance. I want to take a month off to experiment with it. During this month, this instinct will run the show. That is the only way I can find out what that is. Only when I find out can I integrate it back into my life and profession."

He felt a much stronger sense of congruence with this new frame: giving himself a month of experimentation, which he felt comfortable communicating to his clients. It is as if once he experienced what he feared the most, the fear actually no longer had control over him. He was free to take the next step. "What is the worst that can happen," he asked. "If not now, when?"

Hexagram 44 features Allowing energy on the Dense Plane. Jake's strong urge for self-expression is a hallmark of this pattern. Before the reading, Jake was not consciously connected to this energy. Yet he was aware of signs — physical fatigue, the death of a friend — that highlighted his awareness of mortality. Once Jake consciously connected with this deepest instinct, it immediately wanted to express itself through action, resulting in the Dense Plane shifting into Becoming mode. And this bold, expressive energy was amplified in the context of the Hexagram 1, Pure Potential, where all six channels are in Yang mode, all three planes expressing Becoming energy.

Hexagram 1, Pure Potential, is the "Primordial Father" of the entire 64 hexagrams. The interplay between it and the "Primordial Mother", Hexagram 2, Total Manifestation, gives rise to the entire set of hexagrams. The deeper analysis of all these will be explored in Volume 2. For now, it suffices to say that Hexagram 1, Pure Potential, is a time of total transformation, a system upgrade.

This action turned out to be a radical one. It required Jake to make space for big change so that this energy could be integrated with his existing life structure including his client relationships. He chose to experience what he feared the most, and going through that fear helped him to find the resources to create space for the change.

With this reading, Jake successfully navigated from Renewing Deep Instinct to Pure Potential. He created a full month of space to experience the freedom and joy of his creative impulse. A month later, he returned to his life renewed with a tremendous flow of insights.

On the surface, it may not look like something big has happened. But think about it, how many of us running on the treadmill of modern life crave for a full month for oneself without answering to the responsibilities of life? And what kind of creativity would be unleashed if our society and culture honored this need? On the other side of the coin, some of us are lucky enough to be able to carve out self-exploration time. Rather than becoming self-absorbed, how can we enter a space of emptiness to retrieve sparks of creativity in our desire to serve humanity?

To end this section, I will introduce the two cardinal hexagrams, Hexagrams 1 and 2, the Primordial Father and Primordial Mother, shown on the facing page. They represent the most extreme states of the feminine and masculine modes of the psyche. These are the two most polarized hexagrams, consisting of six Yang lines for the Primordial Father, and six Yin lines for the Primordial Mother. They are the two primordial sources for the entire set of hexagrams. The rest of the 64 can be viewed as their "offspring," resulting from these two passing Yin and Yang lines between themselves.

Hexagram 1, the Primordial Father, indicates the system of the psyche has reached a state where all channels are driven by the Enlightening impulse. This is the energetic state in which one may be in touch with the highest and finest knowledge of the universe. That is why this hexagram is named Pure Potential. Hexagram 2, the Primordial Mother, indicates that the system of the psyche has reached a state where all channels are driven by the Enlivening impulse. This is the energetic state where the currents of wholeness flow through one's body and one experiences herself as an incarnation of the deepest truths of the universe in every minute detail. That is why this hexagram is named Complete Manifestation.

These two hexagrams are simultaneously the most powerful and the most vulnerable. They are the most powerful in that they express the virility of the "sperm" and the fertility of the "egg" of our psyche. At the same time, the extreme Yin and Yang make them unstable and most in touch with their vulnerability. They have to mate with their opposites and resolve their conflicts in order to fulfill their destiny.

Most of the time, our conscious awareness is not prepared to receive their full intensity. Therefore, they may pass through our lives without connecting much to our conscious awareness. However, if one of these two readings appears, you may ask, "How shall I prepare myself for the full intensity of the Primordial Father, or the Primordial Mother, on my evolutionary journey?"

Hexagram 1
Pure Potential

Primordial Father

Hexagram 2
Complete Manifestation

Primordial Mother

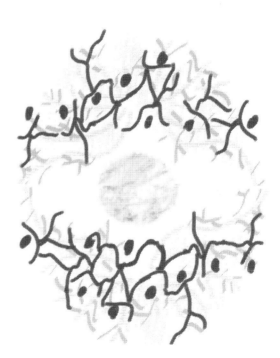

In this chapter, I introduced the hexagram as a six-digit binary symbol to represent the energetic state of the psyche. Through the hexagrams, the architecture of the psyche we built is now connected with the ancient source text of I-Ching. Each hexagram illustrates an evolutionary lesson. With the knowledge of The Resonance Code, one may consciously connect with the evolutionary lessons, and become an active participant in one's own evolution.

I introduced the idea that we can consciously cultivate the vibrational nature of the psyche. This allows us to be conscious and aware as we interact with the informational web of the Inter-Being through a holistic synthesis of all six channels. The Inter-Being is a larger system of life. Its currents of wholeness infuse our daily life. These currents can be detected in the same way a compass can detect the electromagnetic pull of true North.

When we consciously observe a random process, our perception can be used to construct a compass. I introduced the technique of casting a reading by randomly tossing three coins. I provided an example illustrating how to work with a reading.

Together we have traveled to the entrance of one of the oldest, richest, and also most hidden knowledge systems on Earth. Passing through this doorway, you will leave the world you know behind and enter into a new realm of reality. My hope is you will examine how the modern, rational mind lives through you and plant it back into the soil of the Dense Plane, your inner Earth, so that it can grow a wider network of roots. Out of that wider network, your conscious awareness may reach out much higher into the sky, bathing in the infinitely abundant brilliance of the Light Plane. By reconnecting these planes, you may experience the joy, learning, and erotic charge of resonant interplay between your inner Masculine and inner Feminine.

This expedition requires a rigorous approach, teamwork and critical thinking. Plant every step firmly. Integrate and digest the basic vocabulary and practice the skills of increasing awareness. This is the foundation for further study and immersion in the 64 hexagrams to be presented in The Resonance Code, Volume 2.

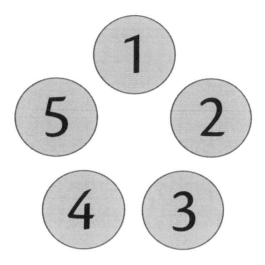

Fieldtuning is a process through which you practice engaging the psyche as a natural "resonator," directly communicating with the Inter-Being. In this exercise you are invited to feel, sense, explore, or experience the influence of subtle energy through engaging non-rational, non-categorical channels of the psyche.

Setting the Frame

*Shown above is a schematic representation of the Field I constructed for this exercise. This Field has five partitions, represented by the five circles. They are key topics discussed in this book. The identities of these topics are presented on the Resonance Path website. **Please do not find out their identities before you conduct Fieldtuning.** Your linear rational mind must be in a state of not-knowing so that it cannot interfere by inserting pre-conceived notions into the Fieldtuning exploration.*

As this book is connected to both the deep history of I-Ching and the work pioneered by the Resonance Code Research Lab, there is a strong field of energy surrounding the five topics included in this Field. You may think of each one of these partitions as a "dialing number" that allows you to connect with an aspect of the Field. In Fieldtuning, you are going to primarily employ the non-rational, non-categorical channels of the psyche to inquire into this energetic field, while your linear rational mind remains completely receptive.

Setting Your Intention

The intention of this Fieldtuning is for you to inquire about your evolution toward wholeness at a personal level. I recommend you hold this question in mind, **"What information is important for me at this point in my evolution toward wholeness?"**

Setting Up the Field

You can set up this field in your own physical space. Find or create a clearly bounded, empty space on the floor. It can be as small as four feet square. Next, take five small pieces of paper or other identical objects and mark them clearly with the numbers 1 through 5. Arrange them within the perimeter to establish five sectors. You do not need to follow the geometric order shown here. Arrange these five sectors in your space guided by your intuition. These markers act as space holders for you to interact with the five partitions of the energy field. Have a notepad and pen ready to take notes. Ideally, invite someone you trust to take notes for you. Now you are ready to begin.

Conduct the Fieldtuning

1. Place yourself somewhere comfortable outside the perimeter. Center yourself using your favorite method. Meditate, take a short walk, stretch, or take a few breaths until you feel you have centered. If thoughts come through or feelings arise at this point, do not push them away. Write them down, (or speak them aloud for your note taker), as faithfully as possible. For example, part of you may protest and say, "This is ridiculous! What hell are you doing!" Or a self-critical part of you may say, "Forget about it! You are not intuitive!" These are all common thought patterns. Your job is not to censor them, but to be a neutral and attentive witness observing whatever arises. Let your inner voices speak. Capture in your notes whatever shows up.

2. After you feel like you have found that neutral witness in you, turn your attention to the five sectors within the Fieldtuning space. Ask them, as if you are asking an advisory board, which one of you would like me to visit first? At this point, you may start to feel yourself drawn to one of the five. If you don't get any clear signal, just randomly choose one. Any random choice is a good choice. Just follow your instincts. No need to take this super seriously. This is only an experiment. Be playful!

3. Move yourself physically to the numbered sector that has "spoken" to you. Take some time to arrange your body. Does this sector want you to sit, stand, or lie down? On top of the paper, around it, or below it — does it ask you to pick it up and hold it in your hands? Try different poses. After you settle your body, again turn your attention inward. What are you feeling and sensing right now? What random thoughts and memories are flowing through your mind? What images or sounds are popping into your awareness? Does your body register temperature, pressure, pain, or pleasure? Does your body feel like moving, shaking, jumping, or dancing? Are any emotions arising in you? Does it feel like you are inhabiting some particular environment while you attend to this field? Note your impressions.

For most people doing this for the first time, this is a very refreshing experience. You are practicing dreaming while awake. The information you are receiving this way is not categorical information. It is qualitative information. This is similar to being blindfolded and led to touch an object. You have to gather as much qualitative information as possible through your senses. When you have enough information, suddenly something clicks in your mind. You realize what it is. Fieldtuning is like blindfolding our linear rational mind, freeing all other channels to operate without censoring and restriction. If you find thoughts of censoring, judgment, or restriction arising, simply include these thoughts too. Write them down or speak them out loud. Then, continue observing what else is arising.

After a while, you will sense that the impressions become quiet and the communication is complete. Thank the Field and step back outside the perimeter.

4. Repeat steps 2 and 3, until you have visited all five sectors. There are two more things to which you can pay attention. First, at any sector, you may inquire, what is its relationship with the other sectors? Following this question, you may perceive forces of connection or repulsion, or additional streams of consciousness coming through. Take a note of whatever you perceive. Second, sectors may want to merge or re-arrange themselves in space. Follow the impulse, rearrange the papers defining the sectors and notice what seems different in their relationships to one another.

5. After you have done all five sectors, leave the perimeter. Again, center yourself using your favorite methods. Capture any remaining impressions, or notice any that you failed to capture in the moment. You can now disassemble the field.

Next check the identities of these five sectors on the website:

ResonancePath.com/fieldtuning-exercise

Each number, 1 through 5, has been assigned to one category of Resonance Code experience.

This time your linear rational mind can take charge. Analyze the qualitative information you have received through Fieldtuning. Match up the information you gathered with the corresponding sectors identified on the website. What associations do you make between these two in each case? What interpretations do you wish to make regarding the complete journey of your tuning adventure? Contemplate how this information informs your personal journey of evolution toward wholeness.

The Resonance Code Research Lab has tuned this field. I include a report of that Fieldtuning for your reference on the website link mentioned above. You are welcome to email your own tuning to me at:

thecode@resonancepath.com

The key to success in this exercise is trust. Trust all those little voices, feelings, sensations, random thoughts, and memories arising in you with your mind in a total state of unknown. Become aware of the censoring influence of the linear rational mind. Even if you think, "Oh this information is irrelevant," or, "This is purely my imagination," or, "This cannot possibly be true," just faithfully record whatever it is, as well as your commentary.

Often, before the final step of involving the linear rational mind, you may feel a lot of energy moving through you. You have consciously reversed a very strong, unconscious pattern of our culture by assigning the linear rational mind the role of follower instead of leader.

Through Fieldtuning, you may experience what it is like to employ your psyche as a resonator with the informational field of Inter-Being. However, to use this information wisely and efficiently requires an ongoing practice of calibration and refining of the resonating function of the psyche. My intention is to continue to provide you resources and information to support this phase of your evolution.

Chapter Six

Introduction to Feelingwork

When the architecture of the psyche remains intact, the currents of wholeness cycle through, sustaining vitality and creativity. The evolution of wholeness requires a timely interplay between the feminine and masculine modes. The feminine mode maintains an original order of wholeness, while the masculine mode disrupts the wholeness to generate space and momentum for new agencies to emerge. As these two modes develop to their extremes, eventually they come back together to resolve the polarity between them in a "conception," the initiation of a renewed cycle.

When the feminine and masculine modes fall out of timely coordination and interplay, each becomes decoupled from one another. In their decoupled modes, the masculine can get stuck in its disruptive and controlling pattern. The feminine becomes inert, as if it falls into slumber and forgets its true creative potential. In its slumber, the feminine either remains acquiescent and submissive or tries to use the tools of the wounded masculine to counteract its domination. The wounded ego carries both of these elements.

In modern times, one of the predominant features of this decoupling is to use the linear rational mind of the Middle Plane to dominate and control the primordial life force of the Dense Plane, while remaining blind to Light Plane subtle energies. To reconstitute wholeness, we need to develop more intelligent interfaces linking the Middle Plane to both the Dense and Light Planes. (The interfaces between the planes are described in detail in Chapter Two on pages 78 to 82.)

Both The Resonance Code and Feelingwork amplify the vibratory nature of the psyche to revitalize the current of wholeness. However, each has a different emphasis. The Resonance Code provides a symbol system that allows the linear rational mind to build a new interface with the subtle energy of the Light Plane. Feelingwork provides tools to establish a more intelligent interface between the linear rational mind and the primal life energy on the Dense Plane.

Feelingwork starts with bringing awareness to the sensory channels on the Dense Plane. It enables one's awareness to find the "exit" at the bottom of the double helix, so that one may experience what is like to "ride the up-soaring wind" of the Enlightening momentum in the unconscious.

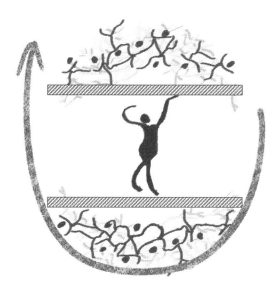

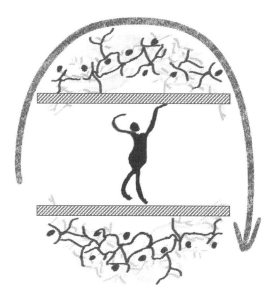

Feelingwork revitalizes the currents of wholeness through facilitating the linear rational mind to build a new interface with the primal life forces of the Dense Plane.

The Resonance Code revitalizes the currents of wholeness through facilitating the linear rational mind to build a new interface with the subtle energy of the Light Plane.

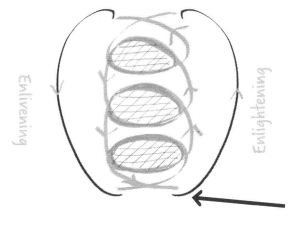

Through Feelingwork, we experience the Enlivening impulse reversing into the ascending outer currents at the bottom of the helix.

Feelingwork allows our awareness to access the feeling mind, the sphere of the psyche which lies outside the scope of the cognitive mind, permeating both the Light and Dense Planes. The feeling mind creates a complex layer of experience between emotion and thought. It influences our perceptions, choices, thoughts, and behavior. And it is distinctively different from what we commonly refer to as emotion in two ways. First, emotion is mainly somatic in nature. In contrast, the feeling mind is an interface between somatic sensation and thought. Second, emotion primarily lives within our body whereas the actual experience of feeling extends beyond the body.

Feeling is endlessly diverse. As we experience feeling through the lens of Feelingwork, we realize that our common vocabulary and categorical way of thinking is woefully deficient at conveying the subtleties and complexity of feeling. As you'll see in the examples that follow, feeling carries highly specific, tangible sensory qualities. For example, a common feeling such as "anger" in one person may take the form of a black, cloud-like substance swirling in their belly. In another person, it may show up as a green, solid mass hugging their feet. Even the same person may experience anger

in different forms in different contexts. Each instance of anger is associated with a complex web of meanings unique to a person's life story.

Through Feelingwork we turn focused attention to the feeling mind, identifying and mapping interrelated, coexisting states. Then we restore the feeling mind to a state of wholeness. In wholeness we can access a felt experience of the architecture of the psyche. Even though The Resonance Code and Feelingwork have vastly different origins, they eventually converge on the same architectural structure. Through each method, we are be able to access this architecture.

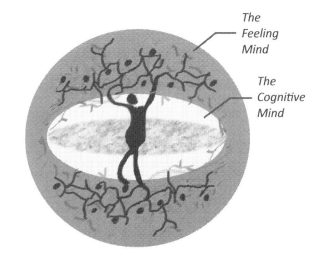

The Feeling Mind

The Cognitive Mind

Feelingwork is my partner and co-author Joe Shirley's life work. He had been developing Feelingwork for two decades when we met in 2012. His journey involved stewarding his masculinity from its deeply wounded family origin toward healing and wholeness.

Joe was born in 1959 in Philadelphia. As a young boy, he was exceptionally sensitive, imaginative, and intelligent. His father was a police officer, both at work and at home. He held an absolute authority over his wife and five children. Joe's mother remained largely submissive to her husband's dominating personality. His father very much wanted to mold Joe, his only son and eldest child, according to his idea of masculinity, tough and disciplined. To him, Joe's emotional sensitivity and intellectual aptitude were obstacles he had to overcome. Starting at very young age, Joe had to develop a lasting strength to protect his gifts from his father's attempts to squash them. This is the paradox Joe had to live with. In order to be true to his sensitive and delicate nature, he had to develop exceptional strength and self-will.

In his twenties, Joe developed severe mood swings eventually diagnosed as bipolar disorder. He took the prescribed pills for one week and decided to throw them away, refusing to be sentenced to a chemical prison for the rest of his life. He resolved to apply all his intelligence and inner resources toward figuring out a pathway not only to his sanity, but perhaps to a bigger truth locked tightly behind the deathly gates of "mental disorder."

For the next seven years, Joe continued battling his inner demons. The volatile and disruptive forces in his psyche swept him from one job to the next, and one relationship to another. Eventually he found his way across North America and settled first in Montana, and finally in Seattle. During this time, he kept searching for a way out of his bipolar prison. He delved into many forms of cognitive psychotherapy, psycho-spiritual and psycho-somatic modalities, hypnosis and New Age self-help that came his way. He undertook an ambitious expedition into the unknown territory of the psyche, being both investigator and the subject of his own experiments.

In 1994, seven years after his diagnosis, Joe had a breakthrough. Here is an excerpt of Joe's writing describing the moment when he made the first major discovery of Feelingwork.

"It was the middle of a sunny summer afternoon, and I was struggling with depression. Focusing my awareness on the space of my heart, where the feeling was strongest, I noted a distinct downward pull from my heart into my belly, like strong gravity.

I wondered what might happen if the gravity were reversed, if instead of pulling downward it pushed upward, and I took a moment to "try it on." In imagining that simple redirection, the feeling itself shifted. Instantly. Dramatically.

From depression all the way to outright cheerfulness, my mood transformed for no good reason. This ridiculous mental trick had done what thousands of hours of deep introspection, journaling, self-hypnosis, cognitive therapy, and all manner of self-help, new age seminars, and mental experimentation had failed to do. In that moment, my depression was nowhere to be found."

Following this breakthrough, Joe started to develop a subtle, yet surgically-precise form of inquiry. Using a set of structured questions, he elicited tangible, sensory qualities corresponding to the actual, felt experience of a feeling state. These qualities would then reveal the unique structure of the state, and they supported comprehensive comparison and connection among coexisting and related feelings. Using this process, Joe would elicit a "set" of feeling states that anchored a particular emotional pattern. These feeling states could range from fear or a sense of annihilation to rage and torrential sorrow. These maps also enabled direct interaction, allowing deliberate shifting of the state toward expressions of greater wholeness. After mapping a set of states, one by one Joe would shift those feeling states toward wholeness, and the set would realign in support of his thriving.

Using this technique, within a year Joe had completely resolved his bipolar disorder and restored his psyche to normal. What he experienced was not considered possible in conventional therapeutic practice. Bipolar disorder is regarded as incurable and patients are put on heavy-duty medication that renders their psyche somewhat flat and lifeless. To reclaim his own life without medical treatment was a miracle.

Meanwhile, Joe realized that his life had been set onto a new track. He had unlocked the deeper truth from the tightly shut gate, and now this deeper truth demanded that he give it everything he had. His discovery was so ahead of its time that he could find no home for it within the existing academic and professional establishment in the fields of psychology or psychotherapy. Instead, he took it upon himself to further his research in this new territory and develop his methodology to its fullest expression. He found a graduate program that offered a Master's degree in Whole Systems Design which supported him to develop this work with the kind of freedom he needed.

For another decade, Joe trudged this lonely path mostly by himself. He developed Feelingwork into a form of practice to work with clients. Meanwhile he devoted most of his energy into understanding the deeper structure of the psyche. After mapping and moving thousands of feeling states in himself and his clients, Joe observed that there was an inherent structure held by how the feeling states relate with one another in a shifted set. He was committed to investigating and refining the most elegant and simple model that arose out of the sea of data he had collected.

Feelingwork and The Resonance Code

I met Joe right around the time I graduated from acupuncture school and started my own clinic. My first experience with Feelingwork was monumental. I felt as if a part of me that had been locked up in the basement of my psyche was finally set free. It was the part that connected with my ancestral knowledge through somatic memories. I had been spending my life trying to free this part of me, and I finally was able to reunite with her. What was most shocking to me was that through Feelingwork, this reunion sparked a powerful qi explosion in my energetic body. Many acupuncture meridians that had been previously blocked burst open. This included the "microcosmic orbit" and "macrocosmic orbit," the most exalted qi circulation experiences at the heart of Taoist alchemy practice.* For thousands of years, Taoist adepts sought this experience through devoting their whole lives to qi cultivation practices. I felt I had been granted a gift bigger than my own life.

At that time, in my mind only modalities like qigong, acupuncture, or techniques from Eastern traditions could induce flows of qi at this level of magnitude and specificity. Yet Joe had little exposure to Eastern traditions. He did not know much about Taoism or Chinese medicine. Listening to his story, I realized that his methodology was primarily a rationalistic inquiry process. Yet with Joe's aptitude for precision and subtlety, this

---

* In microcosmic orbit, Ren and Du, the two energetic pathways of body's central core, connect with each other, circulating energy in a cycle. The macrocosmic orbit extends this circulation to the peripheral channels in the body.

inquiry process felt like a neurosurgery to the mind. As a result, Feelingwork led my awareness to the same territories of the psyche that the ancient Taoists traveled through their deep introspection and clairvoyant vision.

To me, this was a sign that there was a secret trail between the Eastern and Western minds. It lay in the connection between Feelingwork and The Resonance Code. Nothing would be more important, meaningful, and urgent to me than to build this bridge and make its knowledge available to the world. It called upon me to pour everything

I had into the effort. The first stage of building this pathway was a fierce battlefield in which Joe and I fought hard. When we first started working together, neither of our understandings could accommodate the other. The trail connecting Feelingwork and The Resonance Code was steep, treacherous, and broken, and full of blind spots that would trap us going in circles.

We had very strong reasons to attach to what we each believed was true. For Joe, this was his life's work that crystallized two decades of commitment and immense sacrifice. For me, what

I held on to was the only thing I was able to save from my ancestors while so much of our heritage was being annihilated in the collective self-denial that China has been going through. In this battle, we stood in as the representatives of the I-Culture and We-Culture archetypes in a crusade being enacted through our individual personalities. This war was not between Joe and me personally, but between the collective forces acting through our psyches, using our bonds of intimacy and our determination to love each other as their epic battleground.

Six years later, after collaboration with many people, particularly through Joseph Friedman's contribution, the secret pathway between East and West has finally matured into the knowledge system presented in this book. Looking back, both Joe and I are very glad that we fought that "war," not with each other, but side by side. There was nothing more satisfying than knowing that we had each given our best and we had given more than we thought we ever could. We were rewarded with an intimacy that neither of us had ever imagined possible before this relationship. We experienced being held for our most vulnerable and painful parts by the other. And we each found a perfect match who brought out the most powerful parts

of ourselves. We learned that oppositional force, when placed in the context of wholeness, can be the most vitalizing and sexy ingredient in a relationship.

American composer and playwright Jonathan Larson said, "the opposite of war isn't peace, it's creation." I didn't understand it until I experienced it myself. War is the ultimate expression of the oppositional forces of polarities. When we realize that the only "enemy" to fight is ourselves, we can fully embrace the polarity within ourselves. When we fully embody this polarity, we connect with the fountain of creativity within ourselves.

Feelingwork is based on a very rigorous methodology. It sets an example of a new kind of science that turns the beam of observation inward to one's inner territory. In this territory, we are both the investigator and the subject of the experiment at the same time. Many of Joe's writings can be found on *TheFeelingMind.com*. Here I will give a brief introduction to the application aspect of Feelingwork.

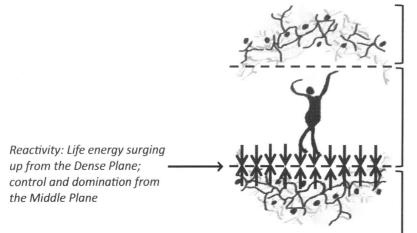

The Feeling Mind

The Language-Based, Cognitive Mind

Reactivity: Life energy surging up from the Dense Plane; control and domination from the Middle Plane

The Feeling Mind

When aspects of the automated circuitry on the Dense Plane need to be programmed or rewired to connect with the upper planes, usually they register in our awareness as basic needs to be met. Examples of such needs are the fundamental senses of safety or belonging. When we are unconscious of them, they show up as felt sensations of emotional distress.

This pain signals that a deeper source of primal life energy wants to be refined and integrated with higher cognitive functions. It is the "fossil fuel" from biological evolution that our psyche can harness as a source of creativity. When our psyche is in state of wholeness, the healthy and generative response to the pain is to open our sensory faculties to fully experience the sensations of pain while maintaining a neutral and curious mental attitude. This way, one can let the richness of the somatic sensations seep through the vast "roots" of the Dense Plane and integrate with the higher levels of cognitive awareness.

This generative response to pain forms the foundation of our capacity for compassion. Compassion means to feel the passion together.

Passion refers to powerful emotions including love, rage and pain. Compassion implies the capacity to feel the intensity of life and the forces of evolution, not just for ourselves but for all beings.

To feel the pain with compassion is different from suffering. Suffering is a non-generative, unconscious activation and distortion of pain. One popular quote captures the essence of this dynamic: "Pain is inevitable. Suffering is optional." But our society does not adequately prepare us with skills required for this compassionate response to pain. On the contrary, it conditions us to find a quick fix so we don't need to feel it. Or it demands us to toughen up and get over it. As the primal life energy surges up from below, and we respond by shutting it down from above, this conflict turns into reactivity which shapes choices and actions. As a consequence, we are confronted with re-occurring life patterns that can both sensitize and numb us to certain frequencies of painful emotions.

Our modern culture is very good at judging, critiquing, analyzing, and creating labels and categories for those who are different from ourselves. At the same time, our collective muscles for compassion are atrophied. We can hardly feel our own pain when it's so deeply buried, let alone reach across the boundary to feel another's. As a result, our society is divided into islands of ideological belief systems separated by fear and even hate.

In a way, the divisiveness is a "healing toxicity," as it forces us to feel the pain so that we have to learn how to transform our response to it from suffering to compassion. To feel the pain of others allows us to transcend our individual selves and experience connection with the larger whole that includes us all. Simultaneously, feeling the pain of each other brings us deeper into our felt sense, our embodied self, and our somatic awareness. Compassion makes us more human by simultaneously stretching us toward higher transcendence and deeper embodiment.

I believe the capacity for compassion is the next frontier of evolution for humanity. Compassion is the current of wholeness flowing through the collective heart and mind. To widen our capacity for compassion, we need to consciously bring our awareness into our felt sense, deeply repressed instinctual impulses, and somatic experience. Let's look at how Feelingwork can help us do that.

Reactive feelings are awareness frozen on the Dense Plane. As raw sensory information and instincts, they are usually below the threshold of the cognitive mind. Our thoughts and behaviors are higher, subtler abstractions of the lower, automated circuitries on the Dense Plane. The reactive feeling states are like broken keys on a piano. Our cognitive mind, thoughts, and controlled behaviors are the music being played on the piano. We cannot fix the piano by playing different music on it. Likewise, it is usually not productive to try to change the reactive feelings by changing thoughts and behaviors. To bring healing into the Dense Plane, we need direct access to Dense Plane awareness. Feelingwork provides a methodology for that.

Science has greatly enabled us to engage with the material world by turning what is invisible visible. The worlds that become visible to us through scientific means range from microorganisms and electromagnetic fields, to the cells and tissues of our own internal organs. Similarly, Feelingwork makes invisible and intangible feelings visible and tangible.

In Feelingwork mapping, we first translate our felt experience of the reactive feeling into a map consisting of sensory information. This information includes location, size, temperature, color, substance, movement, and sound. It can be helpful to think of this practice as applying a part of the brain that is very skilled with imagery in a new way. We're directing its attention toward the feeling part of the brain that is more amorphous and harder to perceive with clarity and objectivity. It's as if we are using this imagery part of the brain the way you would use an X-ray to get a clear image of what's going on beneath the surface of the body, out of sight. We can't look at the feeling directly, but by using the instrument of the sensory questions, we interact with the feeling in such a way as to deliver a tangible image. By doing so, we enable the strength of the Middle Plane, our language capacity, to make a visible and tangible bridge to the otherwise invisible reactive feelings and automated circuitry. See the example map below.

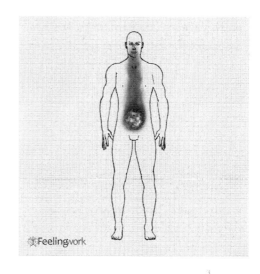

Example: Cranky

Located in the lower abdomen. Like embers, a carbon-like substance, with smoldering fire filling the body. The sound of crackling fire. When the fire rises into the face, the feeling intensifies and becomes Angry.

Associated with Cranky is a generalized irritability at everyone and everything. The thoughts associated with Cranky are, "I want my comfort. Leave me alone." When it turns into Angry, it says, "Damn you. You all suck."

As science made the invisible world of microorganisms visible, biologists started to interact with these microorganisms and acquire new agencies and knowledge. Likewise, after a map is created for a feeling state, one can interact with the map as a handle to restore the feeling from its reactive state to a state of wholeness. This is done through the sensory parameters of the map — the substance, temperature, color, etc. — deliberately shifting one at a time, exploring the spectrum of possibilities and using what feels better as a compass to guide the shift.

Usually in this step, people have distinct sensations of qi moving in or around their body, even those who have never experienced qi or energy before. Entering this space of the psyche tends to be far outside our ordinary daily consciousness, so it is common to experience this as an "altered" or hypnotic state. Yet entering this space is surprisingly easy, and using our awareness in this way is profoundly healing and restorative to the currents of wholeness in the psyche.

After a new map is made, the person can explore what new thoughts or beliefs are arising. To their surprise, they find that new, healthier thought patterns and beliefs, completely impossible from the perspective of the reactive states, naturally arise without conscious effort.

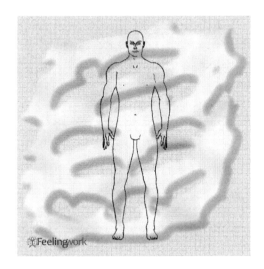

Cranky becomes Connection to Flow

Liquid/water. Gentle flow, little surges, out and back in. Slightly cooler than body temperature, refreshing. Fills me and my immediate surroundings, out to about 10 feet in all directions.

The thought associated with the restored state of Connection to Flow is, "I am connected to the larger flow and purpose of things." Things that were previously irritating are no longer a problem.

Conflict between the controlling force of the linear rational mind and the primal life energy on the Dense Plane. The Light Plane is being tossed aside.

Feelingwork opens a pathway between the Light and Dense Planes, reconnecting the two.

There are three critical ingredients that make Feelingwork potent.

Feelingwork gracefully disarms the incessant, controlling energy from the linear rational mind.

Reactive feelings arise when the controlling forces exerted by the linear rational mind are in conflict with what the primal energy rising from the Dense Plane wants. For example, when we feel anger, our mind might insist us to calm down. Or when we experience sadness, our mind would rather be happy. There is nothing wrong with calming down and being happy. But they are not what most wants to emerge in that moment. The linear mind has to let go of what it wants in order to make space for what wants to emerge.

When the reactive feeling is transposed onto the sensory map and moved according to the guidance of "what feels better," the process is out of the control of the rational linear mind. It has to simply stand by and watch what happens next.

Feelingwork opens a pathway between the Dense Plane and the Light Plane.

When one starts to change the parameters of the sensory map, the agent of change lies at the Dense Plane. We manipulate the parameters of temperature, texture, color and spatial location through our Dense Plane faculty. However, in this exercise, the Dense Plane faculty is applied toward a subtle energy pattern, instead of a concrete material object. This opens up a pathway between the Dense Plane and Light Plane, reconnecting the two.

As a result of the currents reconnecting the Light and Dense Planes, the linear rational mind on the Middle Plane naturally shifts its thought patterns, becoming aligned with what the currents of wholeness are pointing to. Instead of calming down the anger or clicking into a happy mood, the linear rational mind is now engaged in how to transform the primal life energy to fuel the manifestation of the Light Plane subtle patterns.

Mapping and moving a set of feeling states reconstitutes the experience of wholeness.

While mapping and moving one feeling state is an eye-opening experience on its own, one experiences a powerful state of wholeness when one maps and moves a set of inter-locking and connected feeling states. A complete set consists of a minimum of nine states. This set of nine states anchors the main features of the architecture of the psyche in its state of wholeness. After one restores a set of feeling states, the experience is usually a noticeable, sometimes dramatic shift in how one inhabits one's life.

Looking for the nine (or more than nine) reactive states that anchor a reactive pattern is one of the more technical aspects of Feelingwork. The reason is that our normal consciousness is so used to roaming the Middle Plane. It takes quite a bit of experience and knowledge of traversing the terrain in the Dense and Light Planes to locate the nine or more than nine feeling states required for a shift into wholeness.

In my experience of facilitating Feelingwork, when clients first start, most of the narratives they give about the reactive pattern do not contain explicit information about the feeling states. Most of the time, people are not aware of the feeling states in the set. To locate the feeling states is like a treasure hunt that requires the facilitator to look for clues hidden between the words of the story. Following the clues, the facilitator will probe with questions to direct the client's awareness to a reactive feeling that they are not yet conscious of, and to surface it by giving it a name.

Often, the feeling states point to a deeper fear of losing something that is foundational to one's self identity. For example, a person with a successful career is fearful of losing his reputation built through decades of hard work. He feels torn between the demands of his work and giving himself the nurturing space he needs. A woman who has established her authority and power in a field dominated by men is afraid of facing a vulnerability and weakness she has suppressed deep down. She projects the rejection of this part of herself onto her staff and turns excessively critical to others who demonstrate vulnerability around her. A person in a three-decade marriage is afraid of facing the deep disappointment she holds toward her partner. She distances herself from her husband instead of engaging in authentic conversations.

As facilitator, within the scope of trust I build with my client, I look for feeling states that the person is most fearful of or has the strongest resistance toward feeling. This is a very delicate balance as my number one priority is to respect the client's boundary and not to push too far. Within that boundary, I respectfully ask the client to turn their awareness to something they are afraid of seeing. The ironic thing is that once the most catastrophic fear and unbearable feeling is revealed, named, and brought into the daylight of conscious awareness, people actually feel a sense of relief. The relief comes from not carrying the burden in one's unconscious anymore.

Intense reactive feelings such as fear, anger, or sadness point to ways in which the wholeness of our psyche has been disrupted. In our disruption, we forget or refuse to believe that we have other options. We get locked into our reactive pattern and hold fast to it despite its disruption. Feeling the reactive feelings allows us to turn our awareness to these places of disruption so the currents of wholeness can be restored. When wholeness is restored, we regain our capacity to experience every moment as an emerging present, and thereby open ourselves to an infinite scope of possibilities. We are no longer locked in, but become free to choose our next steps with creativity and a felt sense of inner guidance. As we make new choices from that place of freedom, our path diverges from the old pattern and we find ourselves living more authentically, with more integrity and joy in every day.

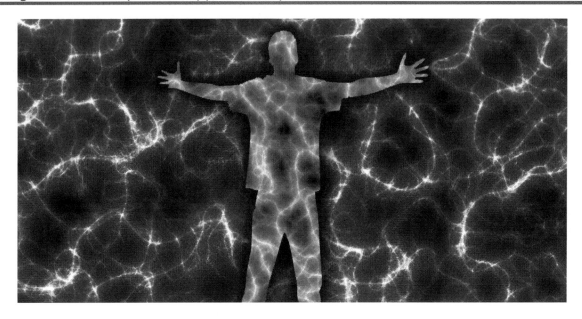

Feelingwork operates with a model of the psyche that is completely different from that of cognitive psychotherapy. Cognitive therapy focuses on dissecting and rebuilding a cognitive model of experience. Feelingwork helps to build new awareness pathways between the cognitive mind and the Dense and Light Planes, facilitating the flow of qi in the psyche. Feelingwork can be engaged as a complementary practice to cognitive psychotherapy.

Feelingwork works best for pioneers and leaders who intend to consciously rewire their automated circuitry of the Dense Plane and engage it as a resource with which to embrace the emerging present. Even though Joe discovered Feelingwork through extricating himself from bipolar disorder, its real strength lies in releasing hidden potential and creativity, and in enlivening one's Light Plane awareness into embodied sensations.

In this exercise, you'll get a taste of how to identify feeling states to map. Think about an area of your life with recent strong feelings, something that's current and alive for you right now. Reflect on your experience. When was the last time you got caught in that loop or found yourself reacting in that old way that isn't how you want to be in the world? Jot down a short list of feeling states you felt in the course of this experience. These feeling state names do not have to be part of the standard lexicon for emotions. Allow yourself to be descriptive and creative. Names people find useful range widely, from descriptions of sensations, to the effects of the feeling, to the intentions of this part, to the behavior it motivates. Here are a few examples taken at random from states people have mapped:

Intimidated	Doubting Myself
Playing It Safe	Disbelief
Threat	Get On With It
Withdrawn	Twisted Stomach
Generalized Hatred	Cutting Ties
Fog / Shut Down	Mental Fireworks
I Want	Catapult
I Can't Have	Heebie Jeebies
Contempt	Bafflement
Quicksand	Shutdown

Please put aside any training you may have had about what constitutes a "real" feeling name. Most existing systems of identifying and working with feelings are semantic in nature. Semantic systems rely on careful definitions in an attempt to categorize what is inherently an infinitely complex field of experience. You want to feel free and supported in defining your experience in whatever way is relevant and meaningful to you.

In addition, semantic systems of working with feelings assume that feelings are a special class of experience, different from cognitions, for example. What we discover in Feelingwork — and this is very important — is that every conscious experience has its foundation in the felt sense. Even if you want to map the experience of "thinking," or "being true," these experiences have at their core a feeling state which can be mapped just as any other feeling state. Even something called "numb" — often interpreted as the absence of feeling — is itself a feeling state fully amenable to the mapping process.

Having named a specific feeling state, you're ready to dive into mapping. Or you might find it helpful to explore and identify related states. Doing so can add more context to any state you choose to map, and helps you start to see the full extent of the issue you're choosing to work on. The following is an exercise you can use to more completely unpack the feeling states embedded in the issue you're exploring.

<u>Creating a List of Related Feeling States</u>

Clear a space, in your mind and on paper. Decide what issue you want to work on, something around which you want greater choice and freedom. Give that issue a name and write that down. Now, write one statement that is true for you about this issue. Get as close to the core of the issue as possible. Here are a few examples:

Jeremy doesn't like me, and that makes me upset.

I procrastinate too much with important projects.

I freeze when I have to give a presentation.

I don't get along with my boss.

I'm confused about whether to stay with Sandra.

Read the statement aloud or say it internally to yourself. Continue by adding the word "because..." and complete the compound sentence with whatever comes to mind and seems to capture something new about your relationship with the issue. Write the second half of the sentence as a new statement. Do this once more, this time using the word "therefore..." after either of the statements you've written. Repeat, going back and forth as you intuit best between adding "because..." and "therefore..." to your new statements until you start repeating yourself or run out of new insights.

Now ask yourself, "What else is true about this issue?" Write a new, different statement if one comes to mind, and repeat the process. If nothing new comes to mind, stop there. Here is an example list of statements to give you an idea of what you're going for.

I don't get along with my boss.

He's a jerk.

I'll never succeed in this job.

I'm stupid for taking this job in the first place.

I'm a failure.

I don't deserve this.

There's nothing I can do about it — I'm stuck here.

I'm not happy.

The whole thing makes me angry.

I need to stay small.

I'm afraid to call attention to myself.

When you've finished generating statements, review them one at a time. What is the feeling connected with each statement? Write a name for the feeling beside each statement. Now review your feeling names to identify any duplicate feelings, even if they have different names. For example, "timid" and "hesitant" might be two different names for the same feeling state. Choose the best name or write a new name for that feeling state and circle it. Circle all the names of unique feeling states.

To decide which one to map first, consider choosing whichever one feels closest to the surface of your experience in the moment. Pick a feeling state that will be easy for you access right now, or easy to remember what it felt like in a specific, preferably recent, moment.

Now you are ready to map your feeling state. You may go to:

TheFeelingMind.com/feelingwork-resources

There you will find extensive instructions and audio files to guide you in mapping the feelings into a sensory information map, and for moving your mapped states and sets toward wholeness.

To the right is a collage of feeling state maps from one person's journey. On the next few pages you'll detailed examples of mapping from Joe's experience. You'll find extensive further examples of other people's mapping on TheFeelingMind.com.

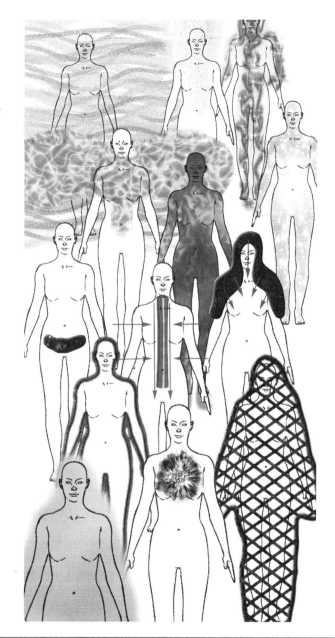

To finish this introduction, I will give you a tour of a set of maps Joe did with himself in 2008. This will give you an idea of the complexity and interconnectivity involved in mapping and moving a set of nine states that will lead to an experience of wholeness.

Background

Joe became aware of a highly reactive pattern in himself that was creating problems in his relationships with other men. A dream helped him surface the feeling states.

I was a prisoner, lying bound on the floor of a bare cell, a tall, jackbooted, masked guard standing over me. I knew the guard was going to beat me and I was helpless to do anything about it. The next day as I reflected on the guard, I recognized his rage as my own. Not only was it mine, but it was familiar, going way back to my teen years.

Vicious-Confused-Fear Triad

Among others, Joe identified a triad of states: Vicious Enforcer, Confused Paralysis, and Fear. Following is the edited version of Joe's account of mapping these three states.

Vicious Enforcer

Description: *This is the part that would out-vicious my father if it had the chance to go back in time – he would be pathetic in comparison to this. "You are WRONG!! Just get the fuck out of my way!" Snarling, growling, prowling, predatory/cat, active muscles. Images of instantly disemboweling someone with a slash of a paw (not a knife). Vicious. This is scary and it NEVER gets out.*

Mapping Notes: *An intensely powerful firestorm rising 20-30 feet above me. Fire that has incredibly dense substance, incredible power. It moves with lightning speed, swirls, consumes. Extremely hot.*

Reds, oranges, yellows, the colors of out-of-control flames. Very very dense, opaque, highly luminous, blindingly bright. The sound of an inferno combined with a deep, deep cat growl, which can peak into a raging roar. The sound is deafening. Looms, threatening, can strike downward at any time.

This is hell personified. It has no conscience. All about asserting dominance, preserving order. I felt this sometimes in my teens, hating my father, wanting to vanquish him and everything like him.

Thoughts: *"I am the enforcer. Cross me and my fury will know no bounds."*

Analysis: *The Vicious Enforcer is me. Not my father. I have no way of knowing whether my father had anything quite this intense inside of him. His anger had regular opportunity for expression, while mine had been completely suppressed for many years. (Mostly. There were moments when it had leaked out, moments which truly frightened me. I felt certain in those times that given the right conditions I was capable of horrible things.)*

Imagine I had a child. And let's imagine my kid was willful and resistant to my authority as his dad. Is it so difficult to imagine I might have become as bad as my father? In fact, it is easy for me to imagine much worse – again, given the right conditions.

Fortunately, I had a number of compensating states that held this in check. Confused Paralysis and Fear are the primary two.

Confused Paralysis

Mapping Notes: *Like that insulation foam that comes in a can, but more beige colored, and pressurized, before it becomes hard. Soft but pressurized, pushing outward in all directions. This is what contains Vicious Enforcer, with the aid of Fear. Fear doesn't have to do it all by itself. Neutral temperature. No movement except for some slight continuing expansion of the foam, ever-increasing pressure. Headache, body ache, dullness. No sound. Muffled sound. Can't hear myself think.*

This does not enter the head except when highly activated, during close confrontations with

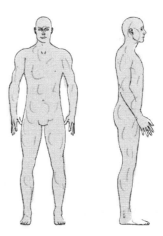

authority, when my own authority is called for, or when I've screwed up.

Thoughts: *"I can't move. The pressure is enormous. The foam is stifling. I am a prisoner in my own body. The fire is completely put out. It's fire-proof foam. I need to figure out what to do, but I can't. Don't know what's what. I'm stuck. Immobile. Inactive. Passive. I don't like this. Must avoid situations which make me feel it."*

Analysis: *Confused Paralysis was the first line of defense against Vicious Enforcer. As long as Confused Paralysis came up in situations where authority was present, I was safe. I avoided all possible situations like this. Employment, for example, was almost exclusively freelance. Having a boss was just not safe, unless that boss was a woman, in which case I could tolerate it.*

Fear
Description: *Confused Paralysis wasn't enough to contain the Vicious Enforcer. In case Vicious Enforcer got too strong, there was a layer of Fear on top.*

Mapping Notes: *A tension in my back and shoulders, holding shoulders and arms back and immobilized. Material is like Brazil nut casing, very hard but not heavy. Rigid, like a kind of armor. About an inch or so thick, maybe less, at skin and*

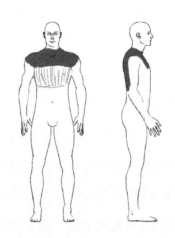

just under it. Feels like my arms are kept immobile. Color of a Brazil nut or a beetle, maybe slightly shiny, smooth, woody tough. Neutral temperature. No movement — resists movement. This stuff is fireproof and is able to contain the Vicious Enforcer, which can't gain its power if it is unable to move. Slight whispering, more like a quiet voice advising caution or good behavior to a child.

Thoughts: *"I have to keep Vicious Enforcer contained. Can't go there. It's very important to keep it contained, because it could hurt someone, or myself. My whole purpose is to reinforce Confused Paralysis, to keep things contained. This is serious business."*

As you can tell, this triad is quite intense. It is a classic example of how the unconscious masculine energy could get passed down from father to son. Joe's father was guided by this notion that a man needs to use force to exert his will and dominate others. He considered Joe's emotional sensitivity as a negative quality to be removed in order to make a man out of his son. As Joe fought to protect his own integrity under the shadow of his father's domination, over time he developed the deeply suppressed Vicious Enforcer, an internal force, equally vicious and forceful against his father. Had Joe not been as conscious in withholding this energy, he might have passed this Vicious Enforcer down to his children or acted it out in the world as his father did.

However, other parts of Joe were determined not to let that happen. Two of them, Confused Paralysis and Fear, took on the job to ensure that he kept the intense energy of Vicious Enforcer within himself. This dynamic was not sustainable and had begun to erupt into Joe's experience, making him aware of the pattern.

At this point, you might be sitting on the edge of your seat wondering what happened when Joe moved the Vicious Enforcer. But when Joe tried to move Vicious Enforcer, it would not budge. He had to turn his attention to two other states and move them first before Vicious Enforcer finally dislodged

from its purchase on his psyche. Those two states were Miasma of Abuse and Powerless.

Miasma of Abuse

Description: *Abusers pervade all space. There is no escape. In my house, my father occupied all the space, all the time. There was threat in the air. You never know when you are going to be seen as "bad" and attacked for your so-called badness. And his logic and perception were so rigidly twisted there was no hope for appeal, no possibility to be seen as who you really were. I received no compassion, no empathy, only reactive hostility, blame, and aggressive humiliation and punishment.*

Mapping Notes: *Like poison. A contaminant. Even when the abuser is not physically present*

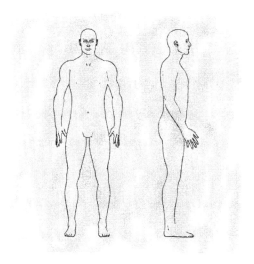

it surrounds you. Their judgment is everywhere. A toxic gas. It can get in you if you breathe, and poison you. A miasma of toxicity; hazy, thick, cloudy, dirty, gray-green-brown, gross, like wafting incense except 1,000 times more dense and it is everywhere. Gets to your core and disables any strength you have, completely rots any resistance, turns it to putrefying jelly, (see Powerless below).

Smotheringly warm, close, choking, overly humid and caustically dry at the same time, like it is moist but chemically incinerates your own moisture. Moving like incense smoke in a still room. Sound of choking sobs, choking because of the toxicity, sobs because of the hopelessness of avoiding it.

Thoughts: *"It is everywhere, in every small abusive communication, disguised in many ways, overt and accepted in many ways, forcibly oppressive in many ways. There's no way to fight back because it is so pervasive, and because it is so disabling. I am too weak in its presence to even put up a fight. I am too frightened to resist."*

Powerless

Description: *I'm in deep shit, terrified I'm not strong enough to resist, to stand up to the idiocy, to fight back, and that I will be subjugated permanently. I am too weak, too slow, too emotional to defend myself against the aggression and mean-spirited abuse. I will cave, and that will mean my life (all life?) is sentenced to permanent subjugation. There is nothing I can do. I am powerless.*

Mapping Notes: *Like jelly, watery, clear, sloppy-gelatinous. It's falling apart and can't hold its shape. Very cold, deathly cold, 35 degrees; whole body; smeary blood-red splotches throughout a translucent haziness. Quivering slightly. Too weak to quiver strongly. Sound is whimpering, crying aloud, me as a child. Wants to wail, but wailing is unsafe, will bring down the mocking wrath of the abuser.*

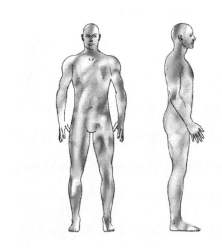

Thoughts: *"I am powerless to stand up to the abusers of the world. Their mindset is crazy, and*

there is no way to reach them rationally. I am too weak to address them directly, they will gut me instantly if I try. I would love to be powerful and rip them to shreds, but I cannot do that because I will not allow myself to become like them. Everything I do is about finding a way to dethrone the Abusers of the world without giving up my own integrity. I want to empower all of the world's oppressed, make them immune to the Abuser's manipulative power. I want to cut the Abusers off at the knees, make the ground they stand on go to quicksand.

"This part contributes to keeping the Vicious Enforcer in check because I don't actually believe I could overcome the abusers even with the Enforcer part. They are much stronger than me."

The Frame for Moving Feeling States

When I soak myself in the descriptions of these feeling states Joe has mapped, I feel as if I have ventured into the bottom of hell. For most of us, without the right tools or guidance, it is not safe to travel there on our own. And why? Why would anyone do that?

Actually, there is a good reason to choose going into hell if the tools and guidance are available. After attaining the state of enlightenment,

Bodhisattva did not stay in the transcended realm. Instead he said, "If I do not go to hell willingly, who would?"

The energetic pathway that exists from the bottom of the inner helix core is an important pathway that completes the flow of wholeness. We cannot become whole without consciously experiencing this pathway. It is through this pathway that we develop the capacity to experience pain while choosing not to suffer, instead choosing joy or even bliss. Developing this pathway is the essence of compassion.

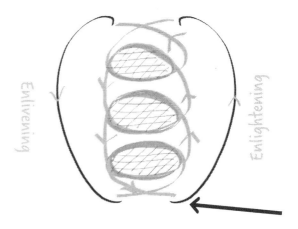

Through Feelingwork, one experiences the descending current through the core reversing at the bottom into the ascending current, linking back to the Light Plane.

Let me share with you the preamble Joe developed to prepare clients when they are ready to move a state. It provides a good outline of an essential frame for this work.

First of all, I want to acknowledge: this feeling you mapped is a part of you that has been expressing itself in a particular way. It took this form at some point in your life where that was necessary to signal something being out of balance for you. At that time, it might have been that you weren't allowed to feel it, and you had to push it aside. Or it might have been, you weren't allowed to act on it, or you didn't have the power to make the changes necessary. Or perhaps you weren't supported in the way you needed, to become aware of what that feeling was trying to tell you and take the action necessary to restore balance and harmony and wholeness in your life. So it had a function, that feeling. But its function was interrupted.

In this process, we want to restore this part's natural functioning so it can signal you, in an ongoing way, about the state of balance in your life. And the way that we're going to do that is we're going to reconnect this part of you with its original or ideal state. This part has a particular feeling state that is what it would feel in an optimal situation, in a perfect world. We want to reconnect with its ideal state. We're going to expand its horizons and reconnect it to the full range of expression available to it.

This is the compassionate voice of the Light Plane speaking to the energies stuck at the bottom of hell. This voice acknowledges that even states as hellish as the ones Joe has mapped here have served life in their own way. All this voice from the Light Plane offers is a freedom to have a difference choice. There is no need to force, knead, shape, correct, punish, or judge. It simply asks with a genuine curiosity, what would you choose differently in a world where your needs can be met? This is why Bodhisattva chose to go down into hell. This voice cannot reach the bottom of the Dense Plane if our awareness only hovers around the upper planes. We have to personally deliver this message through feeling the pain.

Restoration of Wholeness

Now let us see how these intense reactive states were restored to wholeness.

Miasma of Abuse becomes: Shared Light

Description: *I let Miasma of Abuse completely seep into me. I stop resisting it… It begins to dissipate, becomes clearer; becomes fresh and clean air.*

It turns into the light of human goodness, the ability to see the strong heliotropic pull in every human being toward wholeness, and to trust that above all, especially above expressions of shadow, fear, and pain that come out as abuse and control.

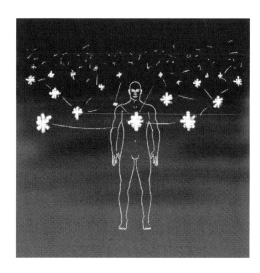

Map of Restored State: *An infinite field of light, with points of light in every person's heart including my own. There is a sense of joyfulness and play about it. The lights are dancing or at least wanting to dance, individually and together. A rhythm unites all the lights, yet each can vary in that rhythm to dance its own dance.*

Warm, white lights in a field of dark, radiant blue, quite beautiful, like half-moon-size stars in a twilight sky, stretching out around the globe. Sounds of light laughter and play, some giggling, some pleasurable sighs, some yeses, many voices.

Now that Miasma of Abuse was no longer a pervasive threat, the other parts were free to begin to move. Powerless was the next to release. To start

the moving process with this state, I chose to use an alternative technique similar to Jungian Active Imagination. I surrendered to the imagery that wanted to emerge from the state and followed it fully throughout the scenario it wanted to create, kept following it, asking what wants to be now, and now, and now. The brief notes from that journey are below. To begin, I returned to my dream of being imprisoned by the abuser.

Powerless becomes: Power Is Connected Flow

Description: *Quivering intensifies - it gets stronger. I am lying on the floor, shaking spasmodically, saying to a tall, jack-booted guard, "Come on, dance with me... you know you want to... go ahead and hit me... as soon as you do, we are dancing, you with me, I with you... you can't escape it; we are wedded by coexistence." I laugh, and my spasms become quakes of laughter. "Yes," I cry out, "you MUST dance with me, because how can you not?" In my laughing I feel powerful; and I see the look of confusion beneath the mask, in the whole body's hesitation, awkwardness. I laugh harder. "And now," I say, "tell me what you really want, and together we shall dance it into being."*

A strong energy, flowing through me, into and out of me, into and out of others. It is an energy of doing, of being together, of our communal dance, our dancing one another's dreams into being.

Map of Restored State: *It flows vertically through me, and out in all directions to flow vertically through others. Sometimes up, other times down, it is not important. Upward is me giving explicitly, and receiving more implicit support; downward is me receiving explicitly, and giving more implicit support. Back and forth, like breathing.*

Lusciously warm, moist and tingly. A juicy, vibrant red, like arterial blood and brighter than that. The energy flows like a liquid, easy and quick at times, gentle and languid at other times. Always there is no resistance, and flow through me instantly connects to flow through one or more others. Sound of deep flow, and something like the breath of the planet... sound of great laughter shared among many people, laughter for its own sake, in naked appreciation for life and our shared experience of it.

Thoughts: *"I am mischievous, playful, and utterly confident in the drive toward joyful wholeness in others. I invite others to dance in many playful and serious ways, always with lightness, always with respect for what I know is the deeper truth in everyone, the desire to belong, to be significant, to matter, to contribute, to participate. At the same time, I have no tolerance for false divisions among people. I can easily challenge such talk and action because I am calling everyone to something more true. They are like children who have been taught poorly, who are only doing what they know in order to feel safe. As soon as they feel the invitation to show up, to drop their defenses, they are glad to do so. It is my job to make those invitations compelling, to reach them where they are, to touch them despite the walls they have put up, and I can do that because I know the purpose of the walls and the manner of their construction.*

"I have a great capacity for compassion and love for every being."

After moving Miasma of Abuse and Powerless, Vicious Enforcer was finally ready.

Vicious Enforcer becomes: Truth Blaze

Description: *In my first attempts to move this I could get nowhere, hardly able to bring my awareness into the feeling for more than a few seconds at a time. To try working around it, I engaged again in the active imagination exercise. My notes on that journey:*

"I am flying above the world, fury, hurling huge firebombs at cities, government, corporate power... dark, all around the globe... then an ease, settling back to earth, to a green village, people, smiling, joyful living, simple, lots of green, much life and laughter... I just want to be one of them... just want a place to call home... As I connect with people, with laughter, with appreciation, I begin taking a leadership role. I am the one who reminds people what they already know. That is what true authority, true leadership, is."

This is about creating harmony, in current form by eliminating disruptions to harmony... Some kind of consolidation is happening, a calming down and strengthening. No need to force it.

Map of Restored State: *A column of light, a pillar of light, as big around as my body, extending above and below me many yards, perhaps as far as 30 feet in each direction. It is anchored by the light within me, which is my personal wavelet/expression of the Shared Light. Provides a kind of photonic "lubrication" for passage of the Power Is Connected Flow through me.*

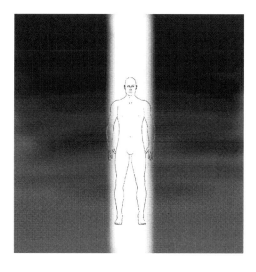

There is a kind of hum, a high-tension vibration like that within an electromagnet or around high-voltage wires. This pillar is rock steady and resists perturbation, although it is flexible, the way a high-density magnetic field would yield movement for an object suspended in it, but would return that object firmly to its centered place. The pillar can flex, but always returns strongly to its vertical position. Top and bottom fade out over the most distal several feet; all around me though is high-density. This

light is almost opaque it is so bright, but is soft, not blinding; you can see through it if you squint. Color is mostly white, glistening.

Thoughts: *"I am me. I am strong. I know what I am here for. I am here to promote dancing among the spirits of all people, to show fighting for the wasteful illusion it is. I represent the light shared by all of us; it is within me and I see it in you. I stand for the sharing of our light, each by all. My light burns through the shadows of illusion, reveals them as simply a mistaken obscuring of the true light within all of us. I am a blaze of wise truth-telling. I shrink at nothing in order to spread my message of shared light, dancing. I laugh in the face of resistance, because I know it is illusory. I laugh with joy to dance with those who might at first disagree with me. How can they know what I represent?"*

Vicious Enforcer was the pivot state this entire set revolved around. As it transformed, the rest of the feeling states followed easily. If you are curious about what Confused Paralysis and Fear eventually turned into, or what were the rest of the four states that are not included here, please refer to Joe's website:

TheFeelingMind.com/feelingwork-examples

This was quite a roller-coaster ride, wasn't it? I want to finish this tour by sharing some important perspectives in Joe's words.

The new states I've shared with you here are the ideal. These are what I aspire to. This set feels true for me as a direction. This inner sense of having a big mission to make the world a better place has been with me from a very early age. It was probably largely responsible for my choosing to trust myself for making sense of the world at age five, rather than look to my parents for that. And it certainly played a role in my continuing to push forward even when things seemed absolutely hopeless in my twenties and thirties.

As an ideal, though, it serves its purpose as a touchstone, as a force by which to orient the vector of creation in my life. At any given moment, my current state of reality will never fully reflect this ideal. As I embrace what is and reach toward this ideal as a pull toward what wants to be, I can embody within myself the difference between the two. This difference between current reality and the ideal possible is the driving force for creation in my life. It drove my discoveries, it is driving my collaboration with Spring now on this book, and it drives my continued development.

When you see the map of the Power-Is-Connected-Flow, does that remind you of the currents of wholeness in The Resonance Code? On the next page, I lay out Truth Blaze and Power-Is-Connected-Flow, side by side with Primordial Father and Primordial Mother. These two feeling states bear a striking parallel with the energetic signature of Primordial Father and Primordial Mother, the two most polarized states in all 64 hexagrams.

It makes sense to me what these feeling states turned into when they were stuck in the reactive mode. When the resonant interplay between Yin and Yang is broken, and feminine and masculine are disconnected, the Primordial Mother sinks into a puddle of powerlessness. Meanwhile, the Primordial Father, instead of blazing a trail of truth, uses its strength as an external force to control and dominate, turning into the inferno of Vicious Enforcer.

Joe mapped this set in 2008. At that time, The Resonance Code was still sleeping in the cocoon of I-Ching. It was another ten years before I would draw the parallel maps through synthesizing patterns from the abstract symbols of 64 hexagrams. Yet, the maps created through Feelingwork, excavated from a deep well of personal experience in the heartland of modern American life, found a connection to the maps in The Resonance Code, condensed from the mists of an ancient cosmology and an ocean of collective wisdom from the distant East.

This is not a coincidence. As Carl Rogers put it, what is most personal is most universal. The corollary of that is what is most universal is also most personal. Your path probably will also be a spiraling trail winding between the personal and the universal. Whatever is pulling you right now, universal or personal, follow its calling and let it take you. And trust its wisdom when it turns and takes you to the other end.

If you choose to use Feelingwork to map the reactive patterns in your life, like other clients we have worked with, you too will experience many of the maps we have introduced here within your embodied sensations. And if you choose to use The Resonance Code to explore the subtle patterns of the Light Plane, be prepared to take a dive with the subtle patterns into the deep pool of enlivenment.

Hexagram 1
Pure Potential

Primordial Father

Hexagram 2
Complete Manifestation

Primordial Mother

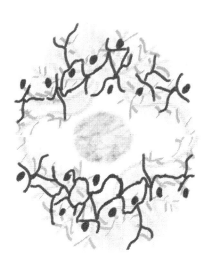

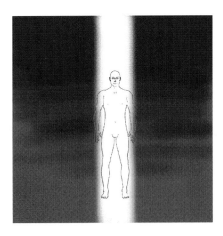

Final Words

Dear reader, at this point, our journey together through this book is coming to an end. I hope the book serves as an introduction to the work done at the Resonance Path Institute, as well as to the people involved in the work. I look forward to hearing from you and possibly, your participation.

To end our journey, I'd like to share my vision of a new arc of our evolutionary journey. This new arc is calling forth a new tribe of people who desire to engage in conscious evolution toward wholeness and to serve humanity from a renewed and strengthened sense of wholeness.

Let us first take a look at the arc of the journey over the last 200,000 years. We started out as scattered clusters of hunting-and-gathering bands separated from each other by the vast landscape of the Earth, including expansive plains, high mountains, and surging oceans.

Today, physical terrain is no longer a barrier separating humans. Most humans inhabit places that are within just a day or two's reach from each other. Among the 7.5 billion people on earth, 4.5 billion are within an instant phone call or text message of one another.

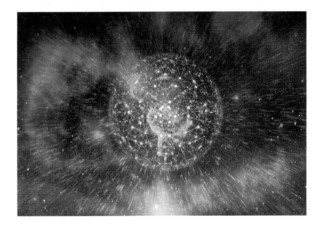

The achievement of modern technology marks the completion of this previous arc of evolution as instant connection has become possible between any two points over the entire physical terrain of the Earth. Meanwhile, we are now at the beginning of a new evolutionary journey to traverse across the terrain of the inner psyche.

In this terrain, we again find ourselves being separated by "plains," "mountains," and "oceans" that divide us in the realm of consciousness. The "plains" of the Inner Earth are the raw sensory experiences of life that have not yet been captured by our existing linguistic lexicons. The "mountains" are the beliefs and cognitive models of life shaped by millennia of culture-specific value systems. The "oceans" are the deep currents of primal life energy and ancestral, emotional imprints in our genetic and epigenetic materials.

In this inner terrain, it may take years, decades or even a whole lifetime of inner transformation to reach those who inhabit a perspective or way of life opposite from where we are. These people may be our neighbors, co-workers, or lovers and family members.

The physical environment on Earth is changing rapidly as we are facing the consequences of disastrous depletion of natural resources, as well as the cascading events of climate change. The social environment we are living in is increasingly diverse and complex. The volatility, uncertainty and complexity of today's world are forcing us to traverse this inner terrain. We have to learn how to build bridges with people who inhabit different "locations" in the inner terrain of the psyche, so that we can solve problems that require a collaborative effort.

In this new arc of the journey, it is most crucial to develop the skill and art of compassion, the capacity to feel the intensity of life and the forces of evolution within ourselves and within humanity, even when they are painful to feel. Often the people with whom we are closest

challenge our capacity for compassion the most, as they present the ultimate paradox between self and other. Between a parent and a child, or intimate partners, often we are caught in a polarized tension where we feel like we must choose between feeling compassion for the pain of others, or our own. Yet we cannot genuinely feel compassion towards others without healing our own pain and addressing our own needs. So, we are caught in a dilemma. Compassion for self or others? There is no formula or the right answer here. Navigation of this dilemma requires an ongoing process and inquiry of self-transformation so that we grow our capacity to

Om Mani Padme Hum, the six-syllable mantra associated with the Bodhisattva of Compassion.

feel and hold another's pain and our own pain simultaneously.

Another place where our capacity for compassion is challenged is in the dynamic between victim and perpetrator. How do we hold genuine compassion for perpetrators while being committed to justice for the victims? That often requires us to change the social system that harbors the root cause of the victim-perpetrator dynamic. To do that, we need to develop a sophisticated intellectual mind to see the system that is otherwise invisible to our eyes. Yet to change the system, our mind has to free itself from rigid conceptual frameworks, so we can develop a sensitivity and fluidity to birth creative solutions. To hold compassion for humanity is a tall order, requiring the rigor of intellectual inquiry, the devotion of an artists' soul, and an ongoing practice to keep our hearts open and supple.

The kind of technology involved in this arc of our evolutionary journey is very different from the technologies we know in today's world. What will enable this new arc of our evolutionary journey is inner technology like The Resonance Code and Feelingwork that interface with psychic "matter" and psychic "energy." For us, the authors, our life-long intuitions from working in this terrain tell

us that there seems to be a realm of materiality and energy associated with our psychological processes. The nature of this matter and energy is beyond the understanding of our current scientific framework. After all, the current knowledge of physics can only explain 5% of the energy and matter in the universe. The psychic matter and energy that we are intuiting may very well lie within the 95% that current physics cannot yet explain.

If what we are intuiting is true, then when we think, feel, sense, intuit, when we read and learn, when we communicate with each other through words, gestures, touch, or movements, all of these processes taking place in our psyche are actively interacting with this unknown source of matter and energy. Just as the previous arc of our evolutionary journey opened us to such abundant knowledge, this new arc will open us to a whole new realm of knowledge and understanding about ourselves and the world around us.

In the previous arc of human evolution, we relied heavily on the material resources of nature such as minerals, plants, or other species of animals. Caught by the urge to develop and progress, collectively we have neglected taking care of the equilibrium that maintains sustainability of the

material resources. We are now living in a world facing serious issues resulting from the depletion of fundamental resources such as soil, water, and energy, along with mismanagement of waste products, not to mention the mass extinctions of animal species caused by human activities.

The Resonance Code, as a form of psychic technology, opens access to a new realm of resources, the Light Plane subtle energies and subtle patterns. This form of resource is abundant and its energy source potent. It requires our utmost care to steward it and use it responsibly. In this new arc of our evolutionary journey, this resource will serve and enable those of us who love planet Earth and all its inhabitants, and who through our love feel committed to restore its beauty and wholeness.

Acknowledgments

The authors: We express our deep gratitude to members of the Resonance Code Research Lab. In the year-long group research, they have midwifed The Resonance Code by staying present with the unknown and being committed to what their hearts and souls know to be true. The work presented in this book blossomed because of their pioneer spirit and passion to explore uncharted territories of humanity.

Resonance Code Research Lab

Alexandra Isaievych

Beth Massiano

Charles Blass

Kris Miller

Riina Raudne

Tong Schraa-Liu

Spring: I want to express special gratitude to Ellen McCord, the chief editor of this book. This book has gone through many rounds of rewriting. Two months before the publishing date, I realized that it needed yet another round of complete rewrite. This final rewrite would not have been possible without Ellen's contribution. Ellen brought in her life-long experience of being a writer, a dedicated seeker and explorer of metaphysical knowledge, as well as her experience as an organizational development consultant, curriculum designer, and trainer. Not only that, she has poured her heart and love into helping to birth this book.

This writing has had several daunting challenges. First, English is my second language. Second, most of the materials presented in this book were ways of thinking and reasoning that were only present in ancient, archaic Chinese, which has been dead for a long time. Much of the information I am sourcing came from my connections with collective unconscious memory. Expressing these ideas in my native language would be difficult. How to express these ideas in modern English in ways that can be related to personally has been dauntingly challenging. I call Ellen my writing acupuncturist. Receiving her comments is like getting healing work on my writing. Sometimes I've felt like Ellen could see the essence of my thoughts without the aid of language. That was how she could help me express my ideas in clearer and simpler ways. The way she interacted with this writing further strengthens my faith that the information presented here is speaking to a universal aspect of our shared humanity.

Ellen McCord, Editor

I want to express my gratitude to the earlier board members of Resonance Path Institute: Victoria Poling, Chris Clark, Jeff Hammerquist, and Marci McReynolds. They helped set the compass for our exploratory work and helped us get off the ground.

Thank you Hilary Bradbury and Dana Carman for your ongoing support. The inquiries and research we have conducted together have generated fertile material for our growth.

I want to thank Marilyn Friedman for her friendship, love, and support for me. She has held an example for the embodiment of feminine wisdom and has empowered and nurtured me with her generous heart. I have grown more whole in her warm embrace.

Finally, I want to thank my music teacher and soul's guide, Kaija. She has led me to my source of creativity and opened my connection to my ancestral wisdom and soul's knowledge through sound and vibration. She has taught me to how to trust that realm of truth that has not found words to express itself in existing language, yet infuses our life with vibration. And she has healed me with her gentle, maternal love and an unwavering commitment to excellence.

The authors: Joseph Friedman, Spring Cheng, and Joe Shirley

Authors' Notes

Spring...

In this book, I introduce how the Inter-Being, as the larger life of being, is ever-present in our lives. When we align our being and actions according to the Tao, the Inter-Being becomes an intimate friend, being both a stern teacher and a loving nurturer. I'd like to share how my interactions with the Inter-Being have led me to this work.

My Dream as a Dancer

The Inter-Being likes to play the game of paradox with me. As a child, my most natural gifts were dancing and acting. However, I was living in a social environment that not only did not recognize these gifts but devalued them. At the same time, I was endowed with a raw aptitude of intellect which the society highly valued but I resisted in myself. This paradox was an endless source of sorrow and struggle in my young life.

Dance and drama are the most embodied forms of knowledge. The intellect is abstract and symbolic. Sir Ken Robinson in an iconic Ted Talk described the hierarchy of education which illuminated my life-long dilemma. Here is how he put it. In our education system, math and science are above the humanities. Within the humanities, art is at the lowest rung of the ladder. Within art, music and painting are higher. Dance and drama are at the bottom levels.

This hierarchy was much more magnified and polarized in China at the time I was in school.

268

China had just started to develop its own science and technology. My father came from a very poor village and my mother from an average family in the city. They both made their careers as astronomers. Their journeys were epic and heroic, built upon enormous personal sacrifice. They beat incredible odds and earned their place among the few members of the elite through much harsh competition.

I inherited a raw intellectual aptitude from them but never enjoyed intellectual work. However, in my formative years in China, my personal liking was inconsequential. Who I would become was defined by the larger community around me. The train of my life was locked firmly onto a track leading to intellectual development despite my resistance.

I launched into a series of intellectual pursuits. A doctoral degree in molecular biology, a masters of biostatistics, career as a data analyst, followed by the pursuit of a Chinese medicine degree.

I sailed through all these. But all the time I was driven by a desire to have the personal freedom I yearned for. That was a big impetus for me to come to the United States. Within the first decade of my life in the US, I did find my personal freedom. With this freedom, I gave myself the gift to develop dancing and acting, not as a professional choice, but as ways to explore my most authentic expression.

I am a person with simple desires. To dance and act in the way I wanted fulfilled my biggest personal dream. But the life force of Inter-Being had bigger dreams for me, even though that meant it had to push through the thick layers of my resistance. But the Inter-Being has its clever way and knows how to lure me into its dream …

Joe

I met Joe through dancing and fell in love with him. It was the first time that I met a peer in the mystical realm. Joe was not at all intimidated by the aura of mystery around ancient Eastern wisdom. I could not just throw archaic terms at him and hope he would submit to its mystical authority. He demanded me to explain what is qi, yin and yang, concepts that were so fundamental to the Chinese mind that few Chinese knew how to define them. But Joe genuinely wanted to know, and find out how these concepts would fit with his conceptual understanding from the western perspective.

Today I am very grateful for his insistence. But when I first encountered that, I was baffled and frustrated. Joe forced me to get off the pedestal of "mystical authority" and drilled into the underlying experience that gave rise to the architectural concepts such as yin, yang and qi. Not only that, to be in intimate relationship means that our deeply held cultural values clashed through everyday life matters, from coordinating cooking to managing finances.

The first three years of our relationship was a constant trial. The gyrating forces of our differences threatened to tear us apart. And the raw power of attraction threw us right back together into the cauldron.

Under such tremendous pressure, we started drilling down to the meanings of most granular concepts such as "I" or "We", or what does someone mean when she says I am ____. What happens in one's mind when he uses the verb "is" to join two concepts together? How does a person know something is true? We were astounded to discover the immense gaps of experience underlying these basic building blocks of language. These gaps are shaped by a combination of collective heritage and linguistic patterns as well as each individual's personality structure.

These discoveries completely transformed how we inhabited our relationship. We deeply

appreciate how vast is the mystery inherent in each person, behind the veil of language. We realized that being intimate with each other does not mean we can know a person with certainty. Instead it means we are granted the privilege to witness the mystery unfolding in our partner. The commitment we have for each other transformed from seeking certainty to enabling our partner to unfold his or her own mystery.

Although the work I write about in this book is abstract and philosophical, the impetus behind it was intimately personal. It was from my desire to communicate with the man I love and respect. It was out of the practical need to share a life and manage a household. Because every communication revolves around concepts such as "I" and "We," and the underlying experience that leads to a statement involving the verb "is."

Joseph

I committed myself to yet another serious intellectual pursuit, learning how to write and communicate philosophical ideas in English. Even then, I vehemently refused to write a book on the subject of Taoism and I Ching. The very idea of writing about the Tao was so against who I thought I was. Not only that, it was against a deep vein of cultural force. Lao Tzu, the legendary author of Tao Te Ching famously said, the Tao that can be named and spoken about is not the Tao. The Tao, to the Chinese mind, is an animated, living being, a trans-human, a being that is more enlivened than the human life we inhabit. The Chinese firmly believed that intellect, no matter how brilliant, was too crude and primitive to capture the essence of the Tao.

I vehemently argued with Joe when he pressed me to write. Why do I bother? Let alone to write in a second language, let alone that I never received any formal training in writing? In the heat of one argument I had with Joe, I drafted a "contract" that indicated the following:

Spring Cheng will not write about philosophical concepts at least until she is 83 years old.

Right after Joe and I signed that contract, a powerful force burst out from my unconscious. The writer part of me suddenly woke up. I was seized by an urge to write. I felt as if the Taoist sages and Confucian scholars of ancient China had risen up from their tombs, feeding streams of consciousness through my mind, demanding me to shape them into words and articles!

That is something we need to be mindful about in our communication with the Inter-Being. The Inter-Being is a great opportunist and tremendous negotiator. I think it must have taken that contract and replaced the number 83 with 42, my age when I did start writing.

The Inter-Being has an uncanny way to stretch us to our furthest limit. And it is thoughtful and considerate. Along with the revised contract, it offered me something else I could not refuse. It led me to meet Joseph Friedman. Joseph is a leadership and organizational consultant, with four decades of experience working in the field of human transformation. And he had a life-long relationship consulting with I Ching, from the time I was only one year old.

This was an encounter destined to happen. We started to converse and exchange ideas about topics we both love, from complexity to leadership, from evolution to Tao, from awareness of time to consciousness. We kept a weekly conversation through video conference nonstop ever since we met in 2016.

So here we are. Joseph, a Caucasian man, well-educated, semi-retired from a prestigious career. Me, a young Asian woman, new to the professional field, struggling to speak about a subject matter with no equivalent English concepts. There is an enormous power differential between us by virtue of our gender and race. The gender differential lies in that philosophy is a field dominated by men. As for the race differential, ever since the 19th century, China has been on the receiving end of an influx of western intellectual ideas and frameworks, including communism. In contrast, the western world knows very little about China's two thousand years of intellectual knowledge, and its rich and diverse philosophical achievements.

In the backdrop of such a power differential, Joseph made a remarkable choice. He chose to give me the listening ear, and his earnest desire to learn. Something magical happened. In his listening and affirming, a "dam" that had built around my heart started to crumble. This dam was held by the karmic forces between China and the West. As a member of my collective culture, my heart was plugged by the cement of shame and devastating pain of disempowerment. The shame arose as a result of being portrayed as intellectually inferior. The devastating pain of disempowerment came from watching the knowledge of my native culture dying off, misrepresented and misunderstood.

With Joseph's listening and his exquisite skill of generative inquiry, a "river" that had been dammed up for millennia started to roar. The knowledge that was frozen as kinesthetic

memories in my body started to unfreeze, seeping through the cracks of my mind, flowing into channels of thinking I never had, eventually converging into the words and drawings that I have now laid out in this book.

Meanwhile, I formed this most beautiful friendship with Joseph. It was the kind of friendship akin to the bond shared by climbing partners who venture into uncharted territory together. We "belayed" each other to climb the steep faces on the mountain of knowledge. Through this experience, we can trust each other with our lives.

Gifts from the Inter-Being

This book crystallizes two most precious gifts I received from the Inter-Being. One gift is the love and partnership I have with Joe. Another gift is the friendship and partnership I have with Joseph. These two men have modeled a mature form of masculine power that has lovingly awakened and courted the feminine knowledge sleeping in my unconscious. They have modeled how to use one's power and privilege wisely, and how to replenish the source of power by enabling those who are disempowered.

The kinesthetic memory of the ancient knowledge does not just belong to me. It is sleeping in every one of us. This river of feminine knowledge, which is melting off, is flowing through all of our consciousness. In our fear of chaos and desperate grasping for certainty, we don't recognize it, and we push it away. I hope through our effort of naming it, describing it, giving it form, and embodying it, we will welcome this river to flow back into our collective heart.

I also made peace with my ancestors. It is true that the Tao that can be named and spoken is not the Tao. Knowing this architecture of the psyche only makes me peek into the wider web of mystery and the unknown. It raises more questions than it answers. The knowledge presented here is imperfect and partial. But that is precisely why I want to present it. Because it is through this kind of partial, imperfect knowledge that we can build a pathway towards the Tao. We build this pathway not for the purpose to reach the Tao, but to provide a foundation so we can experience deeper love and more exquisite friendship, and to savor the finer tastes of both the sorrow and beauty of human life. After all, Tao, in Chinese, in its simplest sense, means the way.

Seattle, Washington, March 2019.

Spring Cheng, PhD, Co-Founder of Resonance Path Institute

Spring has lived a life that embodies an integration of cultures and dance between polarities. She spent the first half of her life in traditional, pre-industrialized China and the latter half in the US. In her first career, she received a doctoral degree in molecular biology and masters in biostatistics, and worked as a data scientist for the pharmaceutical industry. In her second career, following a spiritual awakening to her ancestral lineage, she took a 180 degree turn and practiced acupuncture, Chinese medicine and Taoist cultivation. In seeking an integration between the Eastern and Western ways, Spring met Joe Shirley as both life and professional partner. Together, they founded the Resonance Path Institute aimed at teaching, researching and practicing innovative social technologies of transformation and leadership development. Spring invented Resonance Code Technology, which systematizes the perception and navigation of the inner terrain of the psyche. With this systematized knowledge, one may begin to consciously cultivate the wholeness of consciousness to dance with the complexity of our times.

Joseph...

On May 4, 1974 — when the lead author of this book was one year old! — I cast my first I Ching reading. I was in the midst of many life changes, including a divorce. The next day was a court hearing to settle a disagreement between my soon-to-be ex-wife and me about a small amount of money. I had never expected to be divorced and certainly never to have to go to court. I was vexed and confused. So I cast the coins. The reading: # 6 Conflict. There was very specific instruction about the right frame of mind to enter into a conflictual situation and about trusting an impartial judge to help settle it, "an arbiter who is powerful and just, and strong enough to lend weight to the right side. A dispute can be turned over to him with confidence." Wait, how

did this reading come up on this day?(!) And so as my relationship with my first wife was changing I began my relationship with the Book of Change.

In the years since that reading, I became close friends with the I Ching, using my contemplation, journaling, and generating readings as my most consistent inner practice. The readings were frequently as apropos as on that initial day, but also often opaque and testing my ability to abstract meaning from the strange archaic language of the Wilhelm translation. As I travelled the road of my life, at important crossings and meaningful times I would always pause to inquire of the Oracle, as I then called it, the deeper meaning of the year, the birthday, the loss, the journey, or simply the day.

An astrologer said to me many years ago, "This is the chart of a mystic Argonaut of the inner realms." This startled me, because I did not show that side of myself publicly. I have spent most of my life intensely engaged in what The Resonance Code calls the Middle Plane, what the Hindu tradition calls the "householder phase" of life. Starting and running successful businesses, while simultaneously spending many hours a week intensely working as a volunteer leading programs for a human potential seminar program. Marrying again and starting a family rather late in life extended the householder phase through my sixties. I was led during these years into complex and challenging relationship and family situations that required attention, emotional intelligence, (as much as I could muster), and energy... all requiring external focus and affording many, many opportunities to consult my growing library of I Ching texts.

For example, in 1989 at the same time I was focused on the ordinary efforts of stewarding a rapidly growing consulting company that I had recently co-founded, my family life took an unusual turn and I stepped into living with my wife, our two young sons, her new lover and my new partner which, as you can surely imagine, required a great deal of effort as well. A stable rudder in the whitewater of my life, was my relationship with I Ching.

Shortly after my seventieth birthday three major events signaled the end of that phase of life with its intense outward focus and complications ensuing from my family life. My youngest child "fledged," left our home for college and other adventures. I left my employment at JMJ, the company I had founded thirty years before, and I married my sweetheart, life partner, and immensely patient and loving friend Marilyn.

In this new phase of freedom from "a job," from the direct care of children, and with a lovingly stable home life, I opened myself to discovering what the next phase of life would reveal. I began to offer Reckoning, Renewal and Reinvention programs for leaders in mid-career transitions and included in those programs the use of the I Ching to offer my clients further insight into their situation.

It was at this point that Spring and I were introduced by a mutual friend. I can truly say it was love at first sight. Not the Eros of romance but of creativity. As I have alluded to above, in this life I have walked the path of complex relationship dynamics as a primary means of personal and transpersonal development. And now meeting Spring in this phase of my life, for the first time, as my friend Hillary Bradbury and Bill Torbert write in their book Eros/Power, I experienced the power of a truly erotic friendship with a woman — a relationship filled with erotic, non-sexual, non-romantic and immensely creative energy. And what we set out almost immediately to create was the birthing of The Resonance Code.

Let me be clear. My role in this creation has been and is that of devoted assistant to the lead researcher. My many years of work with I Ching and in many related fields of study and practice had qualified me for this role, most particularly my well-honed capacity to listen deeply and translate what I hear into language that gives the speaker even deeper insight into what it is that they are bringing into the world in their speaking. And what a delight it has been to play this role!

Spring is a mountain climber and we often compared our conversations to scaling a steep pitch, stretching for holds on the smooth face of the unknown we were traversing. As we clarified the ideas together to create a solid "handhold" for our next move, I would feel a growing sense of exhilaration until, when we reached a conclusion of that particular conversation, I would be grinning on the outside and in — filled with a feeling that I had been preparing for this "climb" for a lifetime and fulfilling a deep life purpose of helping to create pathways of awakening for self and others.

The bonus, the unexpected gift that I've received in our collaboration on this book is to have developed a new relationship with my old friend, I Ching. Gradually, over the past two plus years, I've begun to think inside the remarkable intellectual architecture of The Resonance Code as articulated in this volume. Without losing any of the strength and depth of the classical translations and ways of working with the hexagrams, I have begun to approach casting a reading more like writing a poem or creating art than like consulting an oracle.

I've shifted from working in small journals to using a large 11" x 17" artist's pad. I often reflect and write a little as before, but then I will take a colored pencil in my non-dominant hand and begin to make patterns on the pad until I feel it is time to cast the coins. I often integrate the hexagrams into the design. To make meaning and develop a good reading in the timescape, as we have come to call it, I consult classic texts and then The Resonance Code to hear the names of the hexagrams I've cast. Drilling down, I note the trigram names. Then I note the three bigrams relating to the three planes, along with the energies and archetypes they represent. Finally, I step back and let words flow from the field through me to capture the meaning that all these relations and patterns reveal. The experience is more that of charting/creating new knowledge than that of consulting received wisdom.

What a joy it has been and continues to be, to participate in creating this map of consciousness and charting system for consciously engaging in the journey of evolution. May this work be of benefit to all.

Ashland, Oregon, March 2019.

Joseph Friedman, Friedman Consulting. Faculty of Resonance Path Institute.

Joseph has over forty years' experience in consulting and coaching individuals and organizations in communication effectiveness, leadership, high performance teamwork, and creating and enacting strategic plans. He has founded and managed several successful consultancies and has designed and delivered consulting, coaching, and educational programs in Africa, the Caribbean, Japan, India, and Canada as well as within the United States. He has engaged for many years with the wisdom of Taoism as expressed in the I Ching and most recently in Dr. Spring Cheng's Resonance Code. Joseph is a voracious learner and a passionate teacher. In all his work he draws on the two courses of study which have proved the most interesting, challenging, and rewarding of his life — the study of self in intimate relationship with others and the study of what the eye sees when it turns its gaze inward.

Joe...

Many people say we're all the same beneath the skin. I've learned that yes, we may be made of the same stuff, but that stuff can be poured into very different vessels. Over the past six years I've had the wondrous and terrifying opportunity of a profound intimacy with someone very different from me in almost every way. This project has brought us ever closer as it has made more evident the gulf between us.

Spring and I were brought together through improvisational dance, but our improvisation rapidly spread from the dance floor through all dimensions of our lives. In dance, you might choose to echo your partner's movement, or instead go for contrast, separation, or opposition, but you are always in the dance together. You are always co-creating. In our relationship, we have run the gamut from sublime synchrony to epic combat, but have always held the larger frame. Somehow, we knew we were together for a larger purpose, a deeper learning.

As a result, we found ourselves at times enacting dramas much larger than our individual selves. I particularly remember one roadblock about three years ago that seems relevant to

this current project. It was near the time when Spring drew up a "contract" protecting her from expectations to create anything like a conceptual model for the next forty years. We were digging into our work creating Resonance Path Institute, and we kept running into disagreements. These disagreements had a strong charge to them, and,

278

(as is our practice), we turned our ships directly upstream to explore its origin. What we found there surprised us both.

Buried deep in Spring was a drive for revenge against the Western imperialist patriarchy on behalf of thousands of years of lost Chinese heritage, and I was the West's personal representative. Whoa. Now that might have been fine except for my own very powerful drive to disidentify from and find a way to overcome that same Western patriarchy. She was implicitly and fiercely holding me as the representative of the very thing I hated the most and had devoted my entire life to battling. To say my indignation flared would be far understating the matter. Fortunately for us, we had Feelingwork on our side. I honestly don't know how we could have survived without it. We were able to continue engaging, inquiring, and pushing against the current, making progress day by day. It was soon after surfacing this underlying riptide that Spring invented Fieldtuning and my own boat was further rocked.

I had developed Feelingwork over the previous two decades by explicitly and deliberately turning away from anything that smelled to me of "woo," while at the same time rejecting the mainstream theories about feeling, mood, and emotion. For me it was very important to conduct my investigations as a scientist, admitting only the most fundamental data of first-person raw experience into my calculations and hypotheses. My theories took the form of rich description, indicating tendencies and patterns, setting out reliable methods that could be applied by anyone, with anyone.

Although my nature was one of lofty imagination curious about the unseen dimensions of the world, I had bound myself to sensory data in my effort to establish a new science that might one day use the most prized tools of the West to undo the West's rational arrogance and re-establish feeling as a source of wisdom. I considered myself very disciplined in my work and felt that discipline was supremely important if Feelingwork were ever to find traction in the current intellectual environment.

My most essential tool for this effort was what Spring has referred to here as the Middle Plane's linear rational mind, and I was proud of my skills in applying it to pushing the envelope of what was considered the domain of rationality. In fact, looking back from my perspective today, it's clear to me that I was indeed the perfect representative of the West's leverage of and reliance on the rational to colonize new territory.

Fieldtuning asked me to put my linear rational mind aside. Let's just say I was skeptical about the usefulness of this activity when Spring presented her design and suggested we apply it to exploring our differences. But I was willing to give it a try, probably led by my under-expressed intuitive nature. My skepticism quickly took a back seat when I immediately experienced the startling power of the method to bring meaning and insight to an inquiry.

In one of the first of our many explorations, I engaged a kind of map of my inner world, identifying one partition of the field as "mystery." It was something I didn't want to engage, and I placed it outside the perimeter of all I considered important. I don't remember exactly what happened, but I do know that my relationship with mystery changed profoundly that day, and I opened myself once again to a more full spectrum of experience including the unknown (and unknowable).

Up until this point in our relationship I had been quite unsupportive of Spring's early efforts to articulate her explorations into Taoism and the psyche. To me, her attempts seemed crude and clumsy, and I looked down on them as the work of an amateur. Something flipped after this re-engagement with mystery in my own inner world,

and I made more space for Spring's explorations. I can see now that my criticism of her efforts had been a protection of myself from re-opening to the unknown. Anything I was unable to directly observe, name, and thereby nail to the wall felt like an overwhelming threat with the potential to undo all my work to that point and render me powerless to accomplish anything of value with my life. I had been clinging tenaciously to my own security.

From that point forward though, I began to find myself simply supporting whatever Spring wanted to explore, however she wanted to explore it. Now, mind you, it wasn't like I suddenly understood everything she created, but I could (usually) hold it with (some) respect and support. Around this time, I came across a writing course by Bayo Akomolafe and suggested Spring take it. It seemed like a perfect next step for her for reasons I didn't understand but felt strongly. She went for it.

Her participation in that course opened the spigot full-bore, and from that time forward Spring has been living up to that particular meaning of her name — a fountain of delightfully fresh words, thoughts, ideas, and yes, conceptual structures. It's been a virtual torrent, and an amazing thing to witness the emergence of her uniquely original writing talent along with the material of her work itself.

At that time I was still unable to engage her work with a fully open mind, and I am forever grateful for Joseph's arrival on the scene in the role of Spring's sage sounding board and co-developer. I was able to continue a more personal parallel journey for the next couple of years as they assembled the Voyage Lab and developed The Resonance Code. My thread took me further into the maw of the Western beast to further undo my fanatic reliance on my rational ego. I deconstructed and released a powerful sub-personality I called Supreme, for example, that considered itself above and better than all others.

Other aspects of my internalized Western way of thinking that fell to Feelingwork included Inadequacy/Shame, Inner Tyrant, Ruthless Overlord, Sadistic Judge, and Don't Wanna Be Here. The most recent round of Feelingwork, dismantling a profound sense of displacement, as if I was born into orphanhood and had never belonged here in this life, left me open and available in a way I've never been. It was then, this past fall and into the new year, that I re-engaged with my own work in a new way. At the same time I became more open to working on and supporting Spring's work in a way I had never done. Over this

last few months we've experienced a greater joy in collaborating than had ever been possible in the past, and I've been grateful for the opportunity to contribute more explicitly to the creation of this book as it has taken its final shape.

All of what I've written here to this point has been preparation to make my best attempt to share one perspective with you. I have come to The Resonance Code through Spring, and to Spring through my soul's faith in something beyond the rational. That faith faced many obstacles laid in place through my upbringing and education. Those obstacles lived within me, and they were mighty in their ferocious determination to cling to what could be known, observed, proven, measured.

So I want to say, I know what you are up against in your desire to absorb and apply what Spring shares here. In opening to these ideas and practices it can feel as if life itself is under threat. I want to acknowledge that feeling. It is real, and it is a product of a civilization that has leveraged an imbalance in its framing of life to make great strides in the evolution of mind and mastery of the material world.

At the same time, the cost has been catastrophic not only to our collective existence but to each one of us personally. I want to encourage you to notice your discomfort and to choose to walk into it as Spring and I did. To the extent that you are uncomfortable, you are on the edge of evolution, of discovery, and of liberation. I want that edge for you, and I want you to inhabit it for me and for all of us, that we may find our way together into a new life of balance and wisdom.

Over this last month or so I have been applying my highly-valued linear rational mind as a servant to this work, lending my near-fanatic attention to detail to the project of presenting the book with discipline and structure. I've gone page by page to examine grammar, research quotes and image licenses, rearrange layout, tweak typography, and generally make sure, (to the best of my ability), that the presentation of Spring's work is commensurate with the power of the message. This act, putting my mind in service to this ode to the more-than-rational world, feels like a significant marker on my own personal journey.

Also along the way I've been learning from and absorbing the "how" of Spring's birthing of this book. From the way she has involved others and the enthusiasm with which she has welcomed their contributions to the way she has entered the zone of creation without so much as a proverbial map scrawled on the back of an envelope, working

always at the edge of the emerging present, these qualities of her style, (and the results they have produced!), have gradually wended their way as lessons into my own heart. As a result, even though I have been busy up to my eyeballs with this book, I still have found the time to move forward with presenting Feelingwork anew. My website, TheFeelingMind.com is growing in ways that are greater than my conscious control can take credit for. That feels good.

I want to thank Spring for the way she has engaged Feelingwork in this book, the framing she has lent it, and the wisdom she has brought to its presentation. Through her writing I am seeing new things in my own work and gaining a more comprehensive understanding of how Feelingwork performs its magic. Thank you!

Which brings me to a more general expression of gratitude. Spring and I met the first time in 2008, but the timing was off. When we met again in 2012, the stage had been set and we were underway. This most recent journey, the birthing of this book, has brought still others into my life.

To Joseph, my gratitude. What you offered was essential and perfect. To Ellen, my gratitude. You brought the writing to a juicy ripeness to set me up to pluck it for publication. To Riina, my gratitude. You offered me support at a time when accepting support was still new and uncertain for me. To all the Lab folks, my gratitude. You held the frame. To The Resonance Code and the voice of the unknown, my gratitude. Oh!

And finally, to Spring, my gratitude. My love, my challenge, my inspiration, my consternation, my endless joy, and my companion on this journey of evolving souls. Thank you, forever thank you!

One last thing. I am grateful for the fact that never in this journey with Spring have I been able to rest into the illusion that she and I are the same. Whether it is our way of being in the kitchen, our felt experience of the simplest words, or the radical differences in our lineages so obvious in our faces, I am constantly reminded that I can take nothing for granted. I can never assume I fully understand this mysterious being, nor can she assume that of me.

This kept us open always to wondering, to inquiring, to not-knowing. And it is in that place of not knowing that our most fruitful and productive inquiries have begun and ended. In my decades with Feelingwork I have absorbed a bone-deep understanding of this: I can never fully know another human being. Always the mystery of their soul is beyond my ken. With Spring I am fortunate in being able to live and practice that knowledge every day.

My fondest wish for this book is that it reminds people of the profound omnipresence of mystery in one another, and that in being reminded of mystery people find ways here and there to step away from their judgments and appraisals of one another for long enough to sit together with their differences and wonder, "What if?"

Seattle, Washington, March 2019.

Joe Shirley, MA
Developer of Feelingwork
Co-Founder of Resonance Path Institute

It's been a heck of a journey, and there were many times I longed for a "normal" life, free of the burden and responsibility of such an epic undertaking. Today, seeing the scope of what's possible now, I wouldn't change a single step. I invite you to visit TheFeelingMind.com to learn more about what role Feelingwork might have to play in your own dance with the unknown.

... But enough about us. Tell us about you!

Email us at:

TheCode@ResonancePath.com

Appendix I

The Rice Method
and Collective Readings

Casting a Reading Using Rice (or Small Beans)

1. Take a dish of rice (or small beans). Relax into a meditative mood.

2. Randomly pick six small piles of rice and arrange them from bottom to top, in a vertical line.

3. Pick one more pile, the seventh pile, and set it aside.

4. Count the number of grains in each pile.

5. If the number is even, draw a broken line to represent Yin. If the number is odd, draw a solid line for Yang. Now you have the primary hexagram.

6. Count the number of grains in the seventh pile. If the number is six or fewer, then that number indicates the position of the changing line. If the number is more than six, then take away six grains at a time until there six or fewer grains remaining. That number indicates the position of the changing line.

The table on the right shows an example of a reading using this method.

Line	Number of grains	Odd or Even	Odd: Solid Even: Broken
6th	7	Odd	▬▬▬
5th	9	Odd	▬▬▬
4th	3	Odd	▬▬▬
3th	11	Odd	▬▬▬
2rd	5	Odd	▬▬▬
1st	6	Even	▬ ▬

Seventh pile:

- 13 grains total.
- After taking 6 away twice, 1 grain is left.
- Line 1, the bottom line, is the changing line.

Primary: Hexagram 44 Renewing Deep Instinct	Secondary: Hexagram 1 Pure Potential

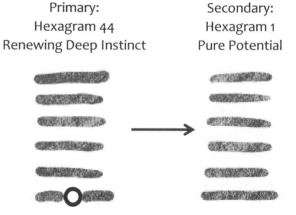

Casting a Collective Reading

The rice method can be easily adapted to a collective reading, which can be particularly powerful. Some of the defining steps of this work emerged out of group readings we did in the Resonance Code Research Lab.

When everyone in the group has counted the number of grains in their piles, the group can build a collective reading using the counts obtained by individuals. For each line, simply add all the individual counts together. Then use the sum to determine whether it is a solid or broken line, based on whether the total is odd or even. Similarly, add all the numbers together for the seventh pile, divide by six, and use the remainder to designate the group reading's changing line.

Using this method, every individual will have an individual reading. And the group will have one collective reading synthesized from all the individual readings.

Appendix II

Endnotes and Image Credits

Overall Practice

Throughout the book, we've made every attempt to document the origins of images and quotes, which you will find on the following pages, listed by page number. Two image sources in particular were most valuable, Unsplash.com and Pixabay.com. Both sources support use for commercial and noncommercial purposes without permission or attribution required. We've chosen to document the artist or photographer when possible, and documented clarifying information about the copyright license when relevant. If an image is not listed in this table, it was created by Spring or Joe.

Images/licenses by source:
- NASA: https://www.nasa.gov/multimedia/guidelines/index.html
- Pixabay.com: https://pixabay.com/service/terms/#license.
- Unsplash.com: https://unsplash.com/license.
- Vectorstock.com: https://www.vectorstock.com/faq (License - Standard)
- Wikimedia Commons: https://commons.wikimedia.org.
- OpenClipArt.org: https://openclipart.org/share
- Creative Commons Licenses: https://creativecommons.org/licenses/
- Flickr.com: See respective Creative Commons License for each image.

Front Matter

- Cover: Four Sisters. Chen Hu. Unsplash user: @huchenme.
- Title Page: Swirl. Pixabay user: PublicDomainPictures.
- p. ix: Image. Alexandra Isaievych. Firmly on the Ground. Used by permission. More at www.isaievych.com
- p. xi: Image. Alexandra Isaievych. Crossing Beyond. Used by permission. More at www.isaievych.com

Introduction

- p. 2: Sunset. Rob Bates, Unsplash user: @inksurgeon.
- p. 3: Prototype DNA Woman. Vectorstock.
- p. 3: Body Ecosystem. Revised Estimates for the Number of Human and Bacteria Cells in the Body. PLoS Biol v(14)8; 2016 Aug.

- p. 4: Neurons. Suzana Hurculano-Houzel, TEDGlobal 2013.
- p. 4: Neural Net. Gerd Altmann, Pixabay user: geralt.
- p. 5: Night Sky. Pixabay user: skeeze.
- p. 6: Leibniz, I Ching. Sam Barlow, https://medium.com/@sam.barlow/the-mystic-in-the-machine-82ab3c3947a9
- p. 7: Luo Shu. Wikimedia Commons, public domain, user: AnonMoos.
- p. 10: Sunrise. Arek Socha, Pixabay user: qimono.
- p. 11: Journey Path. Phạm Quốc Nguyên, Pixabay user: Sanshiro.

Prelude

- p. 18: Experiments Quote. Carl Jung. Synchronicity: An Acausal Connecting Principle, Bollingen 1960, p. 44.

- p. 20: Lao Tzu. Author's translation.

- p. 26: UN Report. The Intergovernmental Panel on Climate Change, https://www.ipcc.ch/sr15/

- p. 26: Bayo Akomolafe. When You Meet the Monster, Anoint Its Feet. Emergence Magazine, Issue No. 3.

- p. 27: Suicides. National Vital Statistics System, National Center for Health Statistics, CDC.

- p. 27: Depression, Mental Disorders. CDC, NCHS.

- p. 37: Macroscopic Quantum Phenomena. See https://en.wikipedia.org/wiki/Macroscopic_quantum_phenomena

- p. 37: Mae-Wan Ho. Science in Society Archive, Quantum Coherent Liquid Crystalline Organism. http://www.i-sis.org.uk/QuantumCoherentOrganism.php

Chapter One

- p. 43: Iceberg. Vectorstock.

- p. 45: Dreamer. Pixabay user:LeandroDeCarvalho.

- p. 45: Einstein. "What Life Means to Einstein: An Interview by George Sylvester Viereck," The Saturday Evening Post (October 26, 1929), p. 117

- p. 47: Spiral. Pixabay user:1239652 (inactive account)

- p. 48: Dance. Robert Collins. Unsplash user: @robbie36.

- p. 50: Confucius (c551-479 B.C.). Chinese philosopher. Gouache on paper, c1770. The Granger Collection. From Wikimedia Commons.

- p. 50: Confucius. Book of Rites, 礼记. Author's translation.

- p. 51: Chinese Painting. Pixabay user: nevermore1990.

- p. 52: Insung Yoon. Unsplash user: @insungyoon.

- p. 53: Huangshan Mountains. Pixabay user: pcsfish.

- p. 54: Etienne Bösiger. Unsplash user: @etienne_boesiger.

- p. 56: Fu Xi. Wikimedia Commons user: Farm. (CC BY-SA 3.0).

Chapter Two

- p. 60: Phylo Tree. Wikimedia Commons user: Madprime. (Public Domain CC0 1.0).

- p. 60: Org Chart. Gerd Altmann, Pixabay user: geralt.

- p. 61: Guitar Hand. Shawn Gaske, Pixabay user: ShawnGaske.

- p. 62: Fractal. Barbara A. Lane. Pixabay user: BarbaraALane.

- p. 64: Automated Fear. Timothy Wilson. Strangers to Ourselves: Discovering the Adaptive Unconscious, the Belknap Press of Harvard University Press, 2004.

- p. 66: Kalachakra thangka painted in Sera Monastery, Tibet, (private collection), photographed by Kosi Gramatikoff, Wikimedia Commons user: Kosigrim. (Public Domain CC0 1.0).

- p. 66: The Rainbow and the Worm, by Mae-Wan Ho, World Scientific Publishing Co, Pte, Ltd, 2008. Image from Amazon.com, reprinted as "fair use."

- p. 67: Face. Alexandr Ivanov, Pixabay user: ivanovgood.

- p. 69. Boys. Robert Collins. Unsplash user: @robbie36.

- p. 69: Steiner. One of those ubiquitous yet untraceable internet quotes.

- p. 70: Tree. Bryan Minear. Unsplash user: @bryanminear.

- p. 76: Cello. Pixabay user: enbuscadelosdragones0.

- p. 77: Tree. Pixabay user: ejaugsburg.

- p. 80: Tree Woman. Stefan Keller. Pixabay user: KELLEPICS.

- p. 82: Fern. Aaron Burden. Unsplash user: @aaronburden.

- p. 83: Woman+Robot/AI. Gerd Altmann, Pixabay user: geralt.

- p. 83: AI Quote: Nilsson, N. (2009). The Quest for Artificial Intelligence. Cambridge: Cambridge University Press. doi:10.1017/CBO9780511819346.

- p. 84: 95/5. Jorge Cham and Daniel Whitson. We have no idea: A Guide to the Unknown Universe, Riverhead Books, 2017. Based on the Planck Collaboration 2013 results.

- p. 84: The Unconscious. Timothy Wilson. See p. 64.

Chapter Three

- p. 90: Tree. Jeremy Bishop. Unsplash user @jeremybishop.
- p. 91: Four Stages. Martin M. Broadwell, 1969. https://en.wikipedia.org/wiki/Four_stages_of_competence.
- p. 92: Water Cycle. NASA. (CC BY 2.0).
- p. 93: DNA. Pixabay user: PublicDomainPictures.
- p. 93: Taiji. Pixabay user: OpenClipart-Vectors.
- p. 94: Woman Qigong. Natalija Tschelej-Kreibich. Pixabay user: Office469.
- p. 94: Woodcut. Xiuzhen miyao, a gymnastic (daoyin/qigong) text of unknown origin, was rediscovered and published with a preface by Wang Zai in 1513 (8th year of the Zhengde reign period of the Ming dynasty). It records 49 exercises. This illustration depicts a technique used for freeing the flow in renmai. Wikimedia Commons / Wellcome Images, (CC BY 4.0).
- p. 99: Data. According to Domo.com's Data Never Sleeps 5.0. https://www.domo.com/learn/data-never-sleeps-5#/
- p. 100: Tree. Marion Wunder. Pixabay user: _Marion.
- p. 100: Suicides. National Vital Statistics System, National Center for Health Statistics, CDC.
- p. 100: Sex Recession. Kate Julian. Why Are Young People Having So Little Sex? The Atlantic, December 2018.
- p. 101: Night Sky. Pixabay user: Reinhardi.
- p. 101: Wealth/Meaning. Residents of Poor Nations Have a Greater Sense of Meaning in Life Than Residents of Wealthy Nations. Shigehiro Oishi and Ed Diener. Psychological Science, December 2013.
- p. 104: Wave. Jeremy Bishop. Unsplash user: @jeremybishop.
- p. 107: Spring Cheng, 2005.
- p. 107: David Abram, Magic and the Machine, Emergence Magazine, Fall 2018.
- p. 109: Lotus. Pixabay user: yyryyr1030.
- p. 110: I/We-Culture. Dr. Janet M. Bennett. From a handout at a training entitled Values, Cultures and Conflicts: Intercultural Complications, at the Dispute Resolution Center of King County, WA, 2016. Adapted and refined by Spring Cheng and Marci McReynolds for a series of cultural competency trainings, City of Bellevue, WA.
- p. 111: Poem. Translated by the author from a WeChat post.
- p. 112: Hands. Josep Ma. Rosell. Flickr user: batega. (CC BY 2.0).
- p. 113: Baby Feet. Benji Aird. Unsplash user: @airdography.
- p. 113: Single-Celled. Libby, Ratcliff. Science, 24 Oct 2014: Vol. 346, Issue 6208, pp. 426-427. DOI: 10.1126/science.1262053.
- p. 113: Sexual Reproduction. Wikipedia: https://en.wikipedia.org/wiki/Evolution_of_sexual_reproduction
- p. 117: Fractal Sun. Stefan Keller. Pixabay user: KELLEPICS.
- p. 119: Magnetic Awareness. Shinsuke Shimojo, Daw-An Wu, Joseph Kirschvink. New evidence for a human magnetic sense that lets your brain detect the Earth's magnetic field, The Conversation, March 18, 2019.
- p. 120: Geodynamo. NASA. Dr. Gary A. Glatzmaier – Los Alamos National Laboratory – US Dept of Energy.
- p. 121: Shame. John Hain. Pixabay user: johnhain.
- p. 123: Leaping. Val Vesa. Unsplash user: @adspedia.
- p. 126: Woman. Candice Candice. Pixabay user: Candiix.
- p. 128: Egg. Wikimedia Commons user: KDS4444. (CC BY-SA 3.0)
- p. 128: Sperm. Vectorstock.
- p. 128: Fetus. Alexei Muzarov. OpenClipArt.org user: azex.
- p. 131: Peak in the Past. Yuval Noah Harari. Sapiens: A Brief History of Humankind, Harper, 2015.
- p. 132: Life's Timeline. See p. 113.
- p. 133: Itzhak Bentov, A Brief Tour of Higher Consciousness, Destiny Books, Revised Edition, 2000.
- p. 133: Arthur Young, The Reflexive Universe, Anodos Foundation, Revised Edition, 1999.
- p. 133: Toroidal Structure. https://en.wikipedia.org/wiki/Stanford_torus.

Chapter Four

- p. 139: Yin Yang Moon Sun Illustration. Flickr user: DonkeyHotey. Adapted for use in this diagram and many others throughout the book. (CC BY 2.0).

- p. 140: Quote. Richard Nisbett. The Geography of Thought: How Asians and Westerners Think Differently...and Why, p. 50. Free Press, Reprint Edition, 2004.

- p. 151: Shell. Sérgio Valle Duarte. Wikimedia Commons User: Ibirapuera.

- p. 152: Tao te Ching. Translated by Stephen Mitchell, Harper Collins, 1st Edition, 1988.

- p. 153: Fire. Cullan Smith. Unsplash user: @cullansmith.

- p. 153: Wood. Victoria Palacios. Unsplash user: @toriamia.

- p. 153: Soil. Paul Mocan. Unsplash User: @paulmocan.

- p. 153: Water. Terry Vlisidis. Unsplash User: @vlisidis.

- p. 154: Crystal. Rob Lavinsky, iRocks.com. Wikimedia Commons, (CC-BY-SA-3.0).

- p. 154: Structure. Wikimedia Commons user: MarinaVladivostok. (CC0 1.0).

- p. 156: Canyon. Tom Gainor. Unsplash user: @its_tgain.

- p. 160: Dam. Originally posted on Flickr by Le Grand Portage, (CC-BY 2.0). Currently on Wikimedia Commons.

- p. 160: Qutang Gorge. Tan Wei Liang Byorn, 2009. On Wikimedia Commons, (CC BY 3.0).

- p. 162: Four Stages. See note for p. 91.

- P. 164: Elephant. Christine Sponchia. Pixabay User: Sponchia.

- p. 165: Star-Gazer. Greg Rakozy. Unsplash user: @grakozy.

- p. 166: Aurora. Pixabay user: GooKingSword.

- p. 169: Neuron Art. Gerd Altmann. Pixabay user: geralt.

- p. 171: Computer Icons. Openclipart user: warszawianka. From the Tango Project.

- p. 171: DNA Man. Openclipart user: GDJ.

Chapter Five

- p. 176: Tree. Pixabay user: skylife81.

- p. 177: Aboriginal Art. Pixabay user: esther1721.

- p. 178: Messier 82. Pixabay user: WikiImages.

- p. 181: I Ching Book Covers. Wilhelm, R., & Baynes, C. F. (1950). The I ching: Or, Book of changes. Princeton University Press; 3rd edition (October 21, 1967). | The Complete I Ching — 10th Anniversary Edition: The Definitive Translation by Taoist Master Alfred Huang. Inner Traditions; 2nd Edition, Revised, Revised Two-Color edition (November 17, 2010). | I Ching: The Book of Change (Shambhala Pocket Classics). Shambhala; 1st edition (March 10, 1992). All three covers shared under common fair use practice.

- p. 187: Most Treasured Hexagram. The Complete I-Ching. Translated by Taoist Master Alfred Huang. Inner Traditions International, 2nd Edition, 2010.

- p. 189: Storm Clouds. John Westrock. Unsplash user: @johnwestrock.

- p. 192: Zha Cai and Meigan Cai. Wikimedia Commons user: Sjschen. (CC BY-SA 3.0).

- p. 192: Cabbage. Doreen Corbey. Pixabay user: bellessence0.

- p. 195: Cellular Signals. Cell phones operate with radio frequencies located on the electromagnetic spectrum between FM radio waves and the waves used in microwave ovens, radar, and satellite stations. https://en.wikipedia.org/wiki/Radio_spectrum

- p. 196: UCLA Study. Rena Repetti, Thomas Bradbury, Belinda Campos, Anthony Graesch. Opportunity for interaction? A naturalistic observation study of dual-earner families after work and school. Journal of Family Psychology, 2009.

- p. 197: Fetus. Alexei Muzarov. OpenClipArt.org user: azex.

- p. 199: Microscope. Wikimedia Commons user: Pleple2000. (CC BY-SA 3.0).

- p. 201: Compass. Aaron Burden. Unsplash user: @aaronburden.

- p. 203: Mae Wan Ho, in Tam Hunt, The rainbow and the worm, Establishing a new physics of life. https://www.ncbi.nlm.nih.gov/pmc/articles/PMC3609844/. Published online 2013 Mar 1. doi: 10.4161/cib.23149. PMCID: PMC3609844.

- p. 203: A. Sutra: 一尘中有尘数刹，一一刹有难思佛. https://en.wikipedia.org/wiki/Avatamsaka_Sutra

- p. 203: Carl Jung. See Synchronicity: An Acausal Connecting Principle, (1960), (for example).

- p. 204: Map. Cam DiCecca. Unsplash user: @camdicecca.

- p. 205: Sailboat. Johannes Plenio. Pixabay user: jplenio.

Chapter 6

- p. 228: Photo by Briana Jones.

- p. 229: Creation Quote. From the musical Rent, by Jonathan Larson. 1996, Mark, end of Act 1.

- p. 231: Pain/Suffering Quote. Indefinite attribution, used many places, most likely arising from Buddhist teachings.

- p. 232: Piano. Thomas Quine. Flickr User: quinet. (CC BY-SA 2.0).

- p. 247: Bodhisatva. Paraphrased from various translations, attributed to the Bodhisattva Kṣitigarbha.

- p. 253: Personal/Universal Quote. Rogers, C. R. 1961. On becoming a person: A therapist's view of psychotherapy. Boston: Houghton. – p. 26

Final Words

- p. 258: Network Earth. Gerd Altmann. Pixabay user: geralt.

- p. 259: Mantra. Pixabay user:ramanbansuri.

- p. 260: 95/5. See note p. 84.

- p. 261: Night Sky. Norbert Pietsch. Pixabay user:PTNorbert.

Acknowledgement & Authors' Notes

- p. 265: Ellen McCord. Photo: Robin Mallgren.

- p. 268: Sir Ken Robinson Ted2006, "Do schools kill creativity?" https://www.ted.com/talks/ken_robinson_says_schools_kill_creativity, at 8:28: " Every education system on earth has the same hierarchy of subjects... At the top are mathematics and languages, then the humanities. At the bottom are the arts. Everywhere on earth. And in pretty much every system, too, there's a hierarchy within the arts. Art and music are normally given a higher status in schools than drama and dance."

39161736R00175

Printed in Poland
by Amazon Fulfillment
Poland Sp. z o.o., Wrocław